THE PINBALL MACHINE

The Family Separation Industry and Parental Alienation

TREVOR COOPER

The Pinball Machine: The Family Separation Industry and Parental Alienation
© Trevor Cooper 2019

ISBN: 978-1-925935-18-9 (Paperback)
         978-1-925935-19-6 (eBook)

 A catalogue record for this book is available from the National Library of Australia

Lead Editor: Kristy Hoffman
Editors: Peta Culverhouse & Beverley Streater
Cover Design: Trevor Cooper and Ocean Reeve Publishing
Design and Typeset: Ocean Reeve Publishing
Published by Trevor Cooper and Ocean Reeve Publishing

Printed in Australia by Ocean Reeve Publishing
www.oceanreeve.com

OceanREEVE
PUBLISHING

Based on a true story. Names and locations have been changed to provide anonymity for the guilty, the author from litigation and comply with the legal requirements of the relevant Australian laws.

Contents

Dedication

To my daughter. I hope that life treats you well, you know that the door is always open, and we meet again soon.

Most of all …

Love Always

Dad

Foreword

By Stan Korosi, M.Couns.HS

The Pinball Machine: 'Let's Play the Alienation Game'

As with any good mystery, the story of alienation such as this leaves the reader mystified by the inevitable erosion of a child's loving relationship with their father and at the same time wondering: What has this father has done to earn the opprobrium of rejection? To cut to the chase, you should read this book because you just can't make this stuff up! The reality is indeed stranger than fiction. This is the lived story of parental alienation, a form of coercive family violence and child psychological maltreatment that equally affects the children of both mothers and fathers in all types of families.

I have been a specialist consultant in the field of parental alienation here in Australia for nearly a decade. As far as I'm aware, I'm the first person in Australia to have "put up their shingle" with this specialisation. I'm an accredited facilitator of an evidence-based remediation workshop that provides children who have been psycho-logically abused in the form of severe alienation, with their best chance of a relationship with both parents and where parents and children learn how children's views may be shaped by adult influence. I have therefore worked with many targeted-alienated parents to help them and their children find each other again and to help these parents live a better life when remediation of their relationship is not possible.

Additionally, I was the founding Editor-in Chief of 'Parental Alienation International' a publication of an international, not-for-profit organisation, the Parental Alienation Study Group (PASG). The PASG has more than 550 members, mostly mental health and legal professionals from 52 countries, including Australia, who provide scholarship and thought leadership in the field of parental alienation.

I am currently undertaking doctoral research into parental alienation as a social issue; surveying and interviewing targeted-alienated parents about their social experiences as they navigate society and social institutions, as parents rejected by their alienated children.

Trevor, the author of this book, and I have moved in the same contexts, with Trevor's voluntary work with mothers and fathers through a national organisation to which I also provided professional development to some of their volunteer groups. Both of us, in our own way share similar experiences. Trevor writes of his lived experience of how a child, his daughter, was coerced into the unwarranted rejection of him, as her father, by the depreciation of his identity as a parent. This is the hallmark of a psychologically and emotionally maltreated child, exposed to alienating process by one of their parents. We need more books like this in the Australian context to demonstrate the reality of this type of emotional abuse as a form of family violence hiding in plain sight in our families and in society.

In Australia, 1 in 4 women and 1 in 6 men experienced some form of emotional abuse from a current or former partner. International research indicates that the prevalence of parental alienation is more or less equal between mothers and fathers. That is to say, that men and women are equally the perpetrators and victims of alienation against their children and every one of their children, a victim of abuse. In Australia 8.9% of men and 4.6% of women who experienced emotional abuse by a previous partner had their partner threaten to take their children away from them, and 38.5% of men, 25.1% of women that experienced emotional abuse by a previous partner had their partner lie to their children with the intent of turning them against them[1].

Why Should You Read This Book?

Like so many experiences of parental alienation, the author unfolds a torturous story that ends with the rupture of a loving relationship between a child and a good parent without regard for the child's welfare. The principal character and protagonist in this book falls victim to its plot of parental alienation; where, in the words of well-known researcher Amy J. Baker, they were cast as being "unavailable, unemotional and unsafe".

---

[1] Commonwealth of Australia, Family Law Act 1975, Section 4AB, § 4AB (2012). Retrieved 17 May, 2019, from http://www.austlii.edu.au/au/legis/cth/consol_act/fla1975114/s4ab.html,

It is tempting to offer 'spoilers' about this book. Suffice to say, I suggest that readers not only focus upon the author's autobiographical description of events (particularly in Part 1) but also ask: who's narratives and who's voice are silenced? Parental alienation manifests not only in what is said and what is done, but also in its absence. If there is one message to take away from this book, it is the sheer purposiveness and intentionality of parental alienation as a form of child psychological maltreatment and coercive emotional abuse, and how easily a child and their loving man, parent and father can be enveloped in a distorted, artificial reality created by the other partner. This artificial alienating reality is dangerous to both the targeted parent and their children. Note the threat made by the mother in this story, "I will make sure you never see your daughter again". In my experience such threats are always carried out and not always recognised by our family violence services as the coercive family violence for which they are commissioned to respond. As many targeted-alienated parents report, they are most in danger for as long as they try to keep in contact with their children—a stark contrast to the opposite experience for victims of other forms of family violence; that they are most in danger when they leave the relationship.

'The Pinball Machine' is an appropriate title as the author explains in the preface to this book. It is a metaphor for entertainment and distraction but with a singular purpose: to take your child. Once you are in the game, you cannot get out unless you lose, and even if you stay in to the end, the 'house' always wins. It is stories like this, told with courage, that reveal the nature of the game in which children are the 'ball', and their rejected parent are the 'flippers'. Of course, we know where the 'ball' always ends up.

Beyond This Book: The Winds of Change

In the spirit of 'that which does not destroy us makes a stronger,' Trevor came close, very close to making a lie of Nietzsche's proposition. Trevor's story illustrates how the trauma of alienation infiltrates all parts of their lives. Parental rejection by alienation is worse than any death, not only is there no body to bury but these parents cannot even acknowledge the loss because to do so, validates the means by which their children were taken. As if that is not enough, they also face the judgement of society oblivious to the abuse of parental alienation hiding in plain sight. The author has taken the path of many parents and made a vocation of his traumatic experience, now advocating for parents and their children touched by alienation.

In Part 3, Trevor discusses the issues that need to be considered in the context of the family at the end of the second decade of the twenty-first century. The family is no longer a structure underpinned by social and gender defined roles. Instead, it is fluid, and reconfigurable as a voluntary network of relationships organised into a family. And it can just as easily be dismantled by the intentional processes of alienation. Yet, within Australia's social and legal contexts, parental alienation is narrowly viewed as a type of relationship issue to which children respond by alienating themselves to resolve an impossible loyalty conflict. At the same time this presentation is considered as a form of coercive, controlling family violence, given as an example in the Australian Family Law Act, 1975[2]. This contradiction is highlighted in cases where children are placed with the parent who alienated them, and their targeted parents excluded from a relationship with their children.

This book highlights the need for the Australian family law system to consider children and parent's welfare as a whole, differentiate children's valid voices from coerced choices and develop a more congruent child support system that does not validate alienation as a ticket for financial abuse. Perhaps, this book will inspire you, the reader; get your placards ready because, mothers and fathers, it is time to hit the streets! Only a 'root and branch' review of the family law system in Australia by a Royal Commission can deliver the necessary change.

Stan Korosi.
M.Couns.HS (Latrobe University),
PhD Candidate (University of the Sunshine Coast)

---

[2] Commonwealth of Australia, Family Law Act 1975, Section 4AB, § 4AB (2012). Retrieved 17 May, 2019, from http://www.austlii.edu.au/au/legis/cth/consol_act/fla1975114/s4ab.html,

Foreword

By William Bernet, M.D.

The readers of this narrative know that it has something to do with parental alienation because it says so right on the cover of the book. Parental alienation is an unusual human experience because it may continue for a long time, sometimes years, before the people who are directly involved realise what is happening to them. This is especially true for the alienated parent, that is, the parent whose relationship with his or her child has been stolen by the machinations of the alienating parent. Once in place, parental alienation may last a lifetime.

In this story, the alienating parent is Nellie; the alienated parent is Trevor; and the child is Jasmine. This book should be read by anyone that seeks insight as to how a good parent may be removed from their child's life. It should also be read by professionals such as police, social workers, psychologists, psychiatrists, lawyers, and the judiciary to gain an understanding of this form of child psychological abuse, systems abuse, and how their actions may aid the perpetrator.

The Pinball Machine is a detailed account, in which Trevor and Nellie move between Australia and the Netherlands;

their relationship transitions from blissful to controlling and vengeful; their children are caught up in intense loyalty conflicts; and they have numerous, frustrating legal interactions. During the early part of the story, there are red flags that parental alienation may be in the works. For example, Nellie tends to isolate herself from Trevor, her children, and their extended family. She has no interest in sharing her own past experiences with Trevor and her children. She has no empathy for Jasmine when she is seriously ill. She lies to Trevor about big and little topics.

Try to put yourself in Trevor's shoes and see if you can identify when he could have realized that he and Jasmine were victims of a campaign of alienating behaviours by Nellie. There is a very dramatic and heartbreaking scene in a McDonald's restaurant, and at that point, Trevor must have grasped that his child was severely alienated from him—even if he could not accept what had happened. Statements made by Nellie in court before that scene and information subsequently gathered by subpoenas, eventually reveal the tangled web of deceit and Trevor's acceptance of the reality of parental alienation and the relationship's destruction. In retrospect, it seems like the processes of brainwashing, indoctrination, and alienation had already been occurring for several years.

It is my contention—that parental alienation occurs right in front of us without being noticed—also happens with mental health and legal professionals. In my work as a child psychiatrist, I knew a family court judge in the 1980s, who told me about a psychologist named Barry Bricklin (who developed a psychological test that helps to identify alienated children). In the 1990s, a psychologist colleague recommended that I read a book by Stanley Clawar and Brynne Rivlin (whose book, *Children Held Hostage,* dramatically described how one parent can brainwash the child to fear the other parent). After that, Richard Gardner and I worked together on a project for the American Academy of Child and Adolescent Psychiatry. Gardner wrote extensively about "parental alienation syndrome", and I eventually learned from him to recognise that malignant psychological condition, which afflicts hundreds of thousands of children and families throughout the world. It was only then that I realized that in previous years, I had seen several cases of parental alienation, but I did not understand or recognise what I was looking at. The naïve evaluator simply takes the children's statements at face value, that is, that they hate their father (or their mother) because of the horrible things that parent did; the evaluator does not realise that the children's adamant refusal to see the rejected parent is driven a firmly held false belief, like a delusion.

This failure to recognise and identify the pathological phenomenon of parental alienation goes beyond the experience of individual families and lack of awareness of trained psychologists and psychiatrists—this blindness has persisted on a societal level for many decades. We know that parental alienation was described in British legal records from the early nineteenth century. We know that mental health professionals described parental alienation—using an assortment of names—in the twentieth century. For example, psychoanalyst David Levy in the 1940s, child psychiatrist Louise Despert in the 1950s, and psychiatrist Salvador Minuchin in the 1970s. Eventually, Richard Gardner identified more than one hundred such cases and gave it a name, "parental alienation syndrome", in 1985. Since that time, scholars have published hundreds of articles in professional journals, chapters, and books. Attorneys have successfully litigated cases involving parental alienation in hundreds of courtrooms in many countries.

Despite this widespread acceptance of the importance of parental alienation in mental health and legal domains, there remains considerable ignorance regarding this topic. Although I refer to it as "ignorance", I am not sure whether this lack of awareness of parental alienation results from deficient knowledge or from a pernicious, purposeful refusal to accept the reality of this challenging mental condition. It remains for those of us who are concerned about parental alienation to continue to work energetically in at least four arenas: research regarding the underlying causes of parental alienation; systematic studies of the interventions for parental alienation; education of mental health and legal trainees and practitioners, such as attorneys and judges; and advocacy with legislatures and the judiciary to improve the practices in family courts. This book, *The Pinball Machine,* is a powerful light for raising awareness, and a beacon for guiding our paths toward addressing the misery of parental alienation.

William Bernet, M.D.
President, Parental Alienation Study Group
Distinguished Life Fellow, American Psychiatric Association
Professor Emeritus, Department of Psychiatry,
Vanderbilt University
Nashville, Tennessee, USA

Preface

By Trevor Cooper

first started this book almost a decade ago whilst in the middle of a bitter separation and I experienced various tactics to ensure the relationship with my daughter was severed forever. The trauma of reliving much of what had occurred while writing this book meant that it has been put down several times.

What happened to make me pick this up and complete the production of this book?

The first was my daughter, and that if she ever asks why I was not around, then there is a record and a clear message that she is loved. This intent changed as the book was written as children just want the conflict to stop, and stop reliving it, as it may be as traumatic for her as it was for me. This book will therefore not be sent to her and unlikely to find her due to the use of aliases and geography. Hopefully, the effort taken, and the love may shine through if it ever does find her. Should my daughter come across this book, then the dedication of "Love Always Dad", is the only part of the book that she needs to read and believe. I am hopeful that in the not too distant future, my daughter will appreciate my efforts to communicate, the life I have led helping other children through helping their parents, the effort in writing this book and that "Love Always" will have meaning to her.

The second was a request to participate in a research project to which the interview started with; "I need to advise you that I have the phone numbers of some emergency counselling services if required and I must inform you that if I feel there is any danger to you, then I will call the emergency services." Having experienced a difficult family separation and seeing what happens to men and women associated with traumatic separations and parental alienation, I knew he was talking about suicide. The impact on the displaced and loving parent, frustrated by common tactics by those doing the alienation, whom are often aided by police, government agencies and courts is profound. This situation has such an impact on so many people's lives; it needs to be more openly discussed by more than just the academe and I felt this story needed to be told.

The third was the information provided by experts in the field of parental alienation. While varying in their methods of diagnosis using "The Diagnostic and Statistical Manual for Mental Disorders" (DSM5) or the "International Classification of Diseases" (ICD11), they were all consistent in the devastating impact on children and declaring parental alienation as a form of child abuse. Having facilitated groups in this area, I had also been exposed to those impacted by both; the attempted and deaths by suicides of their children, that were suffering this form of child abuse. I considered that bringing a real case to the attention of the general public as important.

The fourth was the experience of running separated-parent's groups. One therapist doing his second PhD and was on work experience watched me facilitating over several weeks and was astounded that whatever people revealed, I was able to give snippets of my story to build rapport and then have others in the group share their experiences. He became fascinated by what I had experienced and how anyone could cope under such circumstances. For the group participants, knowing they are not "Robinson Crusoe" and that their experience, psychological and physical manifestations are not unique, helped them enormously. Hearing from others and that have successfully navigated the path ahead and learning that there is hope, there is light at the end of the tunnel is crucial for them to continue on in life and maintain or improve their mental health. It was clear that sharing my experience was helping others. To the professionals not exposed to this area, I hope it gives you some perspective, and for those going through a difficult separation, I hope this book assists you in your darkest days.

The fifth reason was a quote from Plato that has been translated as: "Your silence is consent" or "Your silence is complicity" and, I do not wish to give consent or be complicit to what I have seen in terms of the family law industry.

While the experts phrase it in various ways, my personal perspective of parental alienation is essentially to manipulate a child, psychologically, against their parent to cause rejection for no legitimate reason.

Organisations dealing with this phenomenon are finding it is impacting mothers and fathers at around an equal rate, so it is not a gender issue. It can happen even when the relationship between the targeted child and targeted parent was once a very positive one. As such, this book is relevant to every parent, grandparent, brother and sister as this can happen to someone you love.

In the lightest case, it can be that the child simply wants to please the alienating parent. The alienating parent may sigh when the child requests to see the other parent, so the child learns not to ask again. Education of the alienating parent of the impact on the child and how to manage the parent's emotions in these cases may quickly resolve the issue.

In the extreme cases this may be facilitated by phrases such as; "If he/she really loved you, he/she would have sent you a birthday present" (when the present was sent and concealed) or; "If he/she really wanted you, he/she would be here fighting for you, but you can rely on me" (when kept away through court or other actions) or; "I cannot explain to you why you can't have those sneakers, if your father/mother supported you, you would have them" (when money was available) or; "I had to go to court to force him/her to support you" (when reasonable offers were made). The list of scenarios manufactured by the alienating parent is long, but you get the idea.

There is hope. The Centre for Disease Control (CDC) talk about early brain development and health[3] with

---

[3] https://www.cdc.gov/ncbddd/childdevelopment/early-brain-development.html

responsive care for the child's body and mind being the key to supporting healthy brain development and the positive and negative experiences can add up to shape the child's development and can have lifelong effects. While this sounds terrible for abused children, the mainstream psychologists also talk about brain development in many journal articles and that with maturity and personal experience, the child will question things that they once accepted. Eventually, the child may seek understanding and why they were estranged from their parent. One generalist clinical psychologist said to me, "God help the parent when the child realises they were deceived and denied their other parent. I have seen it too often." I am also seeing, that specialists in this area are forming standards of practice and while many courts have traditionally rejected the expression "parental alienation" they are starting to understand the dynamics with several countries even making parental alienation a criminal offence.

What I have learned in my very personal journey in terms of mental health, the family separation industry, the challenges faced that I have either overcome or accepted, form the basis of this book. This may impact how others perceive and cope in their personal situation and an understanding of how government policies and practices, impact the people they represent in their darkest days.

What's in a name and why the pinball machine?

Even now, I cannot explain what happened and why I am left with constant and nagging questions that gnaw away at me at every opportunity. Upon the end of a seventeen-year relationship, Nellie's actions and the documents that were progressively uncovered or presented to courts in those subsequent months and years left me in a continual state of shock. The depth of deception from the first day I met Nellie, was revealed and the type of person hidden under that veneer, was exposed. How could I have been in an intimate relationship with such a person and how could I ever trust another?

Was the path I chose in my attempt to resolve the issues, acting with integrity and the best interests of the children the right approach? How could I have been deceived for so long and dismiss the many signs, that in hindsight, were so obvious? Will the child I treated as a stepson and jointly funded for 17 years appreciate the true situation and how will it affect him? And will our daughter continue to grow and become the good and decent person I raised, or will she learn the art of deception and believe that is how mothers are meant to treat fathers?

Many questions remain that may never be answered and while accepting the situation for what it is, where I must go from here in my quest to discover what is in the best interest of our daughter Jasmine, myself and a good outcome for all concerned will continue.

The abuse of the legal process, the perjury that denied most of the seventeen years together actually occurred was astounding. The impact of being bounced between several court systems in two countries in Nellie's quest to seek the maximum advantage from each of the court systems and reap revenge, meant that it was emotionally and financially draining. There were glaring inconsistencies between statements made in each of the court cases and each document and submission made to the police, courts, friends and even the Lions Club was independently designed to destroy me, eventually exposing the type of person that was Nellie.

The analogy of me being one of those metal balls in an old pinball game is very apt, and I found that I was up against the pinball wizard who assembled teams without concern as to the expense or the damage she would inflict on herself or the children in her quest. Unlike the player with an overview of the game who can see where the ball may be heading towards, you are very much the ball, having no control, no idea what direction and how fast you will be driven.

Those with their fingers on the flippers buttons (being the legal system of judges, lawyers, barristers) are all part of the multibillion-dollar Australian Family Law Industry that requires your ongoing conflict to score points.

The bumpers are those round knobs in the game that push you around (being the process servers and police), they act on complaints and court orders that may be the result of the illogical fear, blatant lies or procedural processes that were put in for good reasons but then never properly assessed as to their impact.

The various holes that you find yourself falling into along the way, trapped for what seems to be an endless time frame before being catapulted out and back into the game, being pending judgement, court-ordered reports or stays (3 months here or 4 months there, waiting for those reports or until the judges next available date) that trap you temporarily.

The slingshots, being the interim orders when unable to defend yourself for whatever reason, that accelerate your dilemma at a pace that you cannot manage. The analogies are endless.

As the ball in the game, there is no readily available roadmap to guide you on the journey that you can initially locate, and the driving forces may make it irrelevant if there was one. The level of depression and fear that become an integral part of the ongoing journey is something that you are never prepared for and cannot manage easily or without assistance. This account is from my personal experience and how my understanding evolved, facilitating separated parents' groups. While the process of grief and loss is different for every person, when I hear and talk to others, talk about their dysfunctional separation, we each find elements of our stories that compel us to relate with one another.

PART 1:

In The Beginning –
A Family Was Made

1

A family is formed, and a history revealed

I had spent many years travelling and working as a professional engineer in the construction sector. This involved managing projects like the construction of a new township to house the workforce for a mine development, gas pipeline, multi-storey city buildings and airport facilities internationally. After more than ten years in ten locations, I felt it was time to work out a way to finally settle down or else I may be travelling forever.

It was 1992, a recession was looming, and it was the opportunity to change direction, so I enrolled in one of the top Australian universities that would eventually result in the award of a Masters of Business Administration (MBA). I had paid off my house and saved some money to fund a year or more as a full-time student. The admittance requirements at the time for that university was an undergraduate degree and ten years' work experience, so all the students were aged in their thirties or older. One of the first subjects was that of Management Information Systems, which is where I met Nellie, whilst undertaking group assignments.

We seemed to have a lot in common, a desire to get ahead, which was why we were both studying, intellectually we connected, both had a down to earth practical perspective on life and while she seemed quiet, she was easy to talk to and eventually asked her to dinner. After a short discussion, we settled on a Taco Bill Mexican restaurant near the university. It was nothing fancy but were seated in a small area where we could see the fireplace and talk. I was a little nervous at first and wondered if eating tacos was necessarily the best first date food choice, as the potential for them to spill everywhere is high.

If there is a standard discussion on a first date then that was it, covering some of our background and what we liked and what we did apart from the university course. A bit of nervousness on both sides, and then Nellie exposed her secret. With a quivering lip and voice, she hesitantly revealed she was a single mother. My response was not of shock or horror but acceptance, with a response something like, "At our age, that is fairly normal," and we talked about her son, Joe, briefly. When I met Joe, it was first at the University and I remember he liked to play on the arcade machines. He was generally quiet and seemed to just accept me when I went to their house. I would often help him clean up his room and put things away and he seemed to simply enjoy the attention. Joe was really easy to get along with. As such, Joe was not an issue that would impede the relationship and we continued to see each other and included her young son in many activities. Joe had apparently never met his father and Nellie had told Joe that his father was an Irishman that was on holidays in Australia and Joe possibly was too young to want to ask more. Nellie told me a different story in that Joe's father was a bank teller that she had met and that she had to take him to court for child support and the judge commended her for her actions in court. The way she expressed herself led me to believe that Joe's father may have been in a committed relationship at the time, but such a subject was simply avoided by Nellie and I did not push the issue. Never the less, Joe's father was never in his life and it was many years later, that I was truly shocked when I discovered more about Joe's father.

Time was spent at each other's houses and the three of us even had a vacation together at the Grampian's National Park in Victoria. The Grampians is a truly magnificent place where you can stay at many places and the kangaroos enjoy their freedom, grazing on the lush grass. We were fortunate enough to see them grazing just outside the back door of the cabin where we stayed one morning. There were lovely walks along the creek and up what they called the Grand Canyon to the Pinnacle which oversees the valley, restaurants, camping, and barbecue facilities. Nellie confirmed that it was the first vacation Joe had ever been on and seeing the kangaroos, the walks around the Grampians soaking up nature was clearly very special and something he seemed to enjoy. I suppose I chose that destination due to my background, as I grew up with family holidays at iconic Australian locations, mainly in Victoria, such as The Grampians, Phillip Island, and Wilsons Promontory, initially in rented houses and later in a caravan. Our family often stayed in caravan parks at Merimbula and Yarrawonga, sometimes with my uncle and his family.

When Nellie and I first met, I lived in a house in the keys estate that I had purchased several years earlier. The house was a nice three-bedroom house and I had converted one bedroom into an office. The estate was in an area that was developed in the late nineteen seventies, some twenty years earlier and considered a nice suburb with a large shopping centre and all the facilities for families, and it was no longer on the ever-expanding city fringe.

At the completion of my MBA, Nellie and I had become very close, and while we had discussed marriage, Nellie made her feelings known that it was only a piece of paper and outdated, saying, "I wouldn't want to change my name," and she seemed happy with entering into a de facto relationship, which she said was just the same as marriage.

As we continued to date, we would often have dinner at each other's places although mainly Nellie's. While Joe seemed to like being at my place and the activities in the backyard, Nellie said that Joe liked being home in his room with his Nintendo games and it is only with hindsight that I realised it may have had more to do with Nellie being in control of the situation. Neither of us had dishwashers in those days and we would always wash the dishes together afterwards. This had been going on for many months until I was finally told, in a sheepish sort of manner, "I normally rinse them after to ensure all the soap is removed." The response was all right and I started rinsing the dishes off. I did ask the question as to why Nellie didn't ask me earlier, to which I never got a response and we continued with whatever we were discussing, and this was probably one of the earliest times that Nellie put off raising issues that concerned her.

I recall one strange communication scenario that resulted from my previously working overseas on a construction job. I had a friend look after my house while I was away, and she had left behind some children's toys near the kitchen, which were for her nephews and nieces to play with. The first time Nellie visited the house she queried them, and I explained how they came to be there. Some years later, Nellie told me that her immediate thought was that I was some sort of monster and pedophile and was using her to get to her son and remained cautious for some time! To this day I wonder if she suspected that, then why she would place her son at such risk?

At one stage, I broke off the relationship, as it seemed everything was the way she wanted it, as Nellie wanted to spend all the time at her place and none at mine which meant being largely in the upstairs two-bedroom unit which I found restrictive and claustrophobic. The vast majority of decisions including what we ate and where we went, all seemed to be made by Nellie. It was as if I was being absorbed into Nellie's life, rather than extending all our lives, and all of us growing together. It simply did not feel like Nellie and Joe were sharing a part of my life as well and I was losing elements of who I was. The separation only lasted a week with Nellie telephoning me and a compromise was reached with more time spent at my place, where I could cook meals; I think Joe actually enjoyed being out in the backyard and the greater level of activity. I would like to think Nellie had recognised that the compromise was essential so that we grew together rather than being absorbed, but in hindsight, it may have been all about her needs for companionship and what it meant to her to be part of a couple. This lasted a while and seemed to gradually drift back to spending most of the time at Nellie's, and when my brother Graham needed to move down to Melbourne, I made him welcome in the spare room. Weekends at my house were virtually eliminated.

My house was some distance from the city and Joe was at an inner-city school that seemed to be more interested in supporting the local arts community that dominated the parents' groups, focusing on painting, unstructured learning and the avoidance or possibly even hostility towards academic assessment. It was not a special school but one that seemed less interested in the basics of English and Maths, and as such he had not even learned the letters of the alphabet and was way behind academically for a child his age. I would play games with Joe while driving in the car of reading number plates while Nellie sat in the passenger seat, encouraging the activity but never really showing interest. I also spent many hours reading books to Joe while Nellie was busy doing other things and that effort seemed to help Joe. His reading skills quickly improved. We had discussed moving to my place, however, with Joe established in his inner-city school and Nellie preferring to live close to work, we waited until the time was right before moving in together as we both seemed happy with the current situation.

Nellie, it turned out, had purchased the unit where she lived, in Smith Street and seemed driven to own property. She worked the weekends for her brother years earlier, while they helped look after Joe, and doing this weekend work covered her huge mortgage and leave enough for living costs. She told me that the place was such a mess when initially purchased and that she would put Joe into his room and spend a couple of hours each night stripping walls and eventually painted the place which was completed some years before we had met. Joe was well fed with nutritious meals which Nellie cooked for him, but she regarded him as a very dirty and lazy boy and told me several times that instead of going to the toilet, he had once peed in the vacuum cleaner along with the terrible tantrums he would throw after crèche. I never saw the tantrums, he responded well to learning to read and the other activities that parents normally do, so my perception of him seemed to be different to Nellie's. It may be that he had grown out of those behaviours, or that he was getting more attention than Nellie was providing when by herself and working, renovating her unit and then the postgraduate course. As time passed, possibly with the benefit of hindsight, I began to realise that Nellie's providing for Joe was limited to the essentials of food, clothing and shelter and his other needs may have been something that I met for Joe.

I never met Nellie's parents as they had both died several years earlier leaving an inheritance that Nellie looked forward to receiving. Nellie told me that it was enough to purchase a house and we started to look for one together in the area she wanted to live. Eventually, we attended an auction and Nellie placed bids. Nellie's final bid was around $30,000.00 over what her stated budget was from the inheritance, and with her bid accepted, she proceeded to sign the purchase documentation. As it was her inheritance, it was only right that the property was in her name.

The property was settled, and we moved in on the Australian rules football grand final day. As soon as I entered the place, Nellie went into a panic. The driveway concrete was largely broken while walking to the front door and upon entering the house, while clean, with all the furniture removed, the really old and broken power points could be seen. The rising damp in the hallway could be seen and it became clear that the place was really a mess and needed a lot of work. Nellie began to panic, held her chest and face turned from joy to tears. "It's not safe and maybe we shouldn't move in," she said, to which I responded, "It's okay. We can run some power leads around until we can fix it," and tried to settle her down. At this point, she calmed down a bit and told me about the purchase and moving into the 2-bedroom apartment. She couldn't move into that property immediately, fell into depression, and stayed somewhere else for a few weeks until she could bring herself to move in and start all the renovation work. I am not sure if Joe was on the scene when that happened or shortly after his birth, but I was dealing with the present and her current anguish. It was clearly an intense reaction that she had experienced in the past and some would say déjà vu for her. It was probably the first time she had spoken about her history of depression, but I did not regard it as serious and just needed some help to deal with the current situation. I was there to help.

The amount of work and the state of the house became more obvious as time went by. The wiring was very old, and many power points had no earthing connection. Wires were often the cotton-covered type which were well known to cause fires and upon realising that, she again wanted to move out. I ran leads around the house, so we used the power points that were good and that calmed her down.

It was countless hours of work, where every weekend seemed to be dedicated to making the place livable. Every spare cent from my wages went into the property, and I was okay with that, as Nellie had invested all her inheritance and we were building our future together.

It was only months after moving into the house that Nellie announced we were expecting a child and getting the house safe and ready in the lead up to the birth became an even higher priority, as was making sure that Joe was part of the process and not forgotten about. During Nellie's pregnancy, there was one scare, which was some bleeding, and I looked after Joe while Nellie went to the hospital for an assessment of a possible miscarriage. Fortunately, there was nothing wrong and things settled down. I must admit that for most of the pregnancy I felt as if I was not part of what was happening, just a bystander and at times, as if it was simply not real. It was not until Nellie began to show and could feel the baby kick that things started to seem more real.

With the birth a few months away, I decided to purchase a mobile phone. It was not one of the modern smartphones, but more like a slender brick and nearly as heavy (and barely what you may recognise as a mobile phone nowadays); it was 1994 after all. I always kept the phone with me and only a few people had the number, so that if someone rang the chances were that it was Nellie. I was working only ten minutes' drive from home at the time and avoided any travel where possible.

It was not until Jasmine was a week overdue that the doctors decided that she should be induced. An appointment was suggested by the doctor for the following Monday, however, Nellie explained that if they made it on the Friday (three days earlier), this would allow her to do an MBA exam on Thursday, and another on the following Tuesday and the doctor accepted the Friday. Everything would work out well for Nellie if it all goes to schedule. While the doctor was somewhat perturbed by the request and made the examiners at the university nervous, the subsequent events made even more tongues wag.

Everything was planned for the big day and we had arranged with the school for Joe to have the day off. We just needed to check with the hospital at 6:00 a.m. to ensure there hadn't been a rush of newborn children overnight and there was space in the maternity ward. We would then ring my mother to have her stay at the house with Joe and await the call for them both to come to the hospital.

Even the next-door neighbour, Helen, a nurse and her husband, Paul, had been following the progress and knew the arrangements. They were both home that day as Paul was self-employed and Helen on a night shift. We even had their phone number in case something went wrong with our home phone.

My mother was called immediately after we confirmed there was space in the hospital and arrived around 30 minutes later to look after Joe. Upon her arrival, Nellie and I left and were admitted into the birthing room and met the midwife. He was very professional, but I must admit that both Nellie and I were surprised as we were probably conditioned to expect a woman. A quick medical check and then the poke around (as Nellie phrased it) by the doctor to induce the birth, the fitting of a TENS device to help relieve the pain that would invariably commence, and the long wait and guesswork started to determine when the "Grandmother" and "Big Brother" should be summoned. The constant checking commenced to ensure all was going well with the amount of dilation along with time between contractions. My mother and Joe had been waiting for the call and even Helen dropped around to check up on the progress and brought some fish and chips to share as knew they would want to stay beside the phone. Finally, it was about time to call my mother and she and Joe would take around 30 minutes to get to the hospital.

Our daughter arrived on the scene with the usual crying, cleaned up, put in the humidicrib, given the vitamin K injection and then attempts to get feeding going.

The proud grandmother and the big brother entered the room and they were allowed to hold Jasmine, and they both beamed with delight.

That afternoon when re-entering the ward, I passed the nurses' station and I heard a strange conversation:

"You want to see what the woman in room twenty-two is doing?" Said one of the nurses.

13

"I know," replied another in a very concerned tone. *What is going on here?* I thought, knowing that was Nellie's room. I thought Nellie would be physically and emotionally drained and either resting or fussing over our daughter.

On entering the room, Nellie was sitting up and reading her textbook with notes and pens at the side, as if nothing had happened hours earlier that day, studying for her exam that was now less than four days away. Although it was only a few words, the nurse's tone showed a concern that I then interpreted as the mother-child bond was absent and what they saw was simply not normal to them. I had never been a father and had no idea what was normal and considered it to be just Nellie, driven to succeed with the exam that would occur in a few days' time, and the birth was not that draining.

It had been more than two years since we had met and yet it seemed like no time had passed at all, as we were so busy. Dating, me finishing my postgraduate course, my new career, moving in together, the significant renovations and now Jasmine were some of our highlights over the past years. We both took the hectic life in our stride, full of hope and aspirations for the future that was being built and from my perspective, love flourished.

None of Nellie's relatives or friends visited the hospital when Jasmine was born, which is something I would have considered normal. While I asked her if any of her family was likely to come, with her parents having passed away, Nellie largely dismissed the question. It actually made sense to me as I had only met one brother and communication with her family was largely absent.

Nellie described her mother to me as a driven person. Her mother had seen an old mansion, approached the owners to sell it to her, showing great initiative to get what she wanted. Nellie seemed to harbour a lot of unresolved resentment towards her mother's passing and several times made statements like, "The doctors let her die because she was overweight and did not try to save her."

Nellie described her father, Harold, as a likeable bloke that had a backhoe and other machinery to get contracting jobs, would turn his hand to anything; making playgrounds for the local government or whatever was required. I was told he would often have issues with people he owed money to and was once in court for sooling his dog onto someone for trying to get the money he owed them, and that he was regularly in court.

When her mother organised the purchase of the stately, but run-down property, it had no electricity or gas. Harold apparently spent years working on the property and put in the marble entry floor, connecting electricity to the house, and progressively made it livable. While the house we lived in was much smaller and the amount of work far less, there seemed to be some parallels with all the work done in getting our family home ready for Jasmine.

Eventually, her parents' marriage failed, Harold remarried and lived in a small block of flats on a busy main road in Dandenong in what the real-estate agents call a six-pack flat. Essentially some on the ground floor and some stacked on the 1st floor and the whole block is shaped, well, like a six-pack of beer on its side. He died of cancer while Nellie's mother lived in the stately home that he financed and renovated.

Nellie had five brothers.

- Joe which her son was named after, had disappeared at the age of nineteen and many years later, their parents still did not know if he was alive or dead when they passed away. Nellie did manage to find him on the internet in New Zealand but never heard more than that and I suspect there was little to no communications.

- Two brothers that lived in the country. She would not even mention their names and treated them with complete disdain, saying things like my parents loaned them money for a farm that failed and "impacted my inheritance" and clearly wanted nothing to do with them. Nellie would change the subject and get angry when asked, and so I quickly learned that subject was off limits.

- Ray was an older brother that worked as a mining engineer (most of his early years in the nearby Latrobe Valley), and was married without children. They lived nearby, however, I only met them once when we went to dinner at their place. I believe it was Ray's wife that organised the evening, perhaps to reunite the siblings, but seemed to have little long-term impact as we never saw them again.

- The final brother, Greg, was separated from his wife and kids. While she lived in the family home, he appeared to live in the bottom of a control tower at the country airfield. I remember visiting the control tower looking for him and saw the camp bed and sleeping bag on the dirt floor that was at the base of the tower and the feeling that he was living like a homeless person. He appeared to work tirelessly, picking up seafood in his plane for local sales, gave flying lessons, maintaining the runway and surrounding fields, but often just socialised with the various pilots that used the airfield and shared his love of flying. We visited a few times and he barely spoke, in fact, we seemed to spend more time with his former wife.

With the father dying in a small apartment, the mother dying in a large mansion, one brother that walked out and wanting nothing to do with the family, two brothers that she despised, another brother that appeared likeable but distant, and the last brother appeared to live on a camp stretcher in the bottom of the control tower, all the siblings seemed distant from one another. I wondered what had caused such rifts, but Nellie would never say. I am therefore not surprised that there were no visitors at the hospital. We had our family now and all was good.

Nellie had always talked about how she was the brightest of all the children in her family and as such was sent to a boarding school where she could get a better education. Nellie often spoke about mixing with children of the social elite, such as daughters of the owners of a major construction company and others.

In contrast, Nellie also told me once about the discussion she had and asking her mother why the person that lived in the little house at the front of their property had a "white wee" and when telling the story with enormous apprehension, insinuating improper behaviour, but what happened or if it was a made-up story, I never found out. The real reason why she was sent away to boarding school be it because she was bright, removed her from danger or another reason I will never know.

My father was the traditional breadwinner and mother the traditional stay-at-home mum that was the rock that made sure everything went well. I had an older and younger brother and, like all families had our challenges. We would go to the tennis courts and my parents would play on the weekends, and all of us got coaching and recall the annual club outing to the grass courts in a country location.

My father's parents had an engineering works that closed before I was born and that was where Dad was apprenticed. When I knew my grandparents, they lived in a house that was owned and next door to my grandfather's brother. This is just one of the examples I followed in helping family. They eventually moved to an old country seaside house. When my father's parents died just weeks apart, my father was so affected he had what was then termed a breakdown and was hospitalised, but whether it was days or weeks, I was too young to remember.

Holidays were often at Phillip Island where you could see the little penguin parade and seal rocks and spend a significant time at the beach, for a couple of weeks, many years in a row. Eventually, holidays were caravan trips to places like the Grampians and Merimbula along with other destinations, broadened the locations that I learned to love.

My parents separated when I was twenty, initiated by my mother who left the family home. My father quickly remarried a lovely lady called Denise and became a family man again, in a relationship that stood the test of time. I visited them rarely as I was travelling with the construction industry and then a stint in Europe, and as such, I did not know my step-siblings well. Three of Denise's four children died of cancer and a car accident and I was only in Australia to attend one of the funerals, but I am told my father was the rock that got her through those tragic times and played a major role with helping to raise one of the grandchildren.

My mother on the other hand, never remarried, and I believe, was bitter about her marriage to my father although never said anything bad. I never talked to her or how my father was when I visited her or how she was when visiting him. There was low-level tension, however we, as adult children were never discouraged from seeing our other parent.

Some people talk about nurture versus nature or environment versus genetics, but I believe we all have a background that influences our values and how we react in similar situations. People that are close to us such as parents are possibly our most influential role models and while we often reject what our parents do, for example, I chose to never smoke, other behaviours may be learned without us knowing and influence how we act and react. While our family backgrounds were different, Nellie seemed to like being included by my family and we seemed to share similar values.

2

The early years

Nellie often did not observe things in the same level of detail or reach conclusions about what she saw as I did, and when we got home from the hospital this became more evident.

I remembered when I first held Nellie's cat, that she had gotten for companionship years before Joe was born, I was surprised when I looked at its collar. The name on the collar was Spooky, and I asked the name of the cat again. The comment came back; it is Smoky as it was a lovely dark grey coloured cat. I pointed out the engraving to which Nellie inspected and said, "I have never noticed, but she is Spooky and it suits," and the collar left it as it was.

It was some time after our daughter had been born and was going to crèche that I noticed the cat was sleeping under the lemon tree a lot, not eating wet food and eating a limited amount of dry food, and seemed to be drinking no liquid. While Nellie had not noticed, I became concerned at what to me, were obvious changes and I offered to take the cat down to the veterinarian for a check-up to see if there was something wrong, which I did.

The vet's prognosis was grim. It was most likely severe cancer that was impacting Smoky's ability to pass urine. That was the reason she was only eating dry food and would be in considerable pain. While Nellie had not noticed the change in Smoky's behaviour and seemed indifferent as to me taking the cat to the veterinarian, the prognosis met with a reaction, and Nellie showed significant interest and proceeded down to the veterinarian when she got home. The veterinarian agreed to do an exploratory surgery but only if Nellie agreed that if it was cancer, then Smoky would be put down without being woken from the surgery. That was exactly what happened, and to this day, I still wonder why Nellie had not noticed the change in the cat's behaviour.

Concern for how the kids, and particularly how Joe who had been cuddling into Smoky (who was probably 5 years older than Joe) all his life would react. This led me to ask questions at the crèche where Jasmine attended and sought advice on the children's understanding of death and loss and what to do. Suggestions were made of a little plaque or tree to remember her by outside in the garden. In actual fact, Joe seemed to just accept it as if nothing had happened, Jasmine was clearly a bit young, but then Nellie got really upset when I raised the matter of what to do.

"You are worried about the kids and not me! It was my cat!" she screamed.

I felt terrible at the time; she was right and I had been insensitive to her needs. She had looked after

Smokey for all her life, and was upset. I had talked to others about how to help the kids cope and now, discussing how to manage kids as if not considering or helping Nellie, that I had thought had accepted the loss of the elderly cat. The focus seemed to stay on Nellie's grief, and we finished up not doing anything for Joe as he seemed to have just accepted what had occurred and that Smoky was gone.

I was very heavily involved in all aspects of my daughter growing up. Living near work made that even easier. I attended every maternal childcare check-up and later when Jasmine was sick and not permitted to go to childcare, I simply put her in the baby capsule and took her to work. There was no issue as I had my own office and people (especially the boss), knew how much I worked and what I did, so my actions were never questioned.

I often think it was also a personality thing. Where as I did things such as bringing Jasmine to work, my actions were rarely questioned and that was probably due to the long hours I put in to make the company successful. Also, my general demeanour that would challenge someone if they were to question me and did not agree. Nellie, on the other hand, was more of the "shrinking violet" type and would be very defensive if someone challenged her and would therefore never take the kids to work. I recall coaching her for an interview and telling her she always looked down and to the left when talking to someone and would avoid eye contact, which could be interpreted as she had something to hide. She managed to correct this over time and seemed to become more assertive.

We were both working, and Jasmine was enrolled in a local crèche, very close to our home, my work, and was also the same crèche that Joe had attended years earlier. It was only when we got Jasmine into the crèche Nellie told me that the other parents always felt sorry for Joe as he was the first there in the morning and last to be picked up. This was so that Nellie could work a nine-day fortnight and was so angry when he was picked up each day. It possibly explained the reported behavioural issues that I had never witnessed in Joe, but with the two of us that wouldn't happen to Jasmine; I even became involved and on the parent's management committee.

While living in Australia, Sunday outings with the children and I was a regular thing. Nellie was still doing the course at university and whenever we discussed if she would join us there was usually assignments to do and therefore kept her Sundays reserved for assignments and exam preparation. I would pack up the kids, Joe, six years old, and Jasmine (not even one) when these outings started, and would take them to various places including the zoo. I had purchased a family membership with Zoos Victoria which comprises of three zoos, being the one near the city of Melbourne, Werribee Open Range Zoo, and Healesville Sanctuary, which specialises in native Australian animals. All were a relatively easy drive, and with packed sandwiches for lunch, it was an enjoyable and cheap day out for the three of us. While I am sure Joe would remember the Sunday outings, Jasmine would have been too young to remember Australia. All the love and attention she received every day including those Sunday outings and other activities, the smiles she gave to the immediate and extended family, were all the right ingredients to ensure healthy mental and physical development. When she views photos, I hope she recognises that she was well cared for and loved. I would also take the kids to an evening meal on Sundays with my mother and my grandfather. My grandfather really enjoyed the outings from the retirement village and Joe didn't want to miss out on seeing the relatives or playing in the games room.

There was one traumatic incident that Jasmine does somehow remember. The incident was at Healesville Sanctuary and was one of the few times that Nellie did attend. It may have been a semester break with no assignments due, or a special occasion. We had a large family gathering at Healesville Sanctuary which included a picnic. My mother had a plate of food (including potato salad) when an emu walked up behind her and tried to take some food from over her shoulder. The reaction was immediate, with a high pitched and a rather loud scream and the contents of the plate flung high, some of the food landed on Jasmine, who was still crawling. The emu proceeded to peck the potato salad off Jasmine's clothing and she required immediate rescue from the bird, but was never really in any danger. Someone said to me many years later, "If I had a ten-metre chicken pecking food off me, I would remember." Considering the relative size and proportions of my daughter to a fully-grown emu, it was a reasonable analogy! It was probably not the incident itself, but the recalling of the story whenever she saw an emu or even a picture of an emu, that they are still bigger than her and has remained apprehensive around emus for many years and may still be. In any case, I loved the Sunday outings with just the kids and myself and sometimes my mother.

There was also one incident that has always stuck in my mind as strange that occurred when Jasmine was around 18 months old at a shopping centre. I was at a toy shop with Jasmine while Nellie had wandered into another shop with Joe. Jasmine needed her nappy changed urgently as it was leaking onto a ride on toy, so I cleaned the toy and took her to the baby change room. Nellie and I both had mobile phones, so if she returned before me then she could easily ring. When I returned, Nellie was frantic, almost screaming "I thought you had kidnapped Jasmine." It was very easy to reassure her and explain what happened, she calmed down quickly, and I simply dismissed Nellie's reaction. Nellie seemed both very driven and other times very insecure but, on those occasions, I always felt that love and patience would win out.

While there were some strange things I observed and with the benefit of hindsight should have reacted differently, things were generally going along well. We had family holidays to the Gold Coast in Queensland where I had borrowed a friend's camper trailer, a trip up to the mountains, Canberra, and my employers had even provided us with a weekend in Sydney for a company Gala dinner with all expenses paid. Life was good and the future bright.

3

The move to The Netherlands

I had started with an innovative road traffic management company while doing the last two subjects of my MBA and had been working there for around 3 years. I had featured in an industry magazine and published some international papers with respect to freeway management systems. The organisation then got taken over by an international company and within months of the takeover, the board changed along with the company's strategic direction, and closed it down; I found myself out of work. Work on the house continued, I did a few subjects at university, continued to chase work and while there were some offers, Nellie would consider the offers unacceptable as it would mean being away during the week and bringing the kids up alone; I actually agreed. I was also working on exploiting a patent that two elderly gentlemen owned, and the three of us had agreed on a company structure. I would have the controlling interest if I could make it viable and as such, I was what they call "a director of a company in promotion." While there was no immediate income, there seemed to be no rush, as I believed we were debt free, except for

Nellie's 2-bedroom unit that tenants rent was covering that mortgage and the potential for my future earnings was huge. It gave me time to spend more time with the kids and the flexibility meant that I was doing nearly everything for the kids much like a stay at home parent, which I enjoyed.

Nellie had also been seeing a therapist for around six months before she told me. She informed me about her history and that she had been on antidepressants as a teenager and was just seeing someone and it was nothing to worry about. When she told me, I wondered has it to do with our relationship? And if so, surely I should be attending? I recall asking her in the conversation if she wanted me to attend in case I could help, however, the response was immediate, very firm and animated in that he was her therapist and she didn't want me to see him. As such, I backed off. I began to wonder more about her history, why was she sent to boarding school? Why she seemed to not like her siblings? And why one sibling had disappeared? All those subjects that were off limits, avoided or dismissed when raised but I was glad she was seeing a therapist.

It was at this stage that Nellie began applying for jobs internationally and had applied for a job as a native English language editor for a software company in Germany. While unsuccessful, she was asked by the recruitment agency if she could be put forward for a similar position in the Netherlands and was granted an interview. I was initially opposed to the idea of Europe as I had spent many years travelling and this would deny me access to my mother, as well as Jasmine and Joe access to their grandmother, which is how Joe regarded my mother by then. These concerns seemed irrelevant to Nellie and demanded that I sign the passport application for Jasmine there and then. The mere questioning and wanting to discuss the signing of the passport application saw her fly into an abusive rant and threaten legal action. I relented and signed the forms in an effort to calm down the situation and after all, a passport does not mean it will be used, she may not get the job and we can discuss matters at a more appropriate time. I looked after the kids while she flew overseas to attend the interview and of course there was a lot of discussions about the possible adventure.

There was of course, some negotiation leading up to the move. While our daughter was too young to have a say, our young boy, Joe, insisted that he goes to a school where they speak English. There are some private schools like the British School however, there is a chain of international schools managed by the government that attract the same subsidies as "normal government schools", which teach all the subjects in Dutch. The main difference being that they teach in English, and have a requirement that they teach Dutch as a subject. These would be perfect, and his requirement could be met.

My requirements were a little more and as leaving a promising start-up venture, I wanted to ensure I could work so that we would all return to Australia as a family after a year if things did not work out for any of us. Due to my involvement with a road traffic management company and the knowledge demonstrated in Australia, this meant some of the big industry players were happy to offer me names and referrals. As such, before Nellie returned from her job interview in The Netherlands, I had used some of my network and made some contacts in the Netherlands. I managed to get three contacts in the Netherlands and interviews were arranged subject to me nominating the date I would be there. The employer that had offered Nellie the position as a technical writer had assured her that I would have no problems securing work due to her permit and as such, if found a job the visa would be a straight forward application and "rubber stamped." This was echoed by the relocation company and the recruitment consultant or at least that was what Nellie told me she was informed. Everything was agreed to.

Nellie and I had been working on the house for years, with Nellie often coming to the rubbish tip or helping me when passing things up from under the house or discussing what next to do, but largely making sure kids were all right while I laboured away. There were some things to do to put in a tenant, so I frantically fixed up the last of the walls in the house, repainted and even landscaped the front garden so that there was space for four cars to be parked. The changes meant that with lots of off-street-parking (a premium in that area as street parking was often difficult to find), a doorway to the study which meant that the property could be let as a four-bedroom house.

The result of that last few months work was that the rental return had increased $100.00 per week. I recall Nellie being so pleased that she said, "That is yours, as you succeeded in securing that." I just dismissed the statement as irrelevant, as we had a joint income. The funds would be available when we eventually returned to Australia, regardless of it being a year or longer.

We modified the bicycles with mudguards (not normal in Australia) and racks with panniers for the shopping. Dutch classes were also one night a week, so we were able to count the local currency (then Dutch Gulden, as Euro was introduced later) and that we could say good morning, although most of that was not needed as the Dutch are generally very fluent in English. It seemed that we had all rallied behind Nellie for this adventure with the possibility of experiencing life in another part of the world and understanding that we could easily return, meant the unknowns and possible downsides were dismissed one by one. Those known downsides included that:

- Joe could lose or gain six months (as the school years align with summer in Northern and Southern hemispheres).

- Joe and Jasmine (although too young to know), would lose the developing relationship with their extended family from their grandmother, uncle and cousins. This was dismissed as with cheap phone systems and video conferencing like Skype was emerging, and there would be holidays if more than a year.

- I would also have to step back from the company in promotion. This was dismissed as getting back to steady work may be better anyway, and I learned that the moment you return to close friends and family, it is like you had never been away.

The downsides were dismissed, and it was just a year if things did not work out. From my perspective, the opportunity of living in Europe for a year or longer was something that was positive, that was something important to Nellie as she often recounted her work experience as a student in Germany, and how easy it would be to adapt. We were all drawn into Nellie's adventure and it became ours. Nellie's real motivation for the move to Europe would not be exposed for more than a decade, concealed and hidden. Finding out would prove to be devastating.

We of course, had barbecues and dinners mainly with my friends and family ready for the big trip. Then the final trip to the airport, seen off by family, with photos taken and the usual family goodbyes. I still have the photos carrying our daughter Jasmine, boxes of bikes, minimal suitcases and backpacks. Jasmine was under 4, so extra things had to be thought through and being the hands-on father, those considerations were left to me.

Jasmine loved stuffed toys and so I had a backpack full of new small stuffed toys that she had never seen to take on the plane. She was given one soft toy by the hostess however, we found she got bored after an hour and I would miraculously produce a new toy that she played with enthusiastically. Between periods of sleep and around 12 stuffed animals, we made it to the Netherlands without any major drama to the relief of many of the other passengers. We did part of the trip in business class which was a bonus with the larger seats and legroom. Even when we both worked, I tended to do a lot of the child raising activities and as such, I took Jasmine to the toilet and that event is something that parents that travel with kids will relate to. Jasmine sat on the toilet and did what you do and when finished, turned so I could wipe her bottom. In the confines of the aircraft toilet, a brown streak suddenly appeared on the wall. As you do, I wiped her bottom and then proceeded to clean up the wall, to the point it could not be seen. However, there was some left in the toilet bowl that would not go even with repeated flushes. The next passenger reported to the hostess who could be seen exiting the toilet cubicle immediately after the complaint and telling the junior hostess that "boiling soapy water always works!"

Having worked in Malaysia, I knew that when you arrive into a new culture, you do not expect things to be the same and there will be differences; the Netherlands would also have its own differences. What I have found in life, is that when things are done differently by another culture, there is normally a good reason for it, so I try to never be arrogant and look harder to understand. While rare, sometimes there is no logic or a history (where something was tried but not done right), but what you see sometimes is blatantly stupid. It is on these rare occasions that you realise, maybe you can help, as long as you are sufficiently diplomatic, and went there with the right attitude.

There were some unusual experiences being in a foreign country, but as an expatriate, there are many benefits. You find you have similar issues as other expats and therefore that commonality gives you something to talk about. They do not have to be from the same country, however, similar cultures definitely assists, and we quickly found that we were mixing with people from the United States, England and other countries.

The taxi from the airport was one of the first of many unusual experiences. The company that employed Nellie had arranged everything. We arrived in the very early hours on a Sunday morning and the driver was holding a name board to get our attention. We were welcomed to the country by the driver, our luggage was eventually unloaded and put into the taxi van. Like most people in the Netherlands who interact with expatriates, the driver's English skills were good, and he started a con- versation. It turned out that he had been there twenty-four hours earlier, as the dispatcher had looked at the date we boarded the plane and had not considered the time difference.

We proceeded to travel to the township where we were to stay. He had never travelled that way before and as prior to GPS and electronic maps I recall looking at the street directory and, in the end, giving the taxi driver directions, "That must be that way!"

Accommodation initially was in a serviced hotel that had nothing near it apart from the adjacent main hotel. There was a kitchen with a dishwasher, laundry for our clothes and tea/coffee making facilities along with a collection of cooking implements. Everything was brand new and in fact, we found we were some of the first guests into the new complex. This was a self-contained apartment block for people that are just arriving in the country or, as with another family, needed temporary accommodation as they were demolishing and rebuilding their house.

It was still relatively early in the morning and we had slept on the plane. As experienced travellers will tell you, it is wise to not sleep when you arrive somewhere but you should struggle through the day and get a good night sleep in that time zone to wake up relatively fresh the next full day.

I unpacked and reassembled the bikes, inflated the tyres, and got them ready for our first outing. Nellie commenced to look for tea and coffee sachets and went across to the main hotel to get some as well as local information on where to go shopping and our first outing in the new country. The answers were a cultural surprise.

In terms of the tea and coffee, reception advised that we were in the apartment complex and that was our responsibility to buy. We also would not have much luck with shopping as they will not be open until Monday afternoon. The shopkeepers were working Saturday morning so naturally had Monday morning off. They did not grab us some of the tea and coffee from the hotel room supplies, which is what I would have expected from a service orientated organisation as an interim measure, however they did have some complimentary maps.

With the bikes assembled, a slight break after the flight, we took off for a ride. Joe realised that we had to push ourselves a bit to ensure we would adjust to the time zone, Jasmine was happy with the prospect of a playground after so long in airports, planes and the taxi, and everyone was just looking forward to what we would discover. At least I could test my navigation skills again and surely will do better than the taxi driver. We did find the supermarket along with the township, a playground for Jasmine which she enjoyed and we did not get lost.

The phone book worked (and yes this was before the era of food order phone apps) and there was a pizza delivery service which led to a well-deserved meal, albeit jet-lagged and we all had a very early night.

While the accommodation was nice, we quickly discovered it was never finished, at least not to the extent or standard that one would expect. The exhaust system over the cooker was not connected, opened a drawer and the front came off, and there were many similar minor issues. Probably one of the strangest was that Joe decided, after hours in a plane, he wanted a bath, so filled the bath with water. All was well until he stepped in and the whole bath dropped around 1.5cm (or half an inch). Fortunately, it did not leak but you could clearly see around the edge where it had dropped! Thank goodness I had a few tools for fixing the bikes so filled in a bit of time by screwing back on the drawer fronts, and a few other things, but resealing the bath and other jobs were progressively done by the builder.

The best problem I recall was the antenna connection would fail constantly and at critical times during a show. The hotel managers at first claimed it must be just the room, then just the apartment block, then it was discovered happening in the hotel as well, and then when they found it to be the microwave transmission connection to the hotel and apartment block they attributed it to unusual atmospheric conditions. How can that be? It is foggy, wet and miserable, and we are in The Netherlands so isn't that just normal atmospheric conditions? The number of different excuses, and weeks it took to fix made me question what was occurring.

The relocation agent picked us up on the Monday and took us all down to the township of Almere and advised us about some of the cultural idiosyncrasies that we had either faced or were likely to face in the coming days.

It was this first trip with the relocation agent who asked what I did. I responded that I had a base degree in Engineering, MBA and one exam which when completed would give me associate membership of the Australian Society of Certified Practicing Accountants (ASCPA) and that I had several interviews lined up. There was no response to what I had said, and the subject was quickly changed as we continued on to be registered and the local government (Gementee) building.

Over the next few days, I arranged to meet up with people who I had lined up to obtain work. The first potential employer was a traffic management company in the nearby town of Almere. It was ideal as that was where we had planned to settle as there was one of the government-funded chain of international schools that met the agreement Nellie had made with Joe. The first job interview was straight forward. The managing director outlined three positions and asked which one I would like. What could be better?

The second was a major Dutch university. This was also a good fit, as it would leverage off the work done in Australia, I would do some tutoring and research into traffic management systems throughout Europe? I left that interview convinced that I would be offered the position, which was something I rarely feel coming out of an interview!

The third was a small traffic signal company that made and installed traffic lights. It was relatively standard manufacturing and they did not seem to have any desire to move into another area of traffic management, and was therefore not a good fit. I thanked them for their time.

Two out of three is not bad, I thought, *but wait until things are confirmed.*

I spoke to the head of personnel of the first company and was offered a position, with a car, starting in two weeks. This would involve a bit of travel to manage design and deployment projects around Europe. Due to me being a non-EU citizen there was some paperwork to do and realised the potential employer was not that familiar with those requirements. They predominately hired from within the EU, and as such, we organised the head of personnel from the company that employed Nellie to spend a couple of hours with whoever they nominated to run them through all the procedures. Nellie was working at an entrepreneurial IT company; they were doing this all the time, so had offered their assistance as they were happy to transfer their knowledge to ensure the whole family settled into life in the Netherlands.

In parallel, the university contacted me, and I was told by the person that interviewed me that, "I have been informed that we are not allowed to hire you", due to a funding restriction for the research position and that it must be an EU citizen in the role. I was disappointed as it would have been an interesting and very stable position, but that was okay. I had one position that was doing what I do best, which is managing projects and people and I was in the township that we planned to live.

Frantically, we organised childcare for Jasmine so that I could start work. As Jasmine was not yet four, which is the age that children start primary school which in Dutch is *basisschool,* childcare would be essential.

This was our first year in a European winter. We had got some old overcoats from a second-hand shop to get by, and I was taking Joe to school and getting him used to the process. We would cycle to the nearby station, which was a few kilometres away, and then ride the train to Almere (one or two stops) and then walk ten minutes to the school.

At first, Joe would ignore the route and follow me blindly, not taking notice of the way we were travelling. Eventually, I said, "Okay, your turn to lead and I will follow you!" The walk home from the school to the station that afternoon took twice as long as normal, as we wound through the back streets and made a few wrong turns and I would not correct him, allowing him to focus on where he was going and learn from his mistakes. We eventually got to the station and then the next time he concentrated a bit more and made it without a mistake. A few more trips like that and I was confident to let him loose on his own. We eventually found that he could catch the one bus that weaved all over the place and took marginally longer, but he preferred travelling that way. It was only for a couple of months and then we moved into a house near the school, so while they were long tiring days for him, it was not that much of a drama.

Jasmine was still small, and I had a baby carrier backpack, so she would sit on my back for the trip. There was a crèche in Almere and I went to ask if they would accept her. At that time of the year it was freezing, with ice forming on puddles and around the edge of lakes. It was a few kilometres from the station to the crèche, and with only the second-hand overcoat and very cheap gloves, I got to the crèche and let them know I had arrived, but I was quite cold. Jasmine, I believe, was rugged up well in the backpack. They talked to her and showed us both around and managed to organise the enrolment to start. I seemed to get priority due to the starting date I had been given for work. This was fantastic because in Australia I recall the drama of getting her into a crèche when Nellie returned to work, and you often have to take a day or two and build up as they are so heavily booked. What a great system I thought, as I waited a bit longer in the foyer to be thoroughly warm before heading out, into the cold again.

It was Jasmine's first day of crèche and we got up early, showered and dressed ready for Nellie to be off to work, Joe to school and for me to get Jasmine to crèche. I was expecting to start work next week so it would be good and I had a week to ensure Jasmine was settled in. I lifted up her pyjamas to dress her ready for school and noticed small sores all over her little body, and she was clearly not herself. Nellie and I wondered what this was?

I notified the crèche that Jasmine would not be in for her first day and rang the doctor and managed to get an appointment. The relocation agent had made sure that one of her first tasks was to register at a doctor and later when other expats had not registered with a doctor, we realised how important it was.

The history of registering with one local doctor in the Netherlands has some basis in logic which is apparently to stop addicts from approaching several doctors to obtain significant quantities of prescription drugs. Apparently, it also means that doctors cannot take on too many patients. The *apotheeks* (chemist) that issue drugs are also registered and track your drugs, so the whole system is quite controlled.

The doctor (*huisarts* in Dutch) revealed she had waterpokken. "What is waterpokken?" I asked. The doctor thought about it briefly and replied, "Chickenpox". Okay, we know what we are dealing with now and he gave us instructions on how to deal with it. *Hopefully, she will be right in a week and can then start crèche,* I thought.

What to do with a sick, miserable little girl when the television keeps cutting out? The purchase of a video, colouring books, some more artist paints was the easy solution as well as lots of calamine lotion to apply to the chicken pox. With a toddler, you can get great value by playing a video over and over again and keep them entertained.

Jasmine recovered from the chicken pox, but with one minor scar above her left eye that would fade significantly in time. I recall her first day at the crèche, when the lady in charge immediately pulled up her top and inspected the scabs to make sure all had healed and did not present a danger of contagion.

Jasmine has very pale skin, which some people describe as Celtic, and is very sensitive and requires a high degree of protection. I recall her getting a condition called hand, foot and mouth disease, a virus common in children in the warmer months, and the lesions were extensive and all over her body (not just the hands, feet and around the mouth). When we took her back to the crèche in Australia after she recovered, they said they had never seen such an aggressive case with such extensive lesions.

I was offered a position by the CEO of the traffic management company personally, signed a contract and even organised training in the paperwork for their staff, so expected to start work the next week or so as agreed. Unfortunately, there was yet another cultural barrier that was put in place.

The head of personnel was a typical Dutchmen, if there is such a thing. The typical Dutchman is able to speak several languages and with the Dutch language lacking the subtleties of the English language will often come across as arrogant, they smoke heavily and drink coffee like it is a competitive sport, although I have met many Dutchmen that are the opposite. He had accepted the offer for a meeting with the personnel manager that recruited Nellie and would attend personally which was a great sign.

Unknown to us, the head of personnel from the traffic company had already resigned, attended the meeting regardless, and then dumped the task without any briefing or knowledge transfer that we had organised for him on the junior staff to process. The two weeks was then extended again and again and continued for months. Finally, I checked with the government to discover that they had or should have the paperwork to proceed with my employment. During these three months, the company had been taken over and the junior personnel staff rang with a new offer which dropped the salary significantly and took the car out of the offer until I had completed a long probation period.

Stunned, I replied politely, "Could you please repeat what you have just said," in case I misunderstood to which they stated, "It is clear you are not happy with the new conditions, so the offer is withdrawn." I never found out if it was because of the massive amount of paperwork and the staff processing it had simply had enough, the takeover that triggered the actions and not wanting additional staff, but it was possibly a combination. I felt cheated, misled and at a complete loss. Jasmine had been in childcare for months as I had expected to start work at short notice and felt their behaviour was unconscionable. It was some time before I noticed a pattern, and it was explained to me by one of my Dutch colleagues that it is normal to renegotiate a contract once the bargaining position had changed, whereas I had come from a culture that considered the obligations of a contract as fixed.

Over the coming months, I struggled to find meaningful work and was rejected interview after interview on average every few weeks, being told, "We are not allowed to hire you." I began to refer to the situation as "Fortress Europe" and while still looking after Joe, Jasmine, and all the household chores, I fell into a sense of hopelessness and despair: later given medication for depression. There was no assistance in dealing with the situation, in securing work in the Netherlands or returning to Australia where it would be possible to secure work, just medication to cope.

I also realised that I had been conned into coming to the Netherlands. There were three organisations that had told me either directly or through Nellie that I would not have trouble getting work and each of them had a vested interest:

- I do not believe the person from the company that employed Nellie deliberately lied, as he was working in a software production house that employed people from all over the world and was used to the process, but that area due to its needs was treated differently by the government to most other occupations.

- The recruitment agency that placed Nellie had a financial interest and when I contacted that recruitment company after having the job offer withdrawn to assist me, they outlined the issues and challenges I was facing so they knew precisely the situation I was in and clearly knew it, before we moved.

- The relocation agent's representative that helped us register at the local government also stated a few weeks after our arrival that she was so pleased and surprised that I had found an employer that would process the permits, that she was surprised what I had been told by her head office and thought it would be difficult to find work in a management role due to EU restrictions. Furthermore, going forward, I was unlikely that I would get the 30% rule (tax reduction that Nellie secured) as was hired from within the Netherlands. She was clearly well versed in the issues I faced and the long silence when I explained my background on my second day, when she took us for registration made sense.

The recruitment and relocation organisations knew I would face difficulty before I left Australia, but both had a financial incentive for me to agree to the move and I believe to this day had acted unconscionably. The cost to me personally was extreme, to say the least. Nellie was funding all of us but was on a good salary with expat benefits that included a 30% tax reduction rule and as it kept looking like I would secure work, Jasmine was kept in the crèche as it would be hard to get her back in if we withdrew her.

Nellie seemed to be going okay at her work. Just as we had been flown from Melbourne to Sydney for a lavish function with my work in Australia, we were treated well at her work celebrations. We occasionally had dinner with expatriate colleagues including the lead editor for the software manuals who was teaching Nellie a lot about writing software manuals and it was clear that she was learning a lot. Nellie possibly felt inadequate as she had never worked as a writer or editor before. As her first 12-month appraisal was approaching Nellie may have feared for her employment and unknown to me, began applying for alternative employment.

It was nearly a year after arriving in the Netherlands, and, constantly being rejected for work, I wanted to relocate back to Australia as per the agreement. I was suffering terribly and recall breaking down regularly and curling up in the corner of a room. Unable to sleep and occasionally watching videos to try and take my mind off of what was happening.

I recall telling Nellie that I wanted us to return to Australia when the year was up. It was met initially with silence and no discussion, no emotion and Nellie seemed to simply ignore what I had said.

It was at this point that Nellie did the unthinkable. She filed in the Netherlands for sole custody of Jasmine. I was served with documents and Nellie explained what they were and gave me an ultimatum. As a de facto couple which was not recognised in the Netherlands, there was no need for divorce. There had been no discussion about this since I had stated we should all return home days earlier. I could move back to Australia and Jasmine would stay, or I could continue to raise the kids and if I agreed she would try to purchase a house with both our names on the title. I was left with the impossible choice of never seeing Jasmine again or becoming totally subservient, trapped in the reclaimed swamp that is the Netherlands and under Nellie's complete control with no say in what would happen. Nellie had in one swift blow utilised the state to perform the ultimate act of coercive control. Culturally, I knew that in the Netherlands I would have no chance at custody as kids were always placed with the mother as best as I could determine, no funds to seek legal advice and in a depressed state, I was beaten. I agreed to her demand as I believed I had little choice as Jasmine was so important to me.

We did not return home to Australia, but the basic trust that I had for Nellie was never regained.

It is only with the clarity of hindsight that what was happening became evident:

- It was nearly a decade later that it was revealed that Nellie had lied with respect to the Australian property and had taken on significant debt, which as a de facto couple I was also liable for.

- The conversations about how she felt marginalised in babysitting clubs and being put down as a single mother meant that I was there mainly to fulfil her perceived needs and perhaps it was never a healthy relationship with mutual benefits and understanding.

- Having me reject some job offers while in Australia that would have seen me working interstate during the week and less able to look after the kids, was to me, now viewed as selfish.

- The move to the Netherlands removed me from friends and family support and isolated me in a country where I did not even speak the language.

I actually will never know if she collaborated in the lies about my likelihood of getting work in the Netherlands and the difficulties I would face, but clearly she lied about the agreement to move back to Australia after twelve months. Jasmine was now in school which starts when they are four years old and I was hoping I would climb out of the unemployment scenario. There was not even sufficient funds to purchase a coffee and I had no say over finances that were concealed. There was nowhere to turn to for help apart from those offering medications, no employment services for those that were not Dutch, I did not understand the dynamics of family violence, and even if I did there would be no services for male victims. The threats to never see my daughter again with the aid of lawyers if I did not do what she wanted was very targetted. Perhaps Nellie had done some legal research, but I knew nothing about The Hague Agreement for repatriation of children and even if I did return to Australia, filed for Jasmine's repatriation, we had become Dutch residents and now know that litigation would have been difficult and the return after twelve months, would have been denied. In hindsight, all of this showed a clear pattern of coercive and controlling behaviour.[4] Unfortunately, the greater control Nellie had, the more brazen the behaviours. The complete lack of empathy for others became more evident over time, and while there was a reprieve, it was only to get worse.

Nellie finally revealed that she had been looking for another job and was interviewed for a job with a telecommunications company. It was a time when telecoms were being deregulated from a monopoly provider and as the Dutch education system tends to focus on business, there was a shortage of technically orientated people. During the interview, they heard of my background and asked for a resume and we were both employed by the same company in separate departments.

---

[4] https://www.womensaid.org.uk/information-support/what-is-domestic-abuse/coercive-control/

4

A new normality in a new home

We had both been working for some time for the telecoms company and the daily commute was substantial. We did the math and if we purchased a house and stayed there for 18 months and sold it, then financially it would be similar to renting, as rent was not tax deductible, however interest on paying off the family home was tax deductible. The reverse of how it is in Australia. As such we began looking at properties and purchased a home together. It was only a few years old and was very close to our employer. There was an international secondary school near the new location so Joe was catered for and I found a new primary school (*basisschool*) for Jasmine. The house we purchased meant that work was around ten minutes by bicycle and Jasmines' school halfway between home and work. Joe's secondary school was another five minutes past our work so he could either ride his bicycle or catch a tram or bus with a short walk to school.

The health system in the Netherlands has some disadvantages that I found out over the years. One of them that I originally thought was good practice was the exclusivity of the general practitioners (in Dutch known as the *huisarts*).

As you can only go to the practice where registered, when they are overbooked, you have a problem. This is common on a Monday morning to remove the backlog of anyone who has got sick over the weekend. The receptionists will always try to put you off and spread the work out over the week and this is common in all the Dutch medical practices.

We woke up one morning and Nellie discovered Jasmine could not get up and was in significant pain. Nellie told me that Jasmine has a stomach bug and not to worry and that I would need to stay at home to look after her. I immediately went into her room to find her in the foetal position curled up in extreme pain. I managed to lay her on her back and pressed her abdomen on the left and right-hand side with greater pain when pressing the left. I had basic first aid training many years ago and back in my construction days was even registered to drive an ambulance on the construction site but knew my limitations and became very concerned and afraid that it may be serious and should call in help. Hopefully, it was just a stomach bug, but I had to be sure.

Nellie dismissed my concerns and repeated, "It's just a stomach bug. I'm off to work and you will need to ring in sick. I would not bother taking her to the doctor as you will not get in on a Monday morning." It took some negotiation, but Nellie did wait for me to go down to the doctors to make an appointment. We had recently moved to Amsterdam and we lived in a four-bedroom, three-level, modern house, and the doctor was only about ten houses down the road on the nearest corner. I returned quickly from the doctors after making the booking, informed Nellie that I would take Jasmine down to the doctors and look after her. Nellie left for work, and I rang in and notified my managers that I would be off for the day.

I dug out Jasmine's pram from below the stairwell (as it had been put away as no longer in use) and got her down to the doctor's surgery with 10 minutes to spare and signalled to the receptionist who nodded. I waited with Jasmines' head on my lap and after seeing people enter and leaving got up and asked how much longer they expect would be the wait, to be told, "You were meant to be here an hour ago and have missed your appointment, so will not be seen today." There must have been a communication issue as half nine means 8:30 a.m. in Dutch but sometimes I think in English and so would be 9:30 a.m. but I had specifically queried them and said, "So you mean between nine and ten o'clock?" They stated, "Yes, when I made the booking." Fortunately, at that point, the doctor walked out of her office. She had only recently qualified as a doctor and had excellent English language skills as she had spent several years in England and excellent communication skills in general; which is what you need even in your own country. I suspect she overheard what had been said. She saw Jasmine lying there in pain and intervened and said to reception, "I will see her next."

I do not recall if I simply carried Jasmine in and or put her back in the pusher, but I remember putting her on the examination table. The doctor explained that she only had this (holding up her stethoscope) and her hands but is concerned. She wrote out a referral and instructed me to proceed immediately to the local ziekenhuis (which is a hospital). Where was the hospital? I had not been in the area long and she proceeded to give directions and advised I would see signs. Nellie's contract included a car, but she rarely drove: our work was so close, so she never got used to driving on the opposite side of the road to Australia and therefore the car was available at home. I got Jasmine home, into the car and off to the hospital and parked the car. Entering the main hospital foyer from the car park, I was looking for signs and was obviously lost and I was approached by a security guard. I showed him the referral and was immediately sent out of the hospital and back on the street to the emergency entrance.

The Emergency Departments in the Netherlands are quite secure and passed the referral through the slot under the bulletproof glass. We were immediately buzzed in and registered in the hospital administration system. I am not sure of the practices worldwide, but as soon as the first physical examination was conducted, I was asked for a urine *monster*. My Dutch was basic, but having seen the container I remembered that *monster* in Dutch is "specimen" in English. After washing my hands, the monster (not my daughter) was handed over and they appeared to fast track the test and got the results back an hour or so later. This confirmed that a blood test was required and again, another long wait that seemed to last forever while pathology analysed that. The blood tests came back: there was definitely something wrong and an ultrasound was required.

Realising I was a bit lost, someone escorted us up to the reception area for the ultrasound. The technician was good and after putting the scanner on Jasmine was able to see how enlarged her appendix was and while unable to offer a medical opinion his four or five words while doing the scan said it all. At the end of the scan, the technician stated, "The report would be given to the person in charge and sent down immediately." I knew before leaving the room that the appendix would need to come out and while concerned, I knew that it was urgent and was relieved that we were in a major hospital.

By the time we got back down to the Emergency room, a young doctor was waiting as I entered the door with Jasmine and bluntly issued the prognosis, "She has appendicitis and we have a surgeon who will stay back and do her next. We have to operate, there is no alternative." There was no argument from me and wondered if he expected an argument or expected me to want more information and lengthy discussions when there may not have been time. Jasmine was in surgery an hour or so later that afternoon.

While this was all happening, I was ringing up work and trying to get hold of Nellie and informing what they were doing, such as a blood test now and how things were progressing. We were not able to use mobile phones in the emergency ward so there was a bit of running in and out and I had to balance leaving Jasmine and keeping people informed. I rang my mother to let her know before the operation, and while she was half a world away, she was still involved. I still recall the last frantic call to work around 4:00 p.m. and they could not find Nellie, rang home and she was not there, then rang back a work colleague and told him our daughter is due to be operated on shortly and if he could see if he could find Nellie, so that Nellie could see Jasmine before she goes under the anaesthetic. My work colleague also failed to find Nellie, however, she finally turned up (after knock-off time) just as they were wheeling Jasmine into surgery.

Nellie had stopped off at home and left a note for Joe, so when he got home, he would know what was going on. As I had been with Jasmine all day, I let Nellie (as only one person was allowed to accompany the patient) to escort her the last few metres toward the operating theatre.

After what seemed an extremely long wait, it was confirmed that Jasmine was out of surgery and okay and we would be able to see her shortly. After quickly seeing Jasmine to ensure all was well, Nellie went home to get Joe his dinner and let him know Jasmine was alright while I stayed behind.

They allowed one of the parents to stay overnight for the next few nights as Jasmine was so young. I, for whatever reason, was the one who stayed in the hospital overnight and then would go to work in the morning and do a short day of work, get some sleep and return to the hospital. The managers at work said not to bother to come in as they all knew what had happened that day from the messages relayed through my colleague. Eventually, after a few days, Jasmine could come home, and Nellie took a week's holiday, or I now suspect was carer's leave. There were new pyjamas from her grandmother with a card and well-wishes and of course, she needed some special food as required after the operation. I was most impressed as they use a glue to close the surgery, innovative at the time and there would not be Frankenstein-type stitches and a scar.

The day after the operation, I asked Nellie to drop into the school personally and tell them that Jasmine would not be in for several weeks. The teacher was apparently a little shocked as it is unusual for appendicitis at such a young age. Jasmine received a card from all the kids in her class and was welcomed back when she eventually returned. Several times over the next few years I recall Jasmine asking me, "Why did I have an appendix?" and then the explanation that everyone has one but yours got an infection and had to be removed, it's very common, but you were very young when it happened to you. I would reinforce how common appendicitis was by telling her of how my cousin had his removed and that I had to get his car and take it home from hospital. I told her of a friend that spent eighteen months in Antarctica and a requirement was that they have their appendix removed before going as it was so common. Every now and then, sometimes months or years later the same question "Why did I have an appendix?" would be raised.

Families are always having medical emergencies and dramas, and ours was no different. Joe, as a teenager had a piece of New Zealand lamb that he had not chewed properly and about the length of a domino became stuck just below his windpipe. Nellie just sat there while I jumped into action and took him to the emergency entrance of the hospital where they eventually called in a specialist to do a gastroscopy to have it pulled out from his throat, saving his life. All these incidents would have been considered standard in a family dynamic, but it was the differences between the levels of emotions and reactions between Nellie and I that always had me confused.

After the incident with Joe and the lamb, Nellie thanked me profusely for seeing the signs of danger and helping her son by rushing him to emergency. The way she expressed herself, I found myself annoyed with her but held back as I usually did. I regarded Joe as a son (which included all the normal things like taking him on holidays, cooking meals or attending some terrible parent-teacher nights) and rushed Joe to hospital as he needed help. I would do the same for a stranger and did not do it for Nellie because Joe was Nellie's son. I do not think it was just how Nellie expressed herself, but I genuinely believe she thought that way. In terms of Joe, I know he regarded me as his father in terms of a family structure and even referred to us as "his parents."

Many years later, Jasmine was told the story about her appendicitis and responded, "I'm not letting Mum ever look after my health." Little did I realise how significant the event was at the time, along with Nellie's reaction to the kids' medical needs. When I finally left the Netherlands nearly 10 years later, my health was not the best and I needed some special documentation and advice for travelling. The doctor replied that, "I have never seen Jasmine or Joe with their mother, it is always you," which was something that just happened. We both worked similar hours at the same company, I was generally the one taking kids to sports and just like with Joe and the lamb or Jasmine and the appendicitis or even years before with the cat, I suppose I was just noticed a little more, tended to act and while I had not noticed the pattern, clearly the doctor had.

Like most families, the household duties were split up evenly if not formally. On the days Jasmine had swimming lessons, Nellie would take Jasmine to school and I would start and finish work early to take Jasmine to swimming lessons. It was on one of those mornings, Jasmine was ahead of Nellie and crashed into another cyclist damaging his bike. Nellie upon catching up provided a phone number so they could sort out the damage and we heard nothing. A couple of weeks later, we were taking Jasmine to school and were both confronted by the man Jasmine had run into: he was extremely angry. The phone number Nellie gave him was wrong which I immediately put it down to a mistake and that she must have been flustered so I took control. I showed him my phone which had the number on the back created with a labelling machine (as I would show this to people at work so they could contact me and ensure there were no issues due to accents), and he agreed to let me get to work and call the insurance company. A short time later that same morning I got an abusive call from the man that Jasmine had crashed into as he must have thought I was not going to reimburse him and not do anything and was wanting immediate payment. I had checked with a Dutch colleague who said based upon what happened we would be liable and also checked with the insurance company. I actually couldn't understand him well and had a Dutch colleague talk to him on the phone who said his Dutch is not good. I explained that I had investigated the insurance and that the amount was too small, so I would simply pay him directly the value of the bicycle. I do not know if he did not believe me or our language skills meant he did not understand, it then escalated into death threats. It was only a matter of hours since giving him my phone number, but over a week since Nellie had given him a false phone number, so his level of trust in us was low; that may have been why the conflict escalated. After the first threat to kill us all, I responded that I would see him at the police station and pay him the value of the bicycle there. I got hold of Nellie and we both left work early and proceeded to collect Jasmine and go to the police station. More frantic calls were received, he refused to go to the police station and still more threats to kill us. I enlisted the help of the police who rang him and helped get his address so I could pay him off, but I must say, they were not that helpful and would not facilitate the transaction in the safety of the police complex. Hours later, I delivered cash to an address he nominated but the person that I paid, and the name of the person we thought we were dealing with, was not the person that Jasmine had the accident with according to Nellie. False identities had been used by the person Jasmine had crashed into. Something was clearly wrong and I wanted to make sure his stand over tactics would not continue so I threatened that if I ever saw either of them again, there would be a full statement made to the police. When we told colleague at work that had spoken to him (that thought he had terrible Dutch), she suggested that he was probably an illegal African immigrant hiding in that area with friends or relatives. All that drama, because Nellie gave out the wrong phone number!

As a family of four living in Amsterdam, we would ride our bikes to work and school; it kept us healthy in many respects. In the last years in Amsterdam, I estimated we were doing around 8,000km by bike (between the four of us) and around 4,000km by car (which could include an annual holiday to France or elsewhere). As such, bike maintenance was reasonably important and I kept in the shed plenty of spare brake pads, tyres and tubes for the constant repairs that I carried out of an evening or weekend.

Some nights in winter I can remember having to go out to the little timber garden shed that I had fitted out with a bike hoist to replace a tyre that had come home with a puncture or on weekends a bit more time to replace brake pads and sometimes cables. If it involved replacing a gear train, I would normally leave that to the bike shop. It wasn't much of a saving doing it myself, but it was one of those things one does and meant the bike was ready for the next day and besides, I always enjoyed working with my hands.

Joe, was getting more mature and so he was expected to do some of the work on his own bike or be present when I did work. While he did not like it, on many occasions, I am sure he learned some things by osmosis. Certainly, he was getting out the tools and replacing wheels on his skateboard and had a shot at things.

Near the end of the relationship, I stopped maintaining Nellie's bike. When you replace a gear or brake cable, they often stretch a little and so it needs to be adjusted a couple of weeks later. Unfortunately, I was being called stupid and useless, and my explanations about the cables stretching went without acceptance. I stopped maintaining her bike and said to just take it down to the bike shop, as they do not charge much more than the parts. What I quickly found is that she would take it to the shop for the initial work, take it back for an adjustment sometimes twice, and then when it was still not quite right, Nellie would plead for me to fix it, as the bike shop were, in her eyes, useless. As the cables had stretched and already been twice adjusted, I would often do the final adjustment and be credited with fixing it. I learned to never fix her bike if it required new gear cables on the first occasion and she never accepted the explanation that the cables stretched, regardless of who did the work but whoever did the job was regarded as useless.

While I was always supportive of the kids, Nellie would put them down just like she did me when fixing the bikes and so many other examples that would need a series of books to recount the incidents. During the relationship, I remember Nellie saying to Jasmine, "I don't know what's wrong with you, I was baking cakes when I was your age." However, Nellie kept Jasmine out of the kitchen and me for that matter, when she was in the kitchen, and I saw it as putting everyone else down, so she saw herself as better. It was something I always tried to compensate for with the kids. Rather than letting Jasmine give up in her A certificate in swimming, I would take her and give her lessons myself and even enrolled her at a different swimming school. She got her A and we were both excited and tried to ensure she learned never to give up, that she could do things when she tried. She went on to get her B, C, played water polo and was in the top one-third of swimmers in the region for competitions. It was activities and encouragement like that, that I hope instilled tenacity and resilience.

I was frequently credited for poor communication during the relationship. Communication may be expressing, understanding, or listening and any of these may have been the problem, but know that we should always strive to improve. In many discussions, I found myself on the receiving end of Nellie's sudden change in demeanor and anger and I would simply avoid the conflict rather than challenge it. There were many similar events to the bikes and threats would ensue if Nellie did not get her way.

In terms of fixing the bikes and similar situations, later in the relationship I now believe that my attempts to avoid conflict were actually an attempt to manage an abusive relationship. If Nellie would start to raise her voice, start yelling or was clearly going that way, which was what happened when Jasmine had appendicitis, and Nellie wanted to go to work, then I would acquiesce or walk away and retreat to the bedroom and rarely confront her even after she had calmed down. Nowadays, many people would classify her behaviour as domestic violence and my inability to do something more constructively, such as positively and effectively confronting her, were skills I lacked and so I avoided conflict.

There were many incidents that in my mind, I simply explained away, rationalised, dismissed and avoided. As was the case with taking the kids to the doctors, I never looked at the whole picture, but the doctor and others did. I am still somewhat dumbfounded of how blind I must have been.

Dinner with some American friends in the first year proved to be quite interesting. I recall the hospitality of a colleague of Nellie's, with us all going to their house for dinner. As part of the dinner conversation, they asked if we would be going home for Christmas to see our families. This was a typical conversation for expatriates, and it was not unusual for a husband or wife to travel back for a funeral or special occasion. In this case, the whole family were heading back for Christmas, booking their tickets well in advance.

The conversation proceeded, and we said that no, we would not be going back as there are four of us and that airfares are related to the distance travelled or time in the air, so would be too expensive as it is around twenty-two hours to home. "But nowhere is that far," they responded. "You could not possibly travel in an airplane for twenty-two hours." Clearly, the distances involved, and geography was not the strong suit for those American expatriates. In any case, it was logical that we did not travel back every year, as the jet lag and costs involved in travelling halfway around the world means that you don't, unless you make a real holiday of it (much more than a week) to get much benefit.

It was some time after that dinner when we were given permission to take Jasmine's friend Ayla with us for an outing on an international trip to Warner Bros Movie World theme park in Germany which was a two-hour drive. The girls loved the trip and went on lots of rides and managed to see the Police Academy stunt show. As part of the warm up the master of ceremonies asked all the people in the crowd:

"Who is from England?" To get quite a few cheers

"Who is from France?" To secure a reaction of more cheers

Several other countries were asked and then:

"Who is from Australia?" To which our daughter sat there motionless without batting an eyelid! Nellie and I waved our hands and yelled yes in the spirit of the show!

Several other countries were mentioned and then:

"Who is from the Netherlands?" To which the two girls jumped out of their seats waving their hands in the air, jumping up and down cheering!

Nellie and I looked at each other, completely stunned and concerned both at the reaction from who came from Australia and who came from the Netherlands. I believe that was the moment we decided it was time to do a trip back to Australia.

The trip that European summer which is the Australian winter was around four weeks long. We flew to Australia and stayed with my mother for a couple of weeks before flying back via Cairns (which is in Queensland, Australia) and Hong Kong.

I had taken Jasmine out shopping before the trip. She had picked out a new suitcase, and we purchased lots of Dutch souvenirs such as cheese cutting boards (without the cheese), salt and pepper shakers, fridge magnets, and many other things. When doing the final pack, I was very pleased at how helpful Jasmine was being, with the packing of many of the presents in her brand-new suitcase.

When we got to Australia, she opened her suitcase and we were able to distribute the presents over the coming days. Unfortunately, we quickly found that her helpfulness had a catch. I had told her that clothes were generally cheaper in Australia and very cheap in Hong Kong. What she had done however is emptied most of her clothes out of the suitcase and brought practically nothing, so we were forced to go out on a girls clothes shopping spree. Some of my friend's daughters thought Jasmine had shown tremendous initiative! We promised her after all, that we would go shopping, as the exchange rate was very favourable and she could get things that she could not get in Europe, so she felt special! In any case, it was cute, and she needed more clothes as she was growing fast!

You need to appreciate that Jasmine was extremely excited about staying with her nana (aka Grandmother). Nana had visited her in the Netherlands and saw her go to school for her first day. We had arrived in Australia at around 4:00 a.m. local time and by 8:00 a.m. the excitement had worn off and all Jasmine wanted to do was sleep and could hardly stand with the jet lag. She did get up for a little while for dinner but spent nearly twenty-four hours in bed and got up the next morning. Nellie and I were given the main bedroom, Jasmine stayed with Nana in the guest room and Joe given a camp bed in the lounge. The next morning, we drove to where my brother lived and then the first, very cautious and uncertain questions started.

Jasmine said with enormous hesitation, "Daaaad."

I responded, "Yes."

Jasmine said again with enormous hesitation—it felt like I could almost hear her processing her thoughts, working out the question or even if she should ask, "Daaaad."

I responded, "Yes, what is it, Jasmine?"

Jasmine then finally responded with, "Daaaad, why are the houses so flat?"

It was good observation as what we had been living in a country and area where multiple story houses are the norm (ground floor, first floor and top floor or in some cultures first, second and third floor) and that was most of the properties in the Netherlands. I can remember seeing single-story houses in some of the country areas but they were not that common. I explained that it was just different and how the houses were more spread out and did not need the multi-storey as people had cars when these areas were developed unlike many of the places in Europe.

The next occasion was on a day trip to Portsea and a walk along the pier, Jasmine said with enormous hesitation, "Daaaad."

I responded, "Yes?"

Jasmine said again with enormous hesitation and it again felt like I could almost hear her processing her thoughts and working out the question just like with the flat house question, "Daaaad."

I responded, "Yes, what is it, Jasmine?"

Jasmine then finally responded with, "Daaaad ... why is the water that colour?"

I often described the North Sea, especially near the harbour inlets where they dredge, as having a colour closer to dirty milk chocolate. The water in the canals is generally just a black colour, although you can see the bottom at certain times of the year. It was an interesting conversation explaining to Jasmine that the water was clean and free of the mud that is typical of the water off the Netherlands.

Jasmine and I visited many of my friends and took along a VHS tape and on one occasion watched it with my friend's daughter that was not much older. She enjoyed going to school one day with her cousin to see what an Australian school was like. Jasmine was very studious and wanted to know what to say to a class full of Australian kids, so we worked on something to tell the kids her age (well actually 1 year older), about the Netherlands. She told them some things and then counted from 1 to 30 in Dutch. The kids were fascinated in that for thirty-one (31), it is een en dertig (or 1 and 30). I am told they asked other questions and Jasmine participated in a Math class as one of the students. She indicated it was easy, but she did come from a fairly good public school in the Netherlands. We also went on an array of outings including family barbecues and trips to the zoo with her cousins.

Clearly, the trip was paying dividends as she began to again experience the love of the extended family and understand some of the lifestyle associated with Australia.

In stark contrast was Nellie. She seemed to try to isolate herself from my family and we only went to see one of her brothers (Greg from the airfield who did not seem interested). We seemed to spend most of the time with Nellie talking to her former sister-in-law. Nellie spent a lot of time with her friend Felicia who was an unfortunate lady with severe arthritis but seemed to get by as a single mum. Felicia was a loud talker which sounds like an episode of Seinfeld, however, was a nice person but even Nellie would walk away after spending time with her with a headache. Nellie would often say that, "Joe is mine and Jasmine is yours," as if she had always predetermined the shape of a separated family and the lack of integration of friends was in hindsight, just another sign of the compartmentalisation of her life.

We then flew up to Cairns and stayed in a self-contained unit and were able to walk around the tourist area and do some trips such as up to the Daintree forest, Kuranda railway, and of course out to one of the islands on the Great Barrier Reef.

The next stop was Hong Kong. This included, "The Big Buddha and Po Lin Monastery", up to "The Peak Tram", various markets, a bus tour and of course, a trip to Macau before returning to the Netherlands.

The holiday was a huge success from my perspective as the kids had got to see a little part of Australia, of which they were citizens, spent time with relatives and generally had a good time. Of course, we stockpiled essentials like some medications that was some trouble to get in The Netherlands such as Phenergan (which was the only thing that helped with Jasmine's reaction to mosquitoes) and of course, "Minties" and "Tim Tams." Even plastics for Microwaves seemed to be difficult to get at that stage in the Netherlands as they seemed to be slow at adopting the new cooking technology.

The second holiday to Australia several years later was also a great trip. Nellie, in her usual style, decided that I should spend time with my family alone, and Nellie and Joe would come later. Jasmine and I took off and had two weeks in Melbourne with my mother and one task, was to help with the purchase of a new car. As my mother was elderly, she believed it would be the last car that she would ever purchase and wanted it to be a new one. She really did not need much help but talked it through with her and test drove a few vehicles and then searched for the best deal. I remember doing the same thing and test driving a car for my grandfather many years earlier. When he was no longer able to drive, he gifted it to my mother and this was the car I was now helping to replace which was best described as "having character". It was of course quite dated, needed a stick to hold open the boot, and with leaded fuel not being sold in the coming months, had to be replaced. We got a good deal, and as a bonus, the salesman said we could have the new car and keep the trade in for a couple of weeks which allowed Nellie, myself and the children to use it for a holiday.

In the first two weeks, the outings were great as Jasmine and I took my mother to places like the Ballarat Wildlife Park where you can purchase bags of food and hand feed the kangaroos. The keeper was cleaning out the wombat enclosure, and for those of you that think a wombat is a slow and docile creature you are very mistaken. The wombat took off at a great pace with the keeper racing after it and Jasmine joining in the chase. There was very supervised patting of a koala whose name was Caramello. Caramello is the name of a very famous chocolate covered caramel treat in the shape of a koala that was popular in the past! A visit to Sovereign Hill (a recreated gold mining town of the 1860's) and of course the other zoos with her cousins were also on the agenda and in the evenings, Jasmine would spend with her Nana or joined me to catch up with friends. Between Nana twice visiting the Netherlands, the holidays in Australia and the regular presents, Jasmine and Nana were very close.

The new car was ready just before Nellie and Joe arrived and after a good sleep to get over the jet lag, we packed up the old car and headed off. For the next two weeks, we managed to get along the Great Ocean Road to see the "Twelve Apostles." There is a great place to go for a walk of a night time in the rainforests of the Otways where you can see the glow worms and once your eyes adjust, it is a wonderland and is like looking up at the stars at night (neither of which you see in the Netherlands due to their atmospheric conditions). Onto Mount Gambier to see the "Blue Lakes" and then to Wilpena Pound in the Flinders Ranges before returning to my mother's. It was probably over 3,000km round trip (2000 miles), but that did not change the value of the car that was probably sent to a wrecker and crushed shortly after dropping it off at the car dealership. It was a good 4 weeks for Jasmine and myself, and a good two weeks for Joe who experienced another part of Australia that even many Australian's haven't seen.

In the last year of Dutch primary education, the children are given a test to determine their academic ability. It is a standardised testing regime and heaven help the kids that are sick on the day and go badly. The standardised test is meant to indicate the secondary school stream that the kids will be placed in the following year, so it is absolutely critical.

The Dutch secondary school system consists of three levels. Essentially the best students go to the top schools and are expected to become doctors, lawyers and leaders; with the second level students are expected to get through and have a reasonable job; while the lowest level are not really expected to get through secondary school and will be relegated to manual jobs whether they be skilled, such as mechanics or bricklayers or garbage collectors. There are ways to go from one level to the other (maybe an additional year), and within the system there are many sub-categories.

I personally feel it was not ideal, as kids mature at different rates. I also experienced firsthand from my tertiary undergraduate degree, that many of the kids in the Engineering course were extremely bright and got through secondary school with minimal work. Unfortunately, several of the extremely bright kids had never really learned to work hard and study, then failed in the second year of university, so I have always been concerned with these, point-in-time assessments.

Jasmine had been educated in Dutch primary schools and was given a few extra Dutch lessons as she had not been brought up in a Dutch household and she excelled. She had done excellent in the testing and was in the top 5% nationally. This was particularly good as she had come from a home where the parents essentially knew little Dutch and had enormous difficulty helping her at school.

It had never prevented me from trying to help her. When she started primary school, I became the source of amusement for other parents, trying to fit in. I would read Dutch books to my daughter like the other parents as I dropped her off at school to help her settle in. I can still recall one book called *De kleine beer ben bang bij de donker* which translates to *The Little Bear is Scared of the Dark* with lots of pictures of a cute little white (polar) bear in a human house with lamps. Who would have guessed that this early effort would help get her to the point where she would be admitted into the best secondary schools in the area?

We had always discussed that Jasmine would go to the International Secondary School for her secondary education where her brother attended. This is a network of schools that are funded to the same level as the Dutch Secondary Schools with the only condition that they teach Dutch as a subject. With Nellie's agreement, I registered our intention to put her in the International School, commonly referred to as IS, and Jasmine was quite excited as we rode together and submitted the enrolment forms.

The IS was, however, having issues and the parents were getting very upset. The management wanted a purpose-built new school rather than the government supplied building and parents were worried about annual enrolment fees spiralling upwards and potential bankruptcy from such over-investment as some had seen this happen elsewhere. The IS was also part of a non-for-profit (*stitching* in Dutch) and another school in the stitching ran at a fraction of the price and many wanted the finance books opened up as suspected cross-subsidisation.

The parents asked me to get involved and stand for a position on a legally mandated parent, teacher and management committee which I discovered at one public meeting had the power to petition the government to remove management if things were not in order. At the second meeting however, the agenda changed as a student had died by suicide and rumours circulated about a note that was found. According to one parent, the suicide note contained the message that, "I don't want to be a man." Joe was one of the less academically motivated students and would get the lecture by the careers counsellor, "You are nearly 18, nearly a man, you have to put some effort in and make something of yourself." It must have been devastating for the parents, and Joe told me that the careers counsellor was dodging all students that were not "academically motivated" that he had been given "the talk" and wondered if the careers counsellor ever got counselling.

The highest of the three levels of Dutch secondary schools teaches lots of languages (French, German) as well as English and Dutch in the first year and then more languages in the second year (Latin and others). The local highest level schools also did most of their teaching in English and if she went there, then Jasmine would mix with the top students and therefore seen as a great alternative to the IS. Jasmine was always going to be more art and humanities focused which I accepted, but must admit, not being involved in the school at either committee level or helping her academically as I was more mathematics, physics, chemistry orientated was something that disappointed me.

There were so many concerns with the IS that I agreed, Jasmine would be better off in the highest level of the Dutch system and that was where she went.

Life continued to move at the usual pace. There was a request to have Nellie's cousins' daughters come for a brief stay. The two girls were with a sports group touring various countries and were uncomfortable with the current host so when their father, Nellie's cousin asked if they could stay with us if he flew them across, of course, I said yes. Jasmine, Joe and I loved having guests; however, Nellie was always less receptive. We loved to have guests and entertain, everybody that is, but Nellie. Maybe it was because of the dysfunctional links with her own siblings or maybe simply the effort involved. Having guests meant preparing the house and preparing for some sight-seeing opportunities. Jasmine loved the idea that she had cousins and as they were a few years older, they were big girls to her! The two girls also seemed to enjoy Jasmine's company and watched several movies from her collection which had grown enormously from the first one we purchased when she had chicken pox. Jasmine and I took them sightseeing to places like Old Naarden Vesting which is a fortress township and the Ijsselmeer which is the great dyke that keeps out the sea. Nellie however, stayed behind saying she had seen it before and just seemed to have no interest in showing them the country she lived in. Even on the day they arrived, I shuffled appointments to pick them up at the airport whereas Nellie stayed at work and was simply not interested in greeting them. While Nellie did most of the work with preparing the room, preparing some of the meals for the larger household, I cannot think of any additional activity she participated in with her relatives.

I have forever been surprised at the (lack of) hospitality Nellie exhibited and the relationship with her family and now her extended family. I often wonder was this her way of distancing herself further, creating isolation and protecting herself? It was something that I had never seen before and still find it strange. Looking back, I now realised that this also extended to us (Joe, Jasmine and myself). Holidays to various European countries were decided against by Nellie with the explanation that, "I have been there before and not be of interest to me." She simply did not want to share something she had experienced in her past such as visiting Poland or Italy with us. It did not seem to matter what others may want, she would either dismiss or would listen and debate against our suggestions and as always, I compromised, and she got her way.

Nellie simply seemed to have a general lack of empathy to process and act upon the needs of others, both an emotional and physical level. Jasmine's appendicitis was one of many incidents and I recall while Jasmine was being toilet trained in Australia, seeing her scream while peeing and I told Nellie that I will take her to the doctor. I had no idea what was wrong, but the diagnosis was a urinary tract infection. It was only after the diagnosis that Nellie said that she had seen that the day before and she had suffered that in her past and it is really painful. Why she did not have the empathy to act upon what she saw when someone was suffering? I still do not understand.

Nellie did however, accompany me to the occasional function with the Lions Club. Because of that association, I would often meet ambassadors and dignitaries and even judges of war crimes tribunals and would have dinner with people that were making the world news. They would join the service club and in that environment were out of the public spotlight and were just normal people doing a high profile and extraordinary jobs. Nellie would always want to attend the more public functions, but in hindsight, it was never to support me, but to be able to say to others that she had met some of the people I called friends.

Nellie didn't seem to enjoy parenting and while I had to admit, parent-teacher nights for Joe were disappointing, she would refer to the kids as a duty rather than how I saw them, as a treasure that we were entrusted to help grow and achieve. The extent of the difference surprised me many times and especially when the time came for Jasmine to go shopping for her first proper bra and although I had in the past purchased undergarments including crop tops, this was different. When I discussed the shopping needs with Nellie and suggested that she take her the response was, "No, you do the shopping with Jasmine so you can do it, this is no different to anything else." Sadly, for Jasmine that mother-daughter bond seemed absent and I was left with the uncomfortable task of assisting Jasmine. In this, and other cases, was something I believe that Nellie should have done all along. It was an enormous relief as we went into one shop and I recognised the wife of a work colleague who was working there. I immediately introduced Jasmine and she attended to her. It seemed my perceptions of what motherhood is, and how a mother should love certain activities with her daughter, were often tested.

What was most surprising was the reaction when Jasmine went to purchase more bras sometime later. She had gone with a friend (thank goodness, as I remained uncomfortable) and her mother … well let's say, her mother's attitude had not evolved. This time she had purchased a "B" cup. Nellie noticed this and within a week she also had a full set of new bras. Normally she was a size "A", but it seemed she suddenly needed to be a "B"! The cause and effect were staggering, as if there was a competition and she could not let her daughter have a larger bra size then her.

These were just some of the events over a period of time which left me questioning what was going on in Nellie's head. On each occasion when I raised the subject of why she thought that way or why she didn't want to do something, there would be some excuse or I would be dismissed and the conversation cut short. Once again, I simply accepted that Nellie was a little different to most and at one end of the normal spectrum.

5

The takeover, broken arms and broken heart

Companies are constantly looking at the benefits of re-organising their structure, outsourcing and acquisitions and our employer was no different. While many people knew we were a couple, more did not, and I recall the funny incidents like both of us being booked for telecoms training in Germany. The person doing the bookings suddenly realised and wanted to put us in the same room to which we responded, don't bother as that would give us a room to accommodate Jasmine's au pair and take Jasmine along. Another incident was when someone saw Nellie suggesting what to get for lunch, and them saying to a friend, "You want to avoid her as a manager as she tells you what to eat." As with many rapidly growing companies, politics was rampant, and I saw one of her colleagues effectively put down Nellie so that he looked better. I truly believe it was politics and not performance, as I saw Nellie in one meeting when I was the IT representative, and she was direct with her responses to her department's needs and appeared to be doing a good job. The politics saw Nellie's future for promotion and growth being curtailed and she was placed in a quality monitoring role with her pay increases and bonuses minimal.

I stayed in my position in information technology and while my title did not change, my performance was recognised. I found out that the systems I set up for radio optimisation saw people within the company group travelling across Europe to see them. I even received a nomination in my area to be the European Centre for Excellence as would often tell suppliers I discuss concerns with my colleagues across Europe and they should ensure my colleagues do not have the same issue we just fixed. In one of those layoffs, a supplier told me, "We know of three organisations that would employ you and should we contact them?" My salary just kept increasing, and I received higher bonuses than was declared possible from the policy released by the CEO.

Redundancies were common and it was not unusual near Christmas time for hundreds to be laid off which seemed to enable the CEO and group management to declare to the share market, "There has been a restructure just before the end of the financial year and based upon that, the profit projections for this current year are excellent." It was in one of these layoffs that Nellie was made redundant and while she lodged an appeal, was sent home on pay while it was sorted out. Nellie applied for many positions but could not secure an interview. The employment scene had changed, and Nellie fell into the role of being at home. Although meals were less rushed, I continued to take the kids to all their sporting activities. At one stage she did secure a six-month contract through contacts in the expatriate community, but even that did not last as there were repercussions with the permanent employer, but successfully argued, she was always available to resume when allowed back into the buildings. She would go through the redundancy case documents and I helped her with the objections and the case to be reinstated. It took nearly two years and while most had found other jobs in that time, the remaining cases were eventually decided in an administrative court which ruled that she and one other person be reinstated.

While Nellie had been on antidepressants since her teenage years with a break from medication that began shortly before we met and lasted around three years, the challenges for Nellie were significant around this time. Possibly being unemployed impacted her and she became more withdrawn and this time, I managed to get her to see the doctor. She later thanked me as the change in medication helped but unfortunately, I believe she needed more than medication and to see things in a different way, but was unwilling to take that step.

Some years later the company decided to outsource the operations and arranged for the transfer of all operational staff to an organisation that would run the network on their behalf. I, and part of my group that was considered operational was to go and Nellie and her group that monitored the operational quality were to remain. It was a typical outsourcing arrangement, however, the team I was in was split into two, being the projects people and a couple of others. I sought legal advice which was that "because the small group was not transferred in its entirety," then there were good legal grounds for me to reject the transfer according to the legislation. The transfer required that I would eventually be working out of an office around 1 hour and 40 minutes from home (rather than the 10 min ride by bicycle) so there was some downside.

One of the other personal factors that I considered was that I had recently suffered eye problems and a cough that I could not shake after some years and while lung x-rays were clear and no signs of scarring, I had been issued a puffer like those for asthmatics. In terms of the eye problem, I was told it was environmental and they did not know why, but required me to wash out my eyes three times a day.

A previous job in transport and instrumentation also meant that I had worked with vendors that measured pollution and had hooked them up to road traffic equipment to show the relationship between traffic flow, traffic volumes and pollution. The pollution close to the source was extreme compared with government monitoring sites which were often out in paddocks to ensure they got an average. What was more horrifying in the analysis was that children in prams, waiting at an intersection, were breathing in many times higher concentration of pollution than the adult pushing the pram, who was further from the ground due to the way the pollution is dispersed. As such, it made great sense that both these symptoms I was experiencing were environmental as we lived near the exit of a road tunnel and some documents showed it may have been a hot spot for pollution. The fact that the symptoms disappeared whenever I went away for a day for work or on holiday reinforced the medical opinion of it being environmental.

The move may offer a significant reprieve and while no one else in the family appeared to be having issues, it may be better for them as well if we all moved. Years later, I would discover that there are were several environmental pollution court cases pending due to the high levels of pollution in the area where we used to live.

We travelled to the new location and discussed the purchase of a house, relocation to where the air was cleaner, out of the city and maybe rent out of our current place. There was an international school at the new location so the kids would be right and I started to think that maybe our relationship may also improve.

After some discussion, Nellie suggested I should take the position but would be best if I did the travelling as the kids were settled. If I agreed to the transfer (without a fight with the new employer) there were some potential career benefits in that I would be servicing several outsourced companies and not just the one, so the opportunities could be greater. With what I believed was genuine support from Nellie and with Jasmine becoming less dependent upon me to take her on activities I took on the new role.

It was October 2008 and our daughter had to do some work experience as part of her careers subject which aimed to give the kids some appreciation of what happens in the work environment and help guide their subject's choice. Nellie and I were both searching for possible placements and I approached two members of the Lions Club that worked for the European Space Agency (ESA). Martin was a senior scientist with the ESA and had a son slightly younger than Joe and another member was also quite senior, so that weekend we decided to go for a ride on our bikes to see how accessible ESA was, as we had never been there and knew little about it.

We often rode together on a weekend. We both had bikes with 21 gears (3 on the front sprocket and 7 on the back) with hand brakes on the handlebars. I would tend to ride a bit harder and faster than Nellie as could get some benefit in terms of fitness out of the ride that way (i.e. get the lungs and heart working). I would often take a break halfway and stretch while waiting for Nellie and then take off again and meet her again near the end. We would often drive to a friend's house and then ride from The Hague to a seaside place called Katwijk and ESA at Noordwijk was not much further. We had got a little past Katwijk and there were the rolling slopes of the sand dunes and were riding alongside a road. Nellie overtook as she claimed to know the way and was to take the lead for the rest of the trip.

Nellie had just overtaken and was travelling fast down a slope only just in front of me when she saw a sign and slammed on her breaks. I slammed on mine even harder to avoid a collision which saw me catapult over the handlebars along with the baguettes and other things we had purchased at the last town. My arms hurt to the point I thought I was going to vomit. Onlookers that saw me offered to call an ambulance, but I managed to move the bike, sit down and compose myself and we eventually decided to ride back. If I was not well, I could get help at nearby town only a couple of kilometres away and otherwise continue on and stop at the hospital around fifteen kilometres away. Hopefully I was right and would make it all the way back to our friends' place and the car.

We made it to the hospital and by then, I could not turn the key to lock the bike, so Nellie did that and proceeded inside to get treatment. While I asked the admissions nurse for ice to put on my arms, that request was ignored and sent to the waiting room. Eventually, two young doctors attended to me and while there was some debate if to x-ray one or both arms, I convinced them to do both. Sometime later the results came back all clear, just sprained and you can go home, take some paracetamol and see your doctor if pain persists. I never did get cold packs.

As I was normally the first up each morning, I would normally feed Jasmines' cat Sooty. That morning, Sooty came to see why she had not been fed and nudged my hand with her wet nose to get up. The pain was intense and let out a loud cry that scared the cat and probably woke others in the house! It was that evening, around twenty-eight hours after seeing the doctor we received a call from the doctor I had seen at the hospital. "I am very sorry to tell you we have reviewed the x-rays and both arms are broken. Can you please come back to the hospital? Does it hurt?" Does it hurt seemed like a silly question from my side but her being inquisitive was probably a good sign for a doctor! I then asked her, "Am I coming in there to get plastered?" While native English speakers and especially Australians would follow the humour, it did not translate at all and there was no reaction to speak of. Nellie helped me have a shower and I felt like I was getting hosed down like an elephant at a circus and thought this could be the last shower for a while, put on a singlet with a jacket over my shoulders, and Nellie proceeded to drive me to the hospital.

The first step when arriving at the hospital was that the doctor showed me the x-rays and pointed out the mark and explained how that is the blood going into your bones which indicated the fracture and how easy it was to miss. Yes, it was certainly not a compound fracture with the bone penetrating the skin, but when I went to a hospital emergency department, I expected a certain level of competence. The doctor will hopefully grow out of her lack of experience but why was she unsupervised I thought?

My background personality is that I am always trying to help people and have held a first aid qualification much of my adult life, so have a basic knowledge of anatomy. As we looked at the x-ray, I asked, "Is that the radius or ulna?" "That is the ulna," was the response. I was then escorted to the treatment room to be plastered. The arms were put in plaster from the biceps to the knuckles with roughly a right angle at the elbow and it was then the nurse started to look very perplexed. She exclaimed, I am not sure how to arrange the slings as never done two arms at once, but she managed.

I had been issued a new phone just days earlier and not transferred the phone contacts so couldn't text and Jasmine helped by sending an email to a work colleague to let people know what had happened. The next morning, we rang the hospital first thing for an appointment with the orthopaedic (aka the bone doctor) department, and managed an appointment for later that week.

Mid-morning, I got a call from work from the department secretary, "Where are you and are you coming to work?"

They clearly did not get the message and explained the situation. The department secretary then asked, "How can you answer the phone if both arms are broken?" to which I responded, "I pushed the answer button and I am leaning over a bench with my ear to the phone." In any case the next day, we had charged the hands-free earpiece and Nellie put it in my ear before leaving to work so I could better manage calls. Just as well, as the boss rang and I repeated the story, advised that I had spoken to the third line support organisation that I had arranged to do my daily checks and when I would know more about my situation. He actually asked for a photo which Nellie took and showed both arms in the plaster and later discovered it was shown around at the team meeting and was even sent to the personnel department as evidence of the validity of the work absence. It was quite an ordeal and the final photos were the type of thing that are used to promote health insurance. Nellie helped set up the work computer and as my fingers worked, I was able to do briefing documents and talk people through what needed to be done in my absence.

Nellie went to work and applied for carer's leave for the times where I required assistance to get to hospital and clearly told everyone that I was incapacitated and that she "had to look after Trevor." Many of the staff knew me, as I had helped so many people over the years with IT related assistance, so news of my injury was well known. Nellie told me how she told people that, "I have to take a long lunch as I have to go home to feed and check on Trevor,"

or "the trip to the hospital," but the tone of her voice and the emphasis was clear that it was all about her and was missing all empathy. Listening to her, I could tell she was trying to engender a reaction of "poor Nellie she has to go home and help someone that is incapacitated." Nellie worked ten minutes by bicycle from our home, so would get home and feed me lunch. Things that were said such as, "If you need to do a number two then you may need to do in your undies and wait until I get home," drove that point of a lack-of-empathy home.

Jasmine would come home from school and see me seated on the couch and would burst into laughter at the sight that greeted her, and she would need to leave the lounge room as she knew she should be compassionate. My hair was not washed for a week and I normally wash it every day and could not even comb/brush it and remained in just a singlet, so in reality, it must have been a funny sight. From Jasmine's perspective, having someone that would pick her up, fix her bike and do lots of other things for her, suddenly looking like that, it would have been a big change.

On Thursday we proceeded to the hospital and eventually found the reception area of the correct department, told them we were there and waited to be called. A young (when you are my age many people seem young) doctor called us into the consulting room and brought up the x-rays. He looked at me and stated, "The doctor was right to put you in plaster as your radius is broken in both arms." "The radius?" I exclaimed and said no more! From there it was explained that the fracture was near the elbow and they have to cut off the plaster, that I was not to pick up anything more than half a kilogram, (around a pound) but must move the arms or I would lose the mobility and never get it back. Apparently, what happens is that you get a bump over the fracture as it heals, and you need to essentially continually move, so the bump doesn't form or grinds it back so movement remains normal.

A quick relocation to another room which had the required equipment, a nurse called in to assist and the process of cutting off the plaster commenced. The movement of the arms while they were bending them and cutting off the plaster eventually made me feel like I was about to vomit and told them so! A pause in the process while the bed was reclined, feet raised and head lowered and the blood returned to my head and quickly felt better and then back to the task at hand (removal of the plaster). Nellie later stated that she would have simply got a bowl for me to throw up in and continued. Nellie's comment that day became just one more example to me of her lack of compassion and empathy.

I spent the next two weeks pretending I knew Tai chi and moving my arms to hopefully prevent a loss in my range of motion before the next appointment at the hospital. On this day it was a tall, attractive blonde lady that was around 190cm (about six foot three inches) tall and towered above Nellie and I. She confirmed it was the radius, measured the range of motion of my arms, expressed that she was pleased with the progress and that it was time to get physiotherapy. One thing that disturbed me was that she thought I could go back to work as basically working a computer, yet she measured that I could not get my hands behind my back. The obvious toileting difficulties that situation can present which you cannot really ask a colleague for help, did not seem to cross her mind. After she left, I said to Nellie, "At least she got the bone right." The doctor must have heard as she opened the door, poked her head back in, laughed and left again!

The physiotherapist was just a couple of streets from our house and I was able to get in quickly. While the treatment was in progress, the twisting of my arms to get the full range of motion back was painful and at times felt like I was going to vomit. Like the nurse who applied the plaster, he also confessed he had to think carefully in designing exercises as he had never worked with someone with two broken arms. While the arms recovered, the wrists did not. Back to the hospital for more x-rays to be told they are good and may take a couple of years to fully recover.

I was actually losing my faith in the Dutch medical system from first being told they are not broken, then the wrong bone, then could return to work and there was nothing wrong with my wrists when there clearly was. My concerns were reinforced by a Lions Club friend that worked for the Dutch Department of Foreign Affairs, and he had been a consular officer in Australia and an ambassador in other locations. He had been assigned the task of giving the world's ambassadors confidence in the Dutch medical system after one Ambassador died only hours after attending a hospital for a possible heart attack with pains up his arms and was sent away with antacid. There were other less tragic issues, and the majority of ambassadors were leaving the country for treatment of even mild illnesses.

I often suspect that the interplay between society and the medical profession, industrial awards and the law has led to a poor outcome:

- The first is the sickness benefits for employees which is not 12 days like many awards in Australia but unlimited in The Netherlands. They really do look after those that are sick and I lost no salary. This in itself is good and admirable.

- The second is the law and it is difficult to sue anyone unless you can show a loss. As I lost no wages and they treated the pain with all the medical assistance they deemed appropriate and was all done without a loss of income. Compensation for pain and suffering, from what I was told, is minimal so there was no loss and no reason for lawyers to pursue doctors perhaps making the medical profession less motivated to get it right.

- The third interplay is that doctors do not seem to take pride in getting it right. While there are exceptions, I found the doctor's ability to diagnose as really poor considering the funding and the availability of diagnostic equipment. Another friend was treated for years for arthritis, when she was advised in the United States to ask for specific tests, those tests showed she actually had motor neuron disease.

The Dutch however, seem to have little incentive to get it right and that is maybe because of the first two factors impact the third. I have to confess, that at this stage I had begun to lose faith in the ability to get a good diagnosis and treatment if anything went wrong!

It was around this time that I began to plan a family holiday and as Jasmine had expressed her strong interest in animation following career discussions at school that influenced our holiday choice.

Nellie and I discussed taking Jasmine out of school a week early and as there are significant penalties in the Netherlands for truancy, I got permission from her form teacher. The plan was to enrol her in four short courses at Stamford University in the United States that would give her a university degree unit in animation. Jasmine was looking forward to it as she loved drawing with a particular love of the Japanese Manga style and I thought a university credit at the age of fifteen would help set up her future if she continued down that route. Jasmine's only concern was missing out if Nellie and I went to one of the nearby National Parks while she was doing the course, but we would work that out and probably stay around the general location and see her each night I thought.

PART 2:

Into The Pinball Machine

6

The separation announcement

They say that in many cases the initiator of the final separation has been planning it for years[5], has prepared themselves for the separation and gone through the emotions of loss and grief. The other party will often have to catch up and go through the grieving process of loss, anger, shock, betrayal and more[6].

As a youngster, Jasmine had always possessed artistic flair. She was stubborn, yet very firm with what she wanted as she got older. She had a love for drawing, and we had taken her to Disneyland Paris in the past and once with her friend, Ayla. Like all kids, she loved the rides, however it was difficult to get her out of the drawing lessons where artists would teach the kids to draw Micky Mouse along with many of the more modern Disney characters.

It really was her passion and that continued and was encouraged while I was still in her life which included the

---

[5] https://www.psychologytoday.com/au/blog/divorce-grownups/200805/the-psychology-divorce

[6] https://www.beyondblue.org.au/the-facts/separation-and-divorce

planned trip to Stamford. It was in one of those discussions about her choice of subjects in secondary school about what she wanted to do and knowing what I did, she very firmly said something along the lines of, "I don't want to be able to design what is in a television, but they need people to design the frame and make it look good in a room as you would not buy one that looks terrible and that is what I want to do." Her artistic flair and stubborn desire to develop that part of her life, was a treasure for a parent to see.

Her love of design continued as she grew older, to her new hair care and appearance and I would take her to the hairdresser and she liked it cut in her way with the long fringe. Cutting her fringe was therefore needed in between the hairdresser visits, and was also something that I regularly did. While not having the skills of a hairdresser, I managed with the two pairs of hairdressing scissors (one thinning scissors and standard hairdressing scissors) to cut and thin out the fringe but had to be careful that it was not too short.

It was a day in early March 2009, shortly before my fiftieth birthday, when I got home from work. I had been back at work from the time since both my arms had been broken, but had a long recovery to go and still suffered wrist pain when opening doors. Jasmine came up to greet me excitedly asking me to cut her pony (which is Dutch for fringe), as her hair was getting in her eyes and she had school tests coming up. It did not take much for me to put off dinner, put my bag down and head upstairs to get the scissors and comb when she asked.

That was the moment when all our lives changed in ways that none of us could ever foresee. The main bedroom was largely empty and certainly no scissors. The spare bedroom was also completely empty, which is where Nellie normally slept as I was going to bed early and getting up early due to the long commute and allegedly snored which prevented her sleeping.

While I can honestly say I was stunned with the way I discovered the end of the relationship, I can say, I immediately accepted it and, it appeared to be more of a relief than anything. I remained calm, composed myself, went downstairs and quietly asked Jasmine if she would go upstairs as I needed to talk to Mum. Jasmine did not question my request and went to her room without discussion. When I think back, maybe it was something in the tone of my voice realising it was something serious.

After Jasmine had left the room, Nellie stated, "I was going to tell you after you had dinner, I am leaving and moving a few doors down the road. You can raise Jasmine and get her through university and live here, but I consider the house is mine and you cannot sell it anyway as my name is also on the title. I have taken half the money out of the joint saving account," (which was around €60,000.00). "As this is new to you, you will need to work out what you are doing. I will go and tell Jasmine what is going on."

I stood there stunned as she proceeded upstairs. Sometime later I went upstairs. Jasmine was not talking to her mother and her reaction to me could only be described as distant. Her world had been shattered.

As Nellie left to go down the stairs to leave the house, how could I have known how long she had planned her departure, or for that matter how long she had put it off. It took years to unravel the facts, but unravel they did over time.

The next morning, I opened up new bank accounts and ordered bank and credit cards in my name. It was then that I noticed that Nellie had transferred the approximately €60,000.00 months earlier and later worked out that it was two weeks after my arms were broken! I realised that she had been planning this for months and the deception was more evident.

Jasmine lived with me and she didn't want to see her mother, but I never restricted her and when I asked, she said she was fine. Over the next few weeks following the separation, Jasmine and I were extremely close. I think it was her sympathy that I had been wrongly treated, perhaps she was angry at her mother for breaking up her family or maybe it was a bit of Aussie culture of supporting the underdog. I think that she felt that we had both been deserted and while Jasmine was not told what I had been told, "You can raise her and put her through university," she was impacted.

I told some friends back in Australia, and locally, including Pamela, who was with the Lions Club and amazingly connected throughout the local and expatriate communities. It was through Pamela that I was able to find a lawyer who normally dealt with commercial matters and advised there are no problems. He quickly concluded that as our de facto relationship was not recognised in the

Netherlands, that the house was both of ours and I was entitled to my half. Something that proved to be correct. I had absolutely no issues with raising Jasmine.

I had also notified my brother Graham. His partner, Lucinda, rang around and discovered this could not be done by a normal divorce lawyer due to the multiple international jurisdictions and was given the name of David, at a large law firm in Melbourne.

The Australian lawyers' initial advice was solid and outlined what would happen if it was taken to court, likely outcomes, and a strong piece of advice: it is much better if can sort out yourselves and not use their legal services, but are available if required.

Both sets of advice were taken on board as I considered the implications which seemed straight forward. I did not want anywhere near as much as the advice suggested financially, very happy to raise Jasmine but wanted a definitive financial separation. One of the retired members in the Lions Club belonged to a mediator's group, so outlined the situation and he asked around if anyone in his group did mediation for family separations and found someone. I figured mediation was the best route.

There were also the other things that should be done, and I visited Jasmine's school and spoke to her form teacher, asking him to contact me if anything out of the ordinary was noticed. Jasmine's form teacher did something that I asked him not to do, which was to speak directly to her to make sure everything was okay. Boy, did I get in trouble from Jasmine for that! It was nearly as much trouble as when I told her form teacher she could not read the board at the front of the classroom and we were organising glasses, so they rearranged the class and had her sit up the front!

I also got the cats' vaccination for rabies updated which was something we had done for many years. It was a mandatory requirement to take the cats to many countries and ensured we were flexible. If we needed to move for work or other reasons even to some countries within the European Union and the United Kingdom with the cats, then there was a significant lead time. I did a cursory check to discover that Australia was around a six-month lead time (or they are in quarantine for that long) and some months for others in the European Union. I was not secretive about the inoculations and simply paid for them with the joint running account which had a little bit of money in it that Nellie had left while I organised and issued my own accounts and credit cards.

I separated some of Nellie's stuff from mine and carried around to Nellie's new house her belongings that I had found, including photo albums from her childhood and other such material. Jasmine helped as we cleaned up parts of the house and I even painted some of the door architraves (which had been annoying me for years as Nellie had done them and made a messy job of it) and did not want to get Nellie upset while we were together by redoing her painting.

Apart from photo albums, I found a range of other documents of which several concerned me.

- The first was a medical referral from the psychiatrist she was seeing in Australia for her to pass to a psychiatrist in the Netherlands recommending ongoing treatment. I had thought before leaving Australia that she was simply seeing a counsellor, but this was a full-blown psychiatrist.

- The second was a letter she had written but never posted and when I began reading it, I thought it was to me but after the first two paragraphs realised it was to Joe's father. It talked about how they broke up, that she was at a complete loss, going around to his work but not entering, and I called it "The Stalking Letter."

- The Third document was about the court case for child support of Joe. While this would not normally be a concern, it was the address that put me into shock. Joe's father had lived at some stage, in a house diagonally opposite from where we had established the family home in Australia. I felt disgusted, as if I had been used to show Joe's father that Nellie had a new relationship and Joe now had a father. Hung out like a piece of meat! The truth was that I never tracked down the timeline to work out whether he lived in that house the same time as Nellie, Joe, Jasmine and myself.

I saw Nellie during this time and suggested that we go to mediation to which she got upset and shouted, "I'm not going to mediation with one of your Lions Club mates." And stormed off. There was to be no mediation as she had already decided how everything was to go and had hatched her plan. In one of the conversations I appealed to Nellie to consider Jasmine's feelings and I said, "Jasmine is a teenager and she is more interested in her friends and her cats. Parents are taken for granted and expected to support her." I initially thought this fell on deaf ears, however clearly the message had not, as later events unfolded!

A couple of weeks after Nellie left, she telephoned to try to sort out transferring the bills from her name to mine in what was the former Netherlands family home. There was no question regarding how Jasmine and I were doing, but was aimed to simply achieve her aim of cutting down her weekly costs. I was probably equally as blunt with the reply of, "Yes, we can organise that and happy to transfer them to my name but would like to sort out everything now that we have split up." Her response was guarded but clearly was not happy with my response.

My thinking was that we paid for the house in the Netherlands through joint accounts and several times paid off around €30,000.00 from the joint saving account so the house without question to me, really did belong to both of us from a moral, financial and legal perspective. I also wanted all the funds back that I had sunk into the property back in Australia, in other words, full financial settlement. As we were separated, this would give not only me, but both of us, certainty. The company I was with was likely to move its operations to another country and I was likely to be made redundant, and regardless of what happened, this would allow a clean start and sufficient funds to put Jasmine through school and university. If Jasmine and I did have to move, then there would be the expenses of flying Jasmine between Nellie and I which could be significant, especially if we did move back to Australia. I was however, thinking of England as it was relatively close, and at least somewhere where the language was English.

Her reply was that she considered the house in the Netherlands as hers and if I wanted to leave, I have a property in Australia that I can go back to, so there is no mediation required. Her next question was, "Are you after her properties?" to which I responded that wanted the share I put into Vautner Street that I renovated to make it a home. Things got heated as Nellie started screaming things like, "They are all mine," and unfortunately told her that I have followed legal advice and put a caveat on both properties until matters are settled and we really need to go into mediation. Between us now we had four properties to contend with: the property in the Netherlands (that we lived in before the separation) and three properties in Australia: Vautner Street (the house we lived in before moving to the Netherlands), Smith Street (the unit Nellie purchased before we met), and a property in the Keys Estate (that I owned outright before meeting Nellie).

Nellie may have considered the initiation of discussions that we sort out a financial settlement as she would need to compromise, give up something, being taken advantage of, but I will never know. All I know is that it triggered a complete change in Nellie's attitude toward both myself and our daughter, that she would ensure "I never saw Jasmine again," and things turned extremely nasty and distasteful. Everything about me that had been saved up for years came out and she hated everything about me.

Things I thought she had appreciated suddenly became the worst thing that ever happened such as when I was taking out the kids on Sundays so that she could complete the postgraduate course were changed to, "I hated you for taking the kids out on Sundays so I could study. I never got anything done as I felt I was just missing out. I hate you!" Why she never said anything at the time escapes me. I was later told by my mother, that Nellie had once rung her up regarding visiting my grandfather to say, "Trevor doesn't have to take the kids out on Sunday night." Joe really enjoyed the arcade room at the location, we went for dinner and I thought Nellie was getting more study done for her postgraduate qualification. Everything was wrong and exposed long-term communications issues and eventually, the deceit was revealed.

What was I thinking? That the relationship was over and that it would evolve into some level of acceptance, possibly even mutual respect, independence, and both monitor the welfare of Jasmine and Joe? I was on the train back from work when I took a call, and the words used and tone of the conversation went extremely nasty. Nellie yelled down the phone with a level of uncontrollable rage that few people could relate to, "All the houses are mine." The rage was such that I felt threatened and in hindsight, possibly did a stupid thing and hung up, hoping that she would settle down and could be rational.

That evening after the phone call, on a Monday late in March 2009, Nellie entered the former family home with her key for the first time since leaving and was repeating the threats of what she would do and repeating the demands including that I could leave, but all the properties were hers. She picked up Sindy, our daughter's first cat, who was clearly frightened by Nellie's demeanour and leapt out of her arms and scurried away so frightened that I cannot recall seeing the cat again that night.

"You want one of my properties. This house is mine as I paid for it!" she screamed at me. "You are the one who wanted a holiday, so the holidays are yours, but the properties are all mine," she continued to screech into my face.

I told Nellie that the financial division would not be dropped as I had put significant money into making the house in Australia livable with rewiring, plumbing, spouting ... and her reply was, "You cannot prove it!" I did not get into the fact that all the money for the house in the Netherlands was from both our salaries or any other details, as this was emotion at an extreme level and it would have been impossible to have a rational discussion, so there was no point.

"I am not leaving. This is my place," Nellie screamed, picking up objects like the frying pan and saying "this is mine," and lifting them up above her shoulders as if she was about to throw them at me before putting down and moving onto next item, claiming everything in sight and making totally irrational demands. It was not so much what she said, but the lifting of the objects that made the adrenalin pump through me, as I expected them to be thrown and ready to dodge them due to her uncontrolled rage and the sheer randomness of the acts. Since the cat fled from her arms when being picked up and then

Nellie's rage had escalated as if she was possessed. She was completely out of control of her emotions and minimal control of her actions.

Jasmine had been staying with me up until that time, and had seen her mother a couple of times. I tried to move the focus of the conversation onto Jasmine. Then the real threat was again repeated as Nellie screamed, "If you want to take any of the properties, I will make sure you never see your daughter again."

This was highly emotive and hoped her stated feelings toward Jasmine were not true (but unfortunately believe it may substantially be the case). Nellie said she was told that the courts in both Australia and the Netherlands would put significant weight on what Jasmine wanted to do. Who told her may have been lawyers, internet chat or some other source, I do not know, but even without checking I knew she was right as Jasmine was fifteen. It was ridiculous that Jasmine should fit into Nellie's bargaining position as if our daughter was simply to be traded away for property and that her anger and vengeance should determine where our daughter should live.

Her next demand was to take all documents out of the house (particularly anything financial) and she wanted the passports. My response was that she could take copies of any documents but Nellie did not respond to that.

The next threat was, "I'm going to tell the police that you have been assaulting me for the last ten years. The police will believe me as it happens all the time in the Netherlands and they will lock you away." And pulled out her mobile phone.

I was not sure if she was pretending or that worked up, that she could not manage to press the right buttons and call the police, however she was so much out of control and I had nowhere to go. She would not leave, I couldn't get her out of the house and in desperation decided I would call the police on my mobile to get them around to calm things down.

As my phone connected to the police, she fled from the house. Perhaps, she was more in control of herself than I thought, not wanting the police to see her like that, but whatever the reason I was grateful and relieved that she had fled. The police did not even come to the house as soon as they knew she had left, but it certainly left a bitter taste in my mouth as to how far a person will go, what they are capable of threatening and seeing a level of rage that I had never witnessed in my life.

The call should have been recorded and probably registered to that address should Nellie return and escalate the situation again. That night I put the internal bar down on the back door and levers on the front door so Nellie could not enter while we were asleep. The next morning, I went to the locksmith and got a new set of tumblers and changed the locks.

I was working from home two days a week. It was the day following the confrontation with Nellie that I wrote down a series of questions to get my thoughts straight and emailed them to the Dutch commercial lawyer and he rang back. He advised that there is no reason why I could not change the locks (which covered most questions) and that she was free to take copies of any document she wanted which is what I had told her.

The following day, Joe, my stepson, stopped by calling that he needed to find a cable for a video camera. He was told I had changed locks over an incident previous night and that nothing should change between us and that I believed things would work themselves out. While he had not lived with us for some time, this was still his home and was welcome to still do his laundry here. He was given a key after he promised me he would not give access to his mother (words were something like she doesn't need to know I have a key and I will not tell her). Also, Joe asked if he could help pack up his mum's stuff and take them to her place and I said that was fine but will be while I was present and that I would help.

I still foolishly believed things would settle down, just as I had told Joe, but they did not and there were things I did not know. Whether it was Nellie's desire for control, fear and insecurities brought on by the lack of control or a genuine fear that I may abduct Jasmine back to Australia, Nellie had covertly hired lawyers both in Australia and the Netherlands. At that stage, I had no knowledge that Nellie's Australian lawyers had written a letter that "if I did take Jasmine back to Australia, Nellie may be powerless to repatriate her back to the Netherlands", fuelling her fears, Nellie had lodged a submission with police that I held the passports.

7

The assault, fear and legal shenanigans begin

My world seemed to be under attack however, I still did not realise what Nellie had done. I was to raise Jasmine and put her through university and could raise her in the family home which was hers, was what Nellie stated when she walked out. I was almost certainly to be made redundant which would involve a significant payout and Jasmine needed to finish her school year. I needed financial closure so that I could plan the years ahead and I could look after Jasmine. If I did not secure work in the Netherlands, I had to be free to look elsewhere and while I considered Australia, I was also thinking England so Jasmine could easily fly or ferry between us, but now it sounded like nothing would be acceptable to Nellie. The thought of leaving sometime in the future had existed from before we arrived in the Netherlands which is why the cats were always vaccinated, but they could not move for many months as the vaccinations had lapsed. Nellie's temper was such that a physical confrontation may eventuate and how can I protect myself?

Suddenly locks were being changed, I felt threatened by Nellie's desire to want to fight, and confused as to how to resolve the situation and even how she could possibly use Jasmine as a bargaining chip. If she wanted this separation so badly, why was she so livid with me? Nellie possibly also felt threatened as it may have been for the first time, I was standing up to her and she was no longer in full control. I could not manage her temper tantrums by walking away, and locking the door was not working either. I took the day off work, so I could try and make sense of what was happening. I was actually relieved when Nellie walked out as I had been compromising on everything for much of the relationship be it where we lived in Australia, if I could accept a job which meant spending some weekdays away from home, the move to the Netherlands, along with the host of little things. If I said anything she disagreed with, she would scream and make threats but nothing like I had experienced in the last few days. I was glad the relationship was over, but I had to have at least some control over my life so I could look after Jasmine. From my perspective, we cannot be separated and still being controlled by Nellie with her making all the decisions. The only thing I knew was that I had to have some control of my life and that was the line that had to be drawn. Hopefully, that line will be sorted out through mediation I thought, but as events unfolded, that was not possible.

Joe rang later that morning and said he wanted to help pack up Nellie's stuff and he would drop around at 2pm to help pack up a few boxes. He did not arrive which I did not regard as unusual as like many teenagers he was not that reliable anyway. I thought it was good as I was busy working remotely, as well as updating my resume, a job search and possibly an application as redundancy was on the table.

The next day was Friday, so I decided as there was only one day left, I may as well take the rest of the week off. Besides, I needed more time to think, and I had a few errands and appointments, so it seemed a better use of my time.

I had been out several times including to the veterinarian to get the cats' blood tested for rabies antibodies and then I went onto Jasmine's school. I went to advise her class mentor that with there had been further changes and due to the separation, Jasmine would not be going to Stamford for the course. Jasmine would holiday in Australia, however this should not impact her subject choices for 2009/2010 school year and that I anticipated that she would continue at that school. I was then rung and asked to go back to the veterinarian, as they missed one piece of documentation from their vaccination records contained within the cats' passports.

Upon returning home from the veterinarian, I was shocked to see Nellie with a packing box down the back lane going to her house with one of Joe's friends and the front door open. I knew immediately what was happening. Rather than getting copies of documents she was taking everything and had been in my house. Joe must have let her in with the key I entrusted to him! I sprinted up to my front door and tried to go in, only to have the door smashed into me from the other side and while I could not see who it was, I thought it was Joe. I could not enter my own house. In a panic, I pulled out my mobile phone and rang the emergency number and advised the police that there was a burglar in the house and to come immediately.

Trying to remain calm in these circumstances is impossible to do. The shock of what is occurring overrides the mind to make good decisions. Now our separation had progressed to stealing documents when she was told she could have copies of anything, my stepson lying to me about not telling his mum he had a key, lying to me by agreeing to remove stuff under supervision and I wondered how the police would react and would they help put an end to this lunacy?

At that moment Joe (who was inside my house) decided to leave and make a run for it with a cabinet full of documents. It was him behind the door, just as I had thought! As he charged out the door I stood in his path, putting myself in the way as a roadblock. He had no choice but to drop the drawer when he bumped into me and then started pushing me. All I could do was block him and refused to escalate matters and raise my hand in anger and probably couldn't anyway with my wrists still in pain since the accident. In a very loud voice, he yelled, "Why did you get lawyers involved?" "I am taking this, what are you going to do about it?"

While no punching occurred, I was knocked to the ground, but I kept getting up and prevented him from taking the possessions. In that moment you don't notice the pain of the falls, but more the shock, that my stepson would take it to this level. A flash of memories ran through my mind at lightning pace about all the things we had done together as father and son, but with each knock to the ground, the memories were quickly reversed from happy times to both anger, distrust and sadness; that he had lied, when I thought he would stay out of it.

While teaching him to read, taking him to soccer in the freezing Dutch winter, one memory more prominent than the others flashed through my mind which was the incident at the Australian Grand Prix. I had a letter from a government minister saying that the school would not be affected by the event, but when dropping him off at school, a big security guard said I cannot enter the lane leading to the school where we park our cars and walk the kids in. The challenge was picked up and I retorted, "I have a letter here that says I can, and you are not authorised to stop me, so you had better call the police." I drove past, parked the car and took Joe into school and returned to complete my journey to work. This is the boy, I stood up for in the past even when threatened and now this.

At one stage I dropped my phone to the ground, while the police were still on the line. Moments later, Joe picked up my phone pulled out the battery and threw it to the ground in an act of defiance and aggression. As is often the case in domestics, no one wants to get involved. Many of my neighbours saw the scuffle and a few times, I yelled out to them to call the police, but do not think any of them did.

Eventually, the police came and as they approached, Joe took off down the street and left. The police quickly ascertained it was a domestic issue and the events that had just occurred. The drawer unit was one that fit under a desk that I had built years before I met Nellie and both Nellie and I knew the contents were all mine. Inside the draw were documents and things that I had got for my twenty-first birthday, along with my scuba diving license cards. I pulled out the contents of the drawer on the ground to show the police and a quick perusal confirmed with the police that the contents were all mine and I wanted other documents back as had no idea what else had been taken!

Angry and embarrassed, I told them I wanted charges laid for assault, burglary, and theft if all documents not returned immediately and could see Nellie and Joe at Nellie's front door. Police mediated the situation and advised that the best they could do is to allow Nellie to sort out documents they had taken and return what was mine. I showed the police the house stating that pile was Nellie's personal stuff and I had purchased packing boxes and that had arranged for Joe to help pack up.

The police advised they could not lay charges as Joe had been welcomed by giving him a key, and it only took a minute or two for me to realise that deep down I did not want to really want Joe charged or even Nellie and told the police that. Joe was under the influence of his mother and what would charging Nellie do? I did not think it would help and all I wanted to achieve was a sensible outcome for us all. I was told by the police officers in attendance after their discussions with Nellie at her front door that both Nellie and Joe had agreed not to enter the house again without my presence and permission, return all documents that were not hers and that agreement with the police would be included in their report. They recommended that we talk and try to resolve issues.

I then requested the police talk to my daughter, who had been in her room on the top floor of the house. At the time it was just to assure them that I was looking after her well and safe. To my knowledge, she was completely unaware of any of the events that had just unfolded. I felt so terrible for Jasmine that this was now what her life was becoming—this was not at all what I wanted for her. It was in hindsight a mistake as I had introduced Jasmine to the escalating conflict.

I resumed a discussion with the police and told them I had called them to prevent further escalation of the situation. I also told them about the previous days and that Nellie had threatened to claim that I had assaulted her for the last ten years and would get her son to support her and I had to prevent that from happening. The police said that they would not believe accusations like that and were not that stupid and things like that needed proof. After that reassurance, I felt just a little more comfortable, but only for a while.

I then changed the lock tumblers again that afternoon, this time Jasmine and I were the only ones with keys, which I was not happy about in case of an emergency.

Jasmine packed up her bag and left around 8:00 p.m. that night to stay at her mother's, and to this day I wonder what the police had said or had her mother pleaded with her on her mobile phone. Earlier in the evening, Jasmine had stated she would be staying with me, so something had changed. Before Jasmine left, I sat down with her and talked. We would still have a holiday in Australia over her summer vacation and would return before any permanent decisions were made. Jasmine had previously been open to moving to Australia especially after our last trip as upon arriving back she found her cat had passed away days before our return. At that time, she begged in tears to return to Australia; possibly to escape the grief; possibly to be with her nana that she loved, and possibly to go to school with her cousin. I meant what I said, and intended not to make any decisions in Australia and was still thinking I would most likely have to apply for jobs in England. Before the separation, I had even floated the idea with Nellie of investing the savings into a bedsitter or student accommodation if Jasmine studies in England. In spite of my request for Jasmine not to go to Nellie's that night, she wanted to, and I felt I had no choice but to let her. I was so uneasy about the situation that had occurred that day, I felt sick to my stomach.

As the door shut behind Jasmine, I locked the door. It was a heavy thud made by the heavy door and new lock made it seem permanent. It was an ominous warning of what was to come.

I often think of Joe and still send him birthday and Christmas messages. After the total betrayal of trust and the altercation with Joe that evening, I had greater trouble relating to him and perhaps, that was something that his mother wanted. He was not living at either of our homes and was a young adult but for him to attack me like that, he was clearly under the very strong influence of his mother and only taking in the one perspective. He blamed me for involving lawyers. Yes, I had got legal advice but not appointed them to do anything more than a caveat and had asked Nellie for mediation, but whatever he was told, I don't know. Perhaps the fears and anxieties that were his mothers', unknown to me escalated by lawyers, were also instilled to him. All I know was that if this continued to escalate, it was only going to get worse to everyone's detriment.

The next morning, I awoke early and it's fair to say I hadn't slept well. The events of the last few weeks and particularly the last few days were beginning to become more and more intense. I could feel a storm brewing, only I did not know when the storm would come and how intense it would be. I tried to roll over in bed and realised how sore my back was becoming. I had long suffered from back problems since I was a teenager and would often go through phases where it would be worse than other times. Right now, the recent broken arms meant exercise was less than normal, and the stress that was building, I suspect was causing me more pain than usual.

I decided to get up, shower and dress. I peered outside the window and the day was overcast, typical of a Spring day. I wondered how Jasmine was doing and whether she was awake and had breakfast. I thought about calling her but that this may antagonise the situation, so I left it.

I decided to go for a walk, that may help ease some of the stiffness in my back and while returning home I saw in the distance police cars and noticed the blue and white checked tape surrounding an intersection and a section of the canal. This was only ten houses away from where we had all lived together. The recent events had heightened my fears of Nellie's uncontrolled rage which was something that I had never seen in a person.

I had been in difficult situations in the past, and had even seen one man tear up an office; throwing chairs at walls, punching and leaving blood on the walls, while another in the office later told me he was petrified with fear, I calmly said to the angry man are you finished now? I had been the first from the management team on a construction site after someone had been shot and killed, surrounded by large men that were fearful for their families and had handled that situation. Nellie's rage was different. I do not think it was because I was personally involved. She wanted vengeance and had shown her inability to control her anger and although I had thought she would settle down, the police presence put me into a panic.

What was in the canal? As I approached the police, the thoughts that *could Nellie have done something to Jasmine?* This thought turned into sheer panic as I broke into a sweat and began to shake at the thought of what Nellie may have done, and then, seconds later that felt more like minutes, regained some sense of reality, turned and started to walk toward Nellie's new home. It was only five or ten paces when I stopped, again frozen with fear. *What would I find at the house?* I just kept thinking of the uncontrolled rage I had witnessed that had taken control of Nellie. *What if she rang the police and made up a story that I had come to the house to get even? What if no-one is at home or refused to answer the door?*

I turned again and walked toward the area, clearly marked by the barrier tape, nervous and unsure of what to say, my heart was racing and feeling like I was about to vomit. Anxiety had taken hold and as I approached the police tape, a constable approached me and he firmly stated, "Misdaad gebeid, ga weg." Not understanding, and full of fear on what may have happened, I paused and moved neither closer or further away. "Misdaad gebeid, ga weg," the constable again repeated. I began to say, "I just need ... " when the constable cut my sentence short, realising I was speaking English and said, "This is a crime scene, move on." I understood. I found myself unable to move on and asked, "Can you tell me what happened?" and the constable's eyes focused upon me, staring and trying to ascertain why I was there and again said, "This is a crime scene, move on now." "What is the crime?" I asked, and he started to pay more attention as he glared at me. Abruptly, the constable stated, "That is a police matter, move on now," very firmly and with all the authority his position held that would have had most people follow without question. He kept staring, possibly to see if that would make me move on. The thought flashed through my head, that *maybe he is trying to work out if I was returning to the scene of the crime and was involved?* He could probably see me shaking slightly, my voice straining and he was watching me intensely, possibly evaluating me when I finally said, "My wife and I split up, I live just down there, and haven't seen my daughter today and I need to know, what is going on and was anyone hurt." My thoughts had returned to the uncontrolled rage that I saw from Nellie and the threat that I would never see my daughter again, had suddenly taken on an entirely new meaning. The constable changed his tone and instead of the firm instructions that were not working on me stated, "We are looking for a knife that was used in a robbery."

The relief was immediate, I had completely overreacted. This had nothing to do with Nellie and Jasmine. I knew that Nellie was driven. She had worked Joe up to such an extent that there was the altercation. I had found a psychiatric referral for Nellie that she never followed up on. Years earlier, when she was depressed with being sent home from work after being made redundant, I suggested she see a psychologist for depression and she had responded, "I'm likely to get an arrogant Dutchman with crappy English and would want to kill him," and she meant it. She had been on prescription medication most of her life and she believed she was dependent upon them and maybe they were not working. It took most of the day to me regain my composure, but the concerns and doubts as to what Nellie was capable of remained. No one knew what Nellie was capable of, as no one else had seen her exhibit the uncontrolled rage. The fear of what could happen never left me, but was reinforced as new events unfolded.

It was April 2009 when I received a summons served at the house, six weeks after Nellie had walked out. Recalling what had happened toward the end of the first year when I wanted us to return to Australia, I retreated and refused to accept the situation I faced. I refused to open the door or touch the document even after it was shoved through the letter slot. It was clear what it was. Suddenly, it was a whole new ball game! The escalation of conflict through perjury, the abuse of the legal process, and the state aiding her to destroy me had commenced.

Being in the Netherlands, it was all in Dutch. I could read some common-use Dutch, but this was legal speak, which is sometimes impossible to decipher even in your native language, so it was completely illegible to me. As such, I contacted a friend from the Lions Club that was elderly and wise and went to his house. He was able to tell me what it was and contacted his daughter that had a legal background and knew family separation specialist lawyers. I went back to the commercial lawyer to also get some advice. The commercial lawyer looked at the document and seemed both horrified and disappointed at how things had escalated. He exclaimed, "This is the lawyer I would have recommended for you. She is the biggest bitch in the Netherlands!" The lawyer's name was Bella. While he did not know someone to refer me to, my friend's daughter did, and contacted the Dutch lawyer Floortje, and appointed her immediately.

What I later discovered was that there was another property in the Netherlands making a total of five: the property Nellie had moved into, that she had actually purchased two years earlier. I was stunned. I had my lawyer get confirmation of the purchase date and check if there were other properties in Nellie's name. Floortje, my Dutch lawyer also asked me to go through the bank statements for the last few years and those investigations showed that Nellie had syphoned out around €60,000.00 from the joint bank accounts including invoices for curtains and other items from 2 years earlier when she purchased the property, solely in her name out of the joint bank accounts to which we both contributed close to equal amounts. I was fortunate in that I discovered how to download the documents from the bank as Nellie, with the aid of Joe, had taken all that evidence. This was something that Nellie later admitted in court that she had done, stating that I could have seen that if I'd looked years ago and that it was not hidden. It was on the shelves. I do not know if she was insinuating it was my responsibility to know what she was doing, or maybe even that I was stupid for not knowing. Perhaps I should never have trusted her and deserved to be robbed for not monitoring the finances. The €60,000.00 taken from the account months earlier, just after my arms were broken, was 50% of the funds in the joint bank savings account at that time, and a logical division of joint property upon separation. However this €60,000.00 from 2 years earlier; shook me to my core. The complete and utter deception was probably the hardest thing to accept up to this point, but worse was to follow.

As time went by, the actions of Bella and Nellie, as they goaded each other into the depraved attacks, became progressively bolder and more protracted. The acts would drain the life out of myself, Jasmine, and even Nellie, while Bella filled her coffers with the financial proceeds of the conflict.

Again, Nellie came to the house in a fury, knowing I had received the documents, demanding the passports of not only Jasmine but her cats as well! When we first got the cats, we had them immunised for rabies so that it was possible to take them out of Europe in case that was needed. The inoculations were updated, along with the passports however it takes close to six months after the injections before you can relocate the pets with minimum quarantine, or an unacceptable six-month quarantine. She had clearly heard me when I said weeks earlier what was important to a teenage girl was her friends and the cats she loves and therefore, the cats had suddenly become important to Nellie.

Nellie tried various tricks, yelling and claiming that the head of the judiciary was concerned at international abduction and to give her the passports, but I stubbornly, and possibly stupidly refused, as why should she have them and not me? I was the one going on holiday with Jasmine in four months' time.

Nellie stated at one stage that she had spoken to a work colleague that had gone through a separation, and insisted Nellie needed a lawyer. I suspect they helped her recruit a lawyer whom I believe prayed on her insecurities, a lawyer that, rather than recommending mediation as I requested, launched straight into immediate litigation. It was years later that I pieced together that Nellie had hired lawyers in both countries and that the letter from Nellie's Australian lawyer was followed by the report to the police that she feared international abduction of Jasmine. The following day, the attempt with Joe to take all documents from the house to conceal evidence, and now the summons was issued.

I progressively learned more about Bella and it was during one trial in the court foyer that Nellie said that her Dutch lawyer, Bella, had told her in the first meeting, "You must fight for all the money and not leave him with a cent as it is for your children's future."

Such a statement showed me that the lawyer recognised that Nellie had no compassion for those she had broken away from, and to focus on her fears and not negotiate a way to alleviate them but to inflame them. In the trials that followed, I heard of nothing from Nellie or the judiciary that remotely related to what is in the best interests of the child, and this included the Dutch Children's court. The tactic to launch straight into legal processes rather than the mediation I requested, I later learned was also a method to escalate conflict and the lawyer's income.

Apart from appointing my Dutch lawyer, Floortje, I also finished up appointing David in Australia, who turned out to be a lawyer that I do not think would have lied for me even if I asked. He acted properly and with integrity. It may not have been what I thought I wanted as I was tempted at times to try to even the score and balance the outrageous claims, but never gave instruction to that effect. I am glad we were able to operate with higher integrity and this was recognised by the various decisions and directly stated in one of the Australian appeals judgement (to paraphrase, "… where the actions of the applicant and her legal team has been appalling and the actions of the respondent and his legal team has been impeccable.").

Floortje (my Dutch lawyer), arranged a meeting between Nellie's lawyer, Nellie and myself and it was quickly agreed that I hand over Jasmines' and the cats' passports for safekeeping to Floortje, and with some negotiation, mediation was agreed to and a mediator was organised, however this would be some months until the first appointment. Jasmine would also be forced to spend more time with Nellie, being week-on and week-off. I had no real issue with that arrangement, although Jasmine had spent minimal time with Nellie, I saw it as appropriate and maybe things may settle down.

Apart from the upheaval with Nellie and lawyers, it was finally announced that my work was expected to finish in three months (in August). The confrontation was significant and with Nellie showing little ability to control herself, so I tried to negotiate to work completely remotely. My manager even asked his counterparts in Australia if I could work out of the Australian office, however the response was that it would not look right as they were about to perform significant layoffs. The situation was getting worse as Nellie ignored the agreement made with the police, and at one stage came to the back glass sliding door which was locked. When I acknowledged her, and went to the cupboard for a key, she began pounding at the door and screaming. Maybe she thought I had simply turned my back, but it was as if she was again possessed. I did not open the door and she left. Again, my fears resurfaced for everyone involved and I again believed if I didn't leave the house and ideally the Netherlands, that lives were at stake—mine and Jasmines'. If Nellie was capable of this in a few weeks, imagine what could happen if it escalates further? I thought, *If Nellie did attack again, it could be worse with one of us injured or dead and possibly the other*

in jail and Jasmine would have no parents. Just as Nellie had threatened, she could accuse me of anything and I would be forced to stay in the Netherlands, the accusations could see me arrested and falsely imprisoned.

The stress was getting to me. I also knew that if I stayed, then I would be constantly and continuously attacked both physically and psychologically, and eventually fully lose Jasmine. I thought, *if this continued, how could Jasmine love such a weakling? And a completely broken person?* If it led to suicide; she would not have me anyway!

Nellie's parental alienation had begun in earnest ever since the threat that, "I will make sure you never see your daughter." How Jasmine felt at that stage, I would never know. Although Jasmine was fifteen, she was still impressionable and I was watching her drift away from me. Nellie was cooking any meal Jasmine wanted, hired an interior decorator for her bedroom and did everything to win her over. I later found out that she confided in her in the typical fashion of parental alienation, telling her about the separation and making out that she was the victim. Nellie and Joe against me—I didn't stand a chance, but still believed that the years of foundation-building would be enough for Jasmine to know how much I love her, and she would not accept what was happening. I saw no way to resolve the impossible if the mediation failed. The barriers to guide and protect my daughter were being stacked against me, and yet she remains the most important thing in my life!

Soon after, the lingering problem in my back went from bad to worse, who knows whether it was from the stress of the situation that tipped me over the edge, but either way, I went from a back pain to a herniated disc. I was told that the disc in my back had not bulged but burst. I found myself unable to stand and even breathing caused pain when I lay on my stomach. That night Jasmine cooked a dinner for me and served it on the floor so that I could lay on my stomach on the couch and eat. While I only took two paracetamol tablets for the two broken arms, that pain was insignificant by comparison. It was then that I made a mistake that I shall forever regret. Unable to get myself even to the toilet without crying in pain and not wanting Jasmine to see me like that, I asked her if she would stay with her mother until I got better and could look after her again. I did ask her to drop by and maybe do some shopping, so I had food in the house. The cause of the pain was verified by an MRI organised by the huisarts as the local hospital said it would take months to schedule an MRI and I was prescribed Oxycontin (a synthetic opioid / narcotic and works on the brain to alter how it feels and responds to pain). It is difficult to believe the pain one can endure. The lack of support when I was really in trouble and the isolation that followed, was difficult to comprehend and represented an extension of Nellie's control that saw us all leave Australia.

I remember feeling excruciating pain that seemed not to be dulled by the Oxycontin, yet the side effects were significant. While lying face down on my stomach on the couch, Nellie had all the services disconnected in the house when she simply could have done what we had agreed to, and have them transferred to my name. Whether it was the sheer cruelness of cutting off basic amenities, being incapacitated, or the medication I was on, the pure desolation I now found myself in was horrendous. I'd lost my family, my basic amenities, my safety and my mind to some degree from the medication. I was going from happy to crying in seconds and it was only strangers from an online back support group that explained what was occurring. The advice that taking food before the Oxycontin will reduce the mood swings and it did help! The doctor had not warned me about this and while the information supplied with the drugs was in Dutch, I had downloaded the English version of the drug information sheet from the manufacturer's site and that did not mention such dramatic mood swings either. Somehow, with the rest on my stomach, medical checks every two weeks by the huisarts (general medical practitioner), I began to make micro-improvements. In the following months, I kept a couple of friends and family back in Australia informed as to my health and legal progress. Graham tried to get a friend from the United Kingdom to visit and have a bit of a holiday and look after me while I recovered, but that did not happen.

It was more than two months before I had begun standing again and off the drugs which meant that the mediation could commence. The mediator would not meet while I was taking those drugs (as they affected the brain) and wanted the meeting in her office. Finally, I was able to go to a mediation session the lawyers had arranged. My stance had changed enormously over what needed to occur. The ability to rehabilitate myself in the Netherlands would be difficult as access to swimming pools where I could swim laps was restricted. Establishing myself in

England while still recovering from the herniated disc when still unable to sit, may be hard and it was increasingly looking like Jasmine had been alienated from me. Later I was informed by Nellie that she had told Jasmine, that "if you go back to your father you will be looking after an invalid for the rest of your life." Perhaps Jasmine felt abandoned by me when I asked her to stay with her mother, and I suspect that was used against me as well. Jasmine would not even assist with shopping now, and all I had been eating for months was toasted sandwiches (before drugs) and a small microwave (normally a rice or pasta) meal of an evening, as that was all could manage in the circumstances. I was worried that I may not be able to secure work in the Netherlands. I did not consider it safe to stay in the Netherlands as Nellie was extremely unstable towards me. I considered that the only choice that was practical was to get back to Australia and establish a home for Jasmine, negotiate that she visits for Christmas and major summer holidays and if she did join me, then would expect her to visit her mother over Christmas (which is also part of the long summer holiday in Australia).

The mediation session did not go how Nellie expected and a week later, she came around one night and I opened the door to see who it was. She pushed me in the chest, screaming, "Are you a man or not?" I think she wanted me to assault her in return and in that case, she could call the police and I would be arrested just as she had said she would do months earlier. I remember some pain in my back as I forced the door shut against her trying to keep it open and was grateful I succeeded. I know that otherwise I would be trapped in the Dutch court system, defending myself against false assault charges. I checked with my Dutch lawyer the next morning who told me I could not get a restraining order as Nellie's name was also on the property title and she was living so close by. There was nowhere else in the Netherlands I could go, friends in the Netherlands upon hearing what had happened told me to get out of there, my brother Graham told me, "Just get out and leave everything, they are only things that can be replaced, but you cannot." It was much easier to leave, to diffuse the situation and negotiate from afar—I was also in fear of my life.

As the days progressed, I visited work and pleaded with them to make me redundant. All my colleagues had already been made redundant weeks earlier as they had moved the operations to an eastern European country but my redundancy had been delayed due to my illness. My employer agreed, providing I took one of their laptops with me and if they could get me the right access permissions, that I would fix the serious issue they had. They knew I could achieve what others could not, as had resolved that issue for my previous employer after being outsourced to them. I packed up a few boxes of belongings including photo albums, posted them back to Australia and purchased the plane ticket.

Jasmine was with me when I purchased the ticket, but she did not know exactly why I was leaving, but I just told her that I cannot stay with what is happening, and she agreed to see me off. I simply did not feel it was right to tell her about the separation; what her mother had done; what her mother had said (that she did not care about Jasmine's future); the attacks; the threats, and the fear of what would happen if I stayed. I thought that with me not being there to be physically attacked, things would quickly settle down and Jasmine would be with me for the coming Christmas holidays or at worst, her next summer holidays. Her mother had threatened court action (which was cancelled when her fear of child abduction was removed with my lawyer holding the passports), so there was hope that backing off, it could be settled. I also believed Jasmine would be well cared for as there was all the money Nellie had taken recently, so there was time to financially and progressively sort matters out. If Jasmine was not looked after, surely, she would come to me where she would be looked after and I would stay in contact. The events that followed showed that I could not be more wrong.

8

Return to Australia and back to the Netherlands

The morning I left the Netherlands, just six days after Nellie pushed me at the front door and screamed "Are you a man or not?" Jasmine was meant to see me off. I had asked her to keep her mobile phone charged up and beside her bed and rang several times but without a response. She slept in and didn't even come to say goodbye. It's possible she was being a normal teenager, or she was deeply upset and angry, or that she wanted to come and say goodbye but the fear of retribution from Nellie stopped her. I don't blame her but there was just so much I wanted to say, but had not had the opportunity, and I was probably inept at expressing myself well. I had planned to leave the country due to the fear of my own life and to defuse the conflict that continued to escalate with Nellie; breaking the agreement made with police, and my inability to get any protection through a restraining order. I had quietly boxed up ten of the typical removals book boxes and packed what I could into them, sending them to Australia by post. The day I left, I left without any furniture and very few possessions. Jasmine was there for some of the packing and she said that she thought she would like

131

to learn the guitar next year at school. I therefore said, if she wanted my guitar then it is now hers and thought what a better thing to give her as it had very special meaning to me. It was given to me by my parents in primary school and I always played it to help me relax. As for anything else, my brother's advice was, "Leave, it's just stuff, it can be replaced, you can't." I knew he was right.

Jasmine did ring, but only after I was through customs and approaching the departure lounge. She had misplaced her phone and it had gone flat and took a while to recharge it that morning. She wanted to come to the airport but by the time she got there, alone by train, it would have been my boarding time. She was clearly upset but then just talked about how to get into the house again to which I said I had changed the tumblers back and everyone had keys. I thought about cancelling the flight as I desperately wanted to see her but remembered why I was leaving in the first place, why I couldn't get removalists, as I knew Nellie would again become violent or call in the police and lawyers based upon lies and possibly have me arrested. I told Jasmine I loved her, but that she couldn't see me off. I am rarely good with my words, but if she had of been there to see me off I had planned to tell her that she can always join me and that I expected to see her for long vacations, but over the phone, I just couldn't get those words out. It was not the departure I had wanted.

The flight home was long, with the typical refuel in Singapore. It was sad wandering through the airport that years ago I had been in with Jasmine on our last holiday to Australia, looking at the jewellery and visiting the many shops. Now I was alone, completely alone, utterly devastated. I had only been able to stand just weeks ago and the pain of sitting meant I carried the potent drugs in case I relapsed and had stood near the toilets for most of the twelve-hour flight and was not only suffering from physical back pain but also lack of sleep. So much can happen in a few short years. I wandered through the corridors like a ghost, empty, soulless, tired, and confused. I managed a few minutes in the pool of terminal one to loosen my back and an hour laying down in the short-term hotel room that I had booked. It was a desperate effort to stabilise my back that, during the rest, had gone into spasms, but recovered before I had to get up and I boarded the flight back home to Tullamarine, Melbourne.

It was now the end of August 2009 and just five months since separation. It felt like an eternity—so much had happened in that time. One horror incident after the next, layers of trauma just stacked upon one another, crushing each layer as a new incident was laid on top of it. After more than a day on the stand, the initial court proceeding was so stressful, I thought I had a major abscess on a molar which was too painful to speak. I went to my dentist and after x-rays, was diagnosed with a muscular problem in my jaw due to stress!

Like all of you who have suffered the loss of a loved one, I should tell you a little bit about the last few years and family grieving.

When I returned from the Netherlands and I came back to Australia, I stayed at my brother's house the first night and the next day visited my father for his 80th birthday celebration with my brother's two adult children.

His Alzheimer's was advancing and he did not realise we had gathered for his birthday, and I will never know if he remembered me. "Look who is here, it is Trevor!" And he acted as if he knew me but was then prompted, "son number two." When people are losing their memory, they often pretend that they know you, and I am sure many of us have done that or realised it was being done to us.

After that, my brother took me to my mother's place and my surprise return was very well received. We all thought I would be there for a couple of months while things were sorted out and I would concentrate on rehabilitation from the burst L4-L5 disc (which is near the base of the spine) with lots of swimming and the gym and then find work and somewhere to live.

While the gym was great, I joined a snorkelling group and found myself immersed (so to speak) in the activity. At first, I had trouble crossing the road and could not carry the weights. Nowadays, I help pick up people from their wheelchairs and assist them into the sea. No need to be alarmed as we help them out and back into the wheelchairs after! I would also catch up with friends and as I found in the past, it was like I had never been away. My old friends became part of my life again, as well as new ones from the new activity.

The week after my return, I saw my Australian lawyer and we were all hopeful that Nellie and I could negotiate a settlement. Unfortunately, the next four years would ensure I would go to hell and back through the court systems. I would appear in front of ten different judges, across two countries and multiple different courts including the *Hoog*

Raad (High Court of the Netherlands) and the Appeals Court in Australia. The family assets would be plundered to the tune of around $750,000.00 in legal proceedings, with the most ridiculous of submissions, blatant lies, and deception to delay any resolution. Every single court case, I would not eat the night before, but still spent most of my time in the bathroom beforehand with gut-wrenching pain so intense that there was no choice but to purge my bowels and vomit.

A letter was sent to Nellie and her legal representative by my Australian lawyers the week after my return to Australia which asked if the custody and property matters could be settled through a mediated process and have that agreement simply stamped by the court. The care of Jasmine was proposed. This ensured her visiting the other parent for the summer vacation, depending upon which hemisphere she finished up in, and to sort out a financial agreement for her future care until she finishes school or is no longer a dependent.

It was then confirmed that Nellie had appointed an Australian lawyer and what they call a "round table conference" was held and an all-party agreement reached to assess the value of all properties and who should be appointed to do the valuation. It appeared the separation could be done amicably and removing myself from danger to dissipate the escalating conflict was working. There was some follow-up correspondence on who should do the valuations.

Appearances proved to be extremely deceptive, which some may say, matched much of the relationship!

Unknown to me, a court case was lodged in the Netherlands and served at the Dutch property where I had been residing. Nellie and Bella, under the full knowledge that I had not received the notice, started proceedings as if I was there. Out of courtesy, they sent a copy to my Dutch lawyer a day or so before the case was due to be heard. The time zone difference, and a communication problem, I was not made aware in time for the case. Even if I did know, there would have been no time to translate the documents and prepare a defence. The first Dutch case was therefore, a sham! Nellie and Bella had abused due process to circumvent a proper hearing. I was eventually served the judgement through an international court serving system and was only then able to lodge an objection and that resulted in a delay of some months.

The international protocols for the serving of the initial judgement was done by the Sheriff's office and without warning. Officers in black flak jackets, complete with pepper spray and sidearms, banged on the door demanding the occupants show themselves. This was the first of what proved to be many documents served on me by the Sheriff's office. As I was staying at my elderly mother's, it proved to be both frightening and embarrassing for her and she was then faced with the task of explaining to neighbours what the show of force at her door was all about. If I wasn't there, then I would receive a frantic call from my mother and tried to settle her down and would be back shortly to work through the latest documents that were often hundreds of pages. One day I was there when the fully armed sheriff's officers came pounding on the door and invited them in and showed them the metres of folders associated with the court cases. Their response was unexpected as they admitted to having read the document and the claims in the documents. I am guessing that they probably read them to ascertain if they were going into a dangerous situation and stated that the documents seemed ridiculous. The frequency became such that it was upsetting my mother and I asked if the Sheriff's office could ring me in advance and I would meet with them to pick up future documents. The response was conciliatory in that they would see what they could do with their sergeant. Like any branch of the public service, they were only doing their job and following procedures. It is pointless arguing if those procedures are right or wrong as they have no say. If they were serving an order for a dangerous criminal, then the flak jacket, side arms and extreme caution may be essential, so they wear them everywhere.

This first document set the scene for what would follow as the court system of the two countries were played against one another, the Australian courts versus the Netherlands courts.

What was fascinating, is that despite there being no defence in the first Dutch case, both Nellie and I lodged appeals. Nellie objected that she had not won a definitive ruling that all properties in Australia should be covered by Dutch law, and our relationship status as registered in the Netherlands (which was not recognised) should be the basis of any decision. To explain, the Dutch register relationships with the government just as we had when first arriving in the Netherlands, assisted by the relocation agent. The Australian de facto relationship has no equivalent, so we were seen by parts of the government as having no relationship at all. Some diplomats, from countries that are allowed several wives, register only one wife and any additional wives as domestic servants and so a mismatch in the government registers for foreigners is not unusual. The system does have some benefits in that the Dutch have for decades registered gay couples as married in the government offices and therefore never had an issue with the church wedding, which is not recognised and considered a ceremony before God. A couple that are "married" in a church, therefore normally then go to the Municipal offices and register (although the exact order is irrelevant) as happened with a wedding Jasmine attended for her teacher. We had simply registered in the way the Dutch administrators and relocation agent had sought fit. They could not transfer a de facto relationship document as no such document exists in Australia. Nellie and I therefore, had no official relationship other than her sponsoring me into the country in spite of a long relationship and our daughter.

The case in the Netherlands had largely stalled the progress in the Australian courts. What should have been simple, was made complex through massive lies, covertly lodging the court case in the Netherlands, submitting documents on the day of cases and a host of tactics that ran up massive legal fees and to me, showed a blatant abuse of process.

The situation was so bad that a year after I left the Netherlands, I wrote a letter for my daughter, Jasmine, and in case of my death, this was to be delivered to her in the presence of a psychologist. I was in a bad way, and was unsure if I could continue:

The original letter has not been altered except for names to ensure authenticity. This was written solely by the author.

Dear Jasmine

I know I cannot send you this but one day you should know the truth. It took me more than a year after your mother left us to find out most of the truth.

When your mother left me in March 2009 she said she would be down the road in case you wanted to see her. You did and that was good but never believed she was well and never capable of the love that you and Joe deserved.

After your mother left, I got some legal advice to organize a formal separation. You would not remember the house in Australia that I fixed up for you and Joe so it was safe to live in, but Joe may, and if you go through my affidavits of some of the work I did they are true. I think there was one mistake in that I negotiated to raise the rental income with the work I had done and think it came out that your mother raised the rent (the previous month before we left to the Netherlands) but otherwise I think it is all right.

Your mother:

- *Refused to cancel the life insurance that was on my life with her as beneficiary (that I thought had been cancelled years before when the bank was beneficiary but no longer needed when I paid off the mortgage).*

- *When she left and walked out, she said a few things to try to continue to control my life (that are outlined in my affidavits). Later she:*

- *Threatened that if I proceeded with trying to formally settle, she would ensure I never saw you again (succeeded in that, but that is not your fault and as I do not blame you, I must insist you never do)*

- *She would tell the police I had been assaulting her for 10 years and have Joe back her up.*

Some threats she followed through successfully and others she could not because I left:

- *Mid-August 2009 she came to the front door and started to push me in the chest saying "are you a man and what are you going to do about it" to try to make me hit back. I am still sure that she was trying to make me hit her, so she could go to the police and doctors to make her position better in court. The other thing is if she was able to show I could be violent, she could ensure I would not have access to you. There was no way I could stay there in those circumstances and I believe I already knew I needed to leave but that sped things up enormously.*

While progressing to trial she signed affidavits and convinced others to do the same (like Joe and Matt) to:

Say she was living at her new house (that she purchased more than two years before she moved out and I never knew). She had reregistered you and her to the new house for six weeks and as we all know, you and her never moved! She had neighbours of new house say they saw her go in and out, and yet another from work, that she had him around for breakfast there around two years before we separated. Joe and Matt were also involved so had them lie, although they specified slightly different dates and durations. It turns out this was the time Graham visited us in the Netherlands, so he was in the small room and mum still in main bedroom with me.

If the legal manoeuvres she is carrying out work, then I may be bankrupt and am not coping well now with all she is putting me through. She has pushed me beyond what I can handle lately (with her lawyers). I have been to a psychologist and helped until recently, but having the Australian legal system not function because of the Dutch, was a serious breaking point on the 10 June 2010. She deceived me for sixteen years and so if you find some difficulties with your mother in the future know that she conned your father all those years (and you are just a child). I am glad for all the years of enjoyment you provided me and hope that I will leave you what you really missed in your life. That is an extended family and a love of Australia.

Love you always
Trevor (dad)

The letter of course, was never sent. Not even my close relatives knew of its existence. The references to Nellie having convinced people, were that of her telling them her version of events that occurred, which was her perspective or her reality. She was able to convince Joe and Matt to assist her with the removal of documents from the house and having them, and others, submit false affidavits.

I had left the Netherlands in genuine fear that Nellie's would carry out the threat to lie to the police that I had been abusing her for ten years and the incident six days before I left, when she pushed me and tried to get me to fight back, that fear was reinforced. I would be trapped in a foreign country, trying to defend myself against the ridiculous claim of abusing her just as she had threatened. I would be held in the Netherlands and forced to defend myself in a foreign language, unable to get medical assistance and set up an exercise regimen to restore me to an acceptable level of health. Such actions could go on indefinitely until finances were depleted, unable to defend myself and isolated without any emotional support. It turned out, that decision to leave was possibly one of the best I ever made, as I now believe that I had under-estimated the danger. I would almost certainly not be alive today and available to my daughter when she starts asking the difficult questions and determining for herself, why I left her. Will she be left with the belief that her father left her and did not care about her rather than the facts of why I left?

In 2010, I recall sitting at my desk in Australia trying to type up a parenting plan. The very concept of this made me sick to my stomach. As time went by, the court documents became larger and larger. My Dutch lawyer once told me she had to purchase a bigger suitcase to carry the file as she had never had a case with this much paperwork, with every lie responded to, with the facts and proof. Such was the Dutch legal system that required so much detail and paperwork. If Nellie had a receipt for my underwear that I was wearing, she could even claim that was her legal property also, and the claims continued to stack up like a skyscraper!

It was around this time that I asked International Social Services (ISS) to become involved. Their role was to defend children and connect families across the world by providing social work and legal services to families and children separated across international borders, with an emphasis on the best interests and rights of the children. As it turns out, they weren't much help in my case. I was dealing with their Australian office who kept me up to date by email and the Dutch office had simply contacted Nellie and asked if they could speak to Jasmine and of course, never got a response. They claimed they could not contact Jasmine directly until she was eighteen and wondered why I bothered even trying to use them, but at least I had tried.

I was now to attend in person, the Dutch appeals and children's court cases. My attendances were no different to the Australian courts and as every case and court appearance came around, I learnt the art of not eating dinner the night before, nor breakfast the morning of the hearing. I would always feel a gut-wrenching pain that would purge my bowels and be so nauseated that would want to vomit before each case and it was easier to have no contents in my stomach. Bent over the hand basin in the courtroom toilets, dry retching and mopping up sweat with a hand towel became a common ritual for me. The anxiety would build for each and every case and never really dissipated until well after they were completed. This went on for four years.

There were three cases to be held in the Netherlands and I had to attend:

- The first was the appeal of the fraudulent case which was mainly aimed at either circumventing the Australian cases or delaying any such Australian proceedings (and were remarkably effective), but would only delay the inevitable. Not attending the Dutch appeal, I was informed, would be considered disrespectful to the court so, I had to attend. Of course, we can all say I could have ended it, however the only way I now believe Nellie's psychological or pathological need for control could have ended it, was with my life. Should I have not gone through the court processes, I doubt that Nellie would have ever backed off. At that stage, the only way to avoid the conflict would have been to have her properly assessed by the mental health community and treated; that would have been near impossible to do. The courts seem to not want to investigate if mental health issues are driving the conflict and perhaps the reason is that if they decided it was a mental health issue, they would then need to work out how this would impact their right to be heard in court.

- The second two cases were to do with Jasmine and to be run consecutively around a week later and therefore a trip was planned. They were mainly about custody and child support. They were essential to my daughters' welfare, so I had to attend.

I was genuinely fearful that Nellie would make accusations that I had assaulted her during my visit to the Netherlands for the court cases and that was enough for my brother to act. In his words, "Trevor believes he is likely to be attacked and needs a full-time witness, then that is good enough for me." Grahams' attitude was that if Nellie saw him, she is less likely to lose control and that way a confrontation would be avoided. He paid for his airfare and we booked into a youth hostel in The Hague. His partner, Lucinda, however, felt left out and decided to join us as well, which made the trip a little more difficult to organise.

As soon as I arrived in the Netherlands would Nellie stalk me, hurt herself and report me to the police? In the time since I had left the Netherlands, I knew of others who have had this happen and one that actually videoed his former spouse hitting herself while bragging how she would tell the police he did it in her emboldened drunken state. In that case, she was staring straight at the camera doing what turned out to be a confession to perjury and thank goodness that evidence was available. Was I just being paranoid?

The stalking did occur as we left the Dutch records office where Grahams' partner wanted to visit. Nellie went past us pushing my bike through the walking only area, the same bike that she said was too big for her when we were together, wearing a bike helmet along with a sun-smart helmet cover from the Australian Cancer Council. It was a completely ridiculous sight, as she covered her face with her hand as if that would shield her identity from us. Looking back years later it was like playing with my baby daughter by hiding my face and saying boo and she would laugh, but this was serious!

It had been many hours since the court case and there is nothing on that side of town that would have had her in that location and it made no sense that she would be there, although if challenged, I am sure she would invent some reason. There was nothing said, no weapons, no threats, just that feeling that your every movement is being scrutinised, and searching for the opportunity to set me up as she had previously threatened. As my brother and I joked about how ridiculous she looked, the serious side emerged and my gratitude that he was there, flashed through my mind. Not knowing what would have happened if he had not escorted me halfway around the world and if he was not present at that moment and there may have been an altercation like six days before I left the Netherlands. This time I may not be able to force the door shut and she could succeed in making out that I am the aggressor based on me being male, larger and stronger. Such an altercation, may have given greater credibility to the other false claim she had previously threatened of "I will tell the police you have been abusive for 10 years." The event that day to an outsider may conclude I was overly cautious, however it was the events weeks later and again years later, back in Australia, that confirmed that I was not paranoid!

In terms of the appeals court, Nellie's Dutch court documents claimed we had no relationship before going to the Netherlands, and that our daughter was the result of a one-night stand. While this was simply a lie and that a child was discussed, Nellie clearly was not thinking straight. She at one stage worked as a laboratory technician and her math skills are normally adequate. The dates she registered with the Dutch courts meant that Jasmine would have needed to be born two months premature. As she was delivered late (and induced) it was pointed out that, that claim was biologically impossible.

The case law of correct serving of documents was also pointed out, and while it required special dispensation to lodge the specific document that outlined the original letter from my Australian lawyer, and the progress of the mediation, it was submitted. This letter made it very clear that Nellie and her Dutch lawyer knew that the address of the service of the first case was ethically immoral, probably illegal, and was considered in the appeal.

I was asked only one question by the panel of three judges. "Is this the first time you have returned to the Netherlands since you left in August 2009?" The answer was "Yes." I now joke with people I travelled over 16,500 kilometres to say "Yes," just one word, but the truth is that there were the other cases the following week as well.

The findings were overturned in the appeal court based upon the facts, that were able to be presented as my lawyer and I had the time to submit a defence and those facts and common sense led to a correct decision. It was a final decision and not referred back to the lower court.

The decision that I shall not be considered a resident of the Netherlands at the time of serving was proven by the document between the lawyers asking for mediation which clearly stated that I had left the Netherlands and wanted to sort out maintenance for Jasmine and living arrangements. The Dutch property was to be equally divided as per the original advice by the Dutch commercial lawyer. As with the lower court, the appeals court confirmed they would not rule on property in Australia and this time stated not just that they wouldn't but legally couldn't as I was not a resident of the Netherlands at the time of the lodgement of the case. Apart from where I was living, it was pointed out the reason the lower Dutch court refused to decide on Australian property was due to sovereignty. A country cannot impose its laws on another country or the citizen of another country without an agreement with that country or person, as it simply cannot enforce a decision on another sovereign nation.

The eventual judgement was an overwhelming victory for legal process and common sense.

The other two court cases listed in the Dutch court were about Jasmine:

- The first was that Nellie wanted a ridiculous amount of maintenance per month to support Jasmine. While both Nellie and I had been on good professional salaries while living in the Netherlands, the claim was around 80% of what I took home per month, meaning I would not have enough for the most basic living expenses, such as food and utilities, let alone accommodation.

- To put this into perspective, my take-home pay was around €3,100 which would normally support a single income Dutch family well at the time and the claim to "mind" Jasmine was for €2,536. Furthermore, Nellie was on a comparable salary and would naturally control 100% of her salary. Therefore, Nellie essentially wanted control of 90% of the joint salary income even after separation. Modern definitions of domestic violence may consider that financial abuse, and as Nellie refused negotiation, the courts, which became the only option, exposed other incomes from properties and costs, which further distorted the income in Nellie's favour.

- The second was that Nellie had applied for sole custody, and it was my understanding that if granted and Nellie died, Jasmine would become a ward of the state. My second fear with the second case was that Nellie would then have Jasmine change her surname to further erase me.

I had made a counterclaim in the second case which was a request to get Jasmine some counselling and independent professional help to discuss her situation with her. This to me was an essential mental health issue that had previously been agreed by Nellie and myself, but not followed through. I had to fight various cases that were lodged by Nellie in the Netherlands, including the appeal and level of child support, however I only initiated this counterclaim and notifications to the court, that Nellie had not complied with their orders.

These two cases were listed immediately after each other by the same judge, so the judge used her discretion and they were not run independently and that was quite okay.

The tactics were almost perverse. I couldn't outline the threats and attacks and why I left the Netherlands, or it could be construed that there was no way Jasmine should be put in the middle of fighting parents. This occurs in some countries and the child is left with the custodial parent and when that person is the abuser, under the abusers' control.

Nellie, being the applicant for the child support, had her lawyer speak first. Bella (her lawyer) told of Nellie's outrage that I had left, not communicated or spoken to her about Jasmine's welfare, and not paid a cent since I left the Netherlands or any other time for that matter. Nellie also got to speak and outlined how she has tried unsuccessfully to explain to Jasmine why her father had deserted her and that Jasmine would never do that to her cats. Nellie continued that, at times she could not purchase toilet paper as there was no child support, and many other similar statements which allowed me to see the real extent of emotional manipulation and lack of focus on our daughter's wellbeing that had occurred since I left. At the time I left, there was around a year of after-tax salary (€60,000.00) that Nellie had taken out of the joint bank account, so how could things be such that she could not afford toilet paper? Most of these statements were in her affidavit to the court but added the emotional impact and extended them somewhat. The judge appeared to be concerned and ready to attack me but had the experience to wait and listen to the other side.

It was then Floortje's, (my lawyers) time to speak. She was clearly good at her job and outlined the conversations that were had, where all Nellie could do was abuse me for ten minutes and hang up and the dates they occurred (which I had written down the contents after those phone calls). Thinking back on those calls I did not mention that I could not believe how anyone could go on for ten minutes hurling all sorts of abuse, without seeming to take a breath.

Floortje then outlined that I had been in contact with Jasmine with calls each week on Saturdays, as Trevor knew Nellie was not normally in the house Saturday morning. Those calls lasted until Nellie had found out and Jasmine only then advised Trevor that it would be better if he did not call. Floortje did not want to mention Parental Alienation as it was such a contentious issue. I could only conclude that by Jasmine having conversations with me, her father, put her in a difficult position with her mother and I am sure from the judge's face she recognised that as well.

In terms of the sole custody, Floortje stated, "This should be rejected as Trevor has never argued a decision made by Nellie over Jasmine and there is therefore, no reason to strip him of parental rights." While this was true, it was because when I asked Jasmine if she opposed changing schools there was no response and I felt generally powerless. My lawyer continued, "Why would the court strip the father of parental rights when he is perfectly capable and willing to take over at any time."

In terms of the child support, "Trevor has kept a bank account in Australia and had been depositing child support into that account from the day he resumed work." Also, "Trevor wants to assist and is happy to provide the full government-mandated schedule back-dated, not only to the date the case was lodged but to the date he left the Netherlands if your honour deems fit. The only other reason that nothing has been paid, is that Nellie has refused to supply a bank account number to which Trevor can pay the child support, and that Nellie and her legal representative have refused to provide documents that are mandatory in this type of case, such as earnings statements and the like so that the government guidelines for assessing the apportionment of child support can be made."

Her honour's demeanour went from concern over me to an almost furious state over Nellie and her lawyer. "Where are the income statements, give them to me now!" in a very forceful tone, with all the authority a judge could muster as she looked squarely at Nellie and Bella! Nellie fumbled and found most of the documents along with how the claim was calculated and they were passed to Her Honour that quickly went through the documents. Her Honour then said "Well, this is ridiculous," and struck out many of the claims such as her repayments on an investment property and not showing the rental income. Nellie had spent an enormous amount of money and credited all the expenditure to Jasmine. Things like new towels, a holiday to Hungary for Jasmine and that I should also pay for Nellie and Joe (that I had known since he was six and I still regard as a stepson) as Jasmine could not go by herself. A trip to the cinema was also in the same bill and included her and Joe with the statement that I should pay for both of them as taking Jasmine to the cinema was something I always did in the past. It was clear to me and I suspect the judge as well, that what Nellie wanted was to pay for the maintenance of both Nellie and Joe as well. The ridiculous claims were struck out and it was clear to me that something sensible would be ruled when Her Honour considered the claims in detail later.

In terms of the request that Jasmine see a counsellor/psychologist, the judge heard that I was willing to fund it and that it was agreed to before I left the Netherlands but never done. The judge demanded to see Jasmine on Monday after she returned from her school year trip.

Later, at a meeting between the two lawyers, myself and Nellie, I recall her lawyer asking me to pay something in advance of the ruling. While I had no objection to providing money toward my daughter, I still hated paying over money that I am sure would all go to Nellie's lawyer. Regardless of my attitude, so be it. If the money I paid to raise my daughter was stolen by her mother and not used to fund her upkeep, then her mother will hopefully one day be held to account by Jasmine.

As part of the judgement, a sensible child support was ruled, sole custody rejected, seeing a psychologist was not enforced and it was recommended that I keep trying to reunite with Jasmine. I suspect that the judge recognised that Jasmine was under pressure not to associate with me, and therefore reject me, but could not rule in a way that would make it right. It is something that reinforced what I was trying to do and have continued to do ever since, be available for Jasmine, when she is ready.

Jasmine never did see a counsellor or psychologist. Nellie had Jasmine write out a statement that she does not want to see her father and sign it for the courts (something that in Australia was at one stage punishable under the Family Law Act) as it is effectively child abuse. Other things that were later discovered was that Jasmine started to work at a supermarket, and one day I may find out if this was like many teenagers to earn money for herself and give her independence. As her mother had said things in court like, "She had trouble explaining to her daughter why there is no toilet paper," it may have been that Nellie was denying the pocket money and making her feel like she had to contribute as I was not. It may have been that she felt obligated to help look after herself and not ask for money as this would increase conflict between Nellie and Jasmine and entrench the resentment towards me for leaving her in that situation. One day I may find out!

There were several things that I learned from these two cases:

- A judge will not rule that a sixteen-year-old do anything that the sixteen-year-old may object to, as how are they going to deal with enforcement? If the court ruled that the child should see a psychologist and the child refuses or attends but refuses to talk, then what can the judge do? The judges like to make orders that they can enforce if they are not complied with and that is hard with a child.

- The second was that anyone can claim anything in court (and regularly do) and it is how you deal with those claims that matter.

- I also learned that the courts are many years away from recognising parental alienation, which is the systematic destruction of the love between a parent and a child (when there has not been physical child abuse etc.) and that something needs to be done about it, but more about that later.

I continued with my weekly calls to Jasmine direct to her mobile. One time, I rang her when she was with friends on the train back from Rotterdam. The call went well but she preferred not to be disturbed with friends and asked me not to call. The communication changed to an e-mail every Sunday night, which went on for many years. Of course, there were the special telephone calls on birthdays and at Christmas, but many times they did not make it through. Maybe Jasmine was away on holidays or out for the day? But it was very different to when I brought her up and we would get up before 4:00 a.m. to speak to relatives while they had Christmas lunch in Australia. In one of those years, shortly after separation, I offered to pay for Jasmine to fly over for Christmas, to only be out-bid by her mother, as she offered an all-expenses-paid trip to Hungary.

I did get to see Jasmine and Joe on this trip. It was a stressful reunion for all involved and difficult to organise as Jasmine had not been communicating. Jasmines had a school trip to Morocco and while it may have been unknown to Nellie, I was on the school mailing list, able to see her school records including attendance and subjects, given consent for the trip, copied into all the details and trip itinerary, the information sessions which I could not attend, the email updates to parents on how the trip was going, so I was closely following her progress in every way possible. Lucinda, my brother's spouse however, wanted to see some of Europe and as Jasmine refused to communicate, rather than waiting in the local hostel, we took off for a few days to do a quick trip through Belgium visiting Bruges, France visiting Villers Bretonneux, Luxembourg and Germany, visiting Trier and driving up the Moselle and showing her castles but as this was the off-season, none were open. It was in Bruges, the first night of the trip, that I got an email from Jasmine, that she would meet me the following week after she returned from the school camp. While I was ecstatic that we would meet up, at the same time disappointed that she was putting it off. I would have packed the car and returned that night if I could see her.

Joe had arranged for us to all meet at McDonald's, which was somewhere neutral and on a Friday evening. Jasmine did not want to see me, but was apparently convinced by Joe at the last minute to attend. She had arrived back from a school camp in Morocco and had seen the Judge. I was at McDonald's with my brother, Graham, and his wife Lucinda, when Jasmine walked in. Her hair was long and unkempt, you could tell from her face that she had been crying, eyes red, the skin on her cheeks patchy. I felt so terrible for her and thought she still could not process what was happening. She had been clearly taught to hate me and that I had abandoned her. I am sure she had no knowledge of Nellie's blackmail, or what some would call coercive control, being that her mother would make sure I never saw Jasmine again unless I did not do what she wanted, the threats to lie to the police and have me locked up, or the final assault, being the reason why I left the Netherlands. Perhaps she felt she was betraying her mother by talking to me and that every word she spoke would be extracted from her by her mother, as such interrogation is common in parental alienation cases. We were so close as a father and daughter, up until the conflict with Nellie which started some weeks after Nellie walked out and maybe, she was made to feel totally betrayed with my leaving. My heart sank, but put on a brave and friendly face.

While I focused on Jasmine, I asked her to help me order everyone's meals and we stood in the queue together, surrounded only by strangers. I asked her if there were any questions she had for me, hoping she would ask me what was troubling her but the answer was "No." I asked her did she enjoy her school trip to Morocco and again a single word answer of "Good." The more open-ended questions like what did you do in Morocco were either dismissed or answered in a way to cut the conversation like "Went to places with the school." Eventually, we took the trays back to the table and gave Jasmine and Joe belated presents, the main ones being her sixteenth birthday present from myself and one from her grandmother that had been returned to Australia unopened, which at the time had put her grandmother in tears. There was also a birthday cake with candles as we had missed being there for her birthday as time raced by. No-one could break through to Jasmine and the conversation moved to Joe who was trying his best to make Jasmine comfortable and talked about what he was doing, and he asked questions about Australia. Jasmine eventually got up and went to the toilet in tears. Lucinda (my brothers' wife) followed a minute or so later. With Jasmine locked in a cubicle crying, Lucinda later told me that she tried to console her. As Lucinda ran a childcare centre, her opinion that Jasmine's behaviour was extremely unhealthy, and her facial expressions that showed deep concern, reinforced my concerns over Jasmine's anguish and mental health. Jasmine eventually returned signalling to Joe as she walked outside. Joe went outside and returned and said they have to leave now, and he took all the presents and cake and said he will try to get Jasmine to meet again over the weekend. Meeting with Jasmine was heartbreaking. Even if she had yelled at me for leaving, at least I could have responded. I just hoped that we would meet over the weekend.

I then got a voice message but did not notice it for some time. It was largely silent but it was from Jasmine. She had either tried to ring me or mistakenly called me just before she entered McDonald's according to the caller ID and it appeared the phone was then in her pocket. The whole meeting was recorded however as it was in her jacket, it was just a very long, very quiet, muffled voices and not a word could be understood although I played it several times to try to glean some information.

I had booked flights for the Sunday so that I could have the maximum availability for Jasmine, but in spite of requests by text and phone calls, she did not want to meet. I found that her mother had left to go to Australia for the court cases before Joe and Jasmine met with us and perhaps that had allowed her the opportunity to meet.

In the lead up to the Dutch cases, back in Australia, Nellie had filed around nine sworn affidavits full of perjury. Some were blatant perjury, while others like the one from her work colleague included that the two of them went to France for a "dirty" weekend in Amiens, while I looked after the kids, were a revelation that may or may not have been true. I actually did not know if that weekend in the Amiens was just another lie to bolster her case that our relationship had ended, was aimed to hurt me or was the truth. At the time, I was told that she went for a weekend reunion with some of her old work colleagues from another department. Whether it was a lie or the truth, the deception and breach of trust either at the time of going on the trip or now in the affidavit, was malicious. That affidavit sent me to the doctors for a check-up and blood tests!

The trip home from the Netherlands with Graham was uneventful. Lucinda had rearranged her travel schedule so she could visit Paris and enjoy its sights. I had organised some "Temaze" tablets to put me to sleep during the trip as I would be in court the morning after I arrived back.

The first court case in Australia went well. I feared that each lie in the affidavits would be believed and had spent significant time on preparation, analysing the affidavits and addressing each item line by line that ensured the facts were presented to my Australian lawyer. The hard work paid off, and if not done then, I may have lost. The court was able to see through all the lies to such an extent, I was given the rights to lodge a claim for costs. The stress of going through this was enormous and costly both in legal fees but also emotionally and mentally. In the early stages of court preparation, it was impossible to work while recovering from the burst disc, the countless hours providing the evidence for the lawyers and when I did secure work, I needed weeks off to attend court, then long hours at night preparing for court. Defending myself had become a full-time job.

9

Fathers' Support on stress and nightmares

When you are under tremendous stress such as with a family breakdown, the events and nightmares of the past can return to haunt you.

I had been in a car accident when I was mid-twenties, and someone had died. That was over twenty-five years ago, but for the first time in decades, I started to have nightmares and seeing the face of the dead person as the event was recalled. I should be quite grateful as a friend that was a refugee from a war zone, had nightmares during his court case of when his head was held and forced to watch his parents being shot and sister raped by soldiers. I have often told about the power of the brain and the neural pathways being reinforced such that even those things that are suppressed or filed away, can be brought back. All I can think is that perhaps the pathways associated with other forms of trauma are strengthened such that horrors from our past come back to haunt us.

Calls from the lawyer that the case was to be delayed were regular and due to the many tactics that were perpetrated by Nellie and her legal teams. It simply meant that the confrontation would be extended, costs would spiral up and not seeing my daughter, knowing she was suffering, was devastating. One such call caused me to have an emotional breakdown while driving on the freeway. Despite having a hands-free kit, the tears were impacting my vision and the emotions so high that I had to stop. The emergency stopping lane on the freeway was put into use and to hell with the police or anyone else that wanted to ask what was going on.

At this stage, I knew that the trauma was at the forefront of my mind as old traumas were reappearing. I knew it was time to seek some professional help and was encouraged by my lawyer during that freeway call, my mother and others, so I did. I not only took up seeing a psychologist, but I discovered a group on the internet called Father Support; they were a peer support group that met weekly.

Initially, I sent Fathers Support an email enquiry before the first Australian case and even the Dutch child custody case. A few days passed when I then got a call from Lawry, who was a facilitator at the local group. Lawry was a colourful character, extremely committed to helping save the lives of men and had a history himself that was as extreme as mine. I would come to the group and share my story and found it helped me personally but also, to not feel alone, to feel supported, that others were suffering in similar ways and I wasn't going mad on the emotional rollercoaster.

The aim of the Peer Support model at Fathers Support was to:

- Explain some of the processes you may encounter along the way.

- Share valuable information and experience and access to resources.

- Provide a safe place to share your story (i.e. unload).

- Provide a community of common circumstances that have experienced what has occurred, challenges of others, understanding and emotional impact.

- Be anonymous.

- Encourage patience—we have all been through this.

- Provide access to mediation, financial, mental health services and more.

- Help find services that are local to where you work and reside at a time when you need them most.

The peer support model helped me immensely and assisted me to stay focused on my daughter's well-being. It helped me understand that I had to help the court by providing the information, so it can make informed decisions. Fathers Support is an organisation that I continue to be active with today.

Following the freeway incident where I became so upset it was dangerous to drive and stopped, I saw a doctor (General Practitioner) that gave me what they call a "General Practitioners Mental Health Plan." It was an approach I preferred as I hated drugs, especially after the narcotics that I was prescribed for pain management caused by the burst disc in my back.

It took some effort to see a psychologist which started around the same time as I started with Fathers Support. I could just picture being put down by Nellie with statements like, "That weakling couldn't manage on his own, and needed to see a head shrink" even though she saw one most of her life! I see it all the time when I talk directly to both men and women as well on confidential Facebook chat groups. They go to court and face the assertion from their former partner or their partner's lawyer, that the children would be unsafe with them and should not be allowed to see the children as they are mentally unstable and in the care of a psychologist or psychiatrist. The fear of repercussions from seeking professional help can be insurmountable for some. Maybe this is part of the reason that when broken down by gender, the successful rate of suicide is around three times higher in the Australian male population than it is for the female population[7] but I doubt it. My personal opinion of the difference in suicide rates is that it is more likely related to the lack of male-friendly services, as many men want to be able to hear from others, be able to share for a purpose which may be to learn new skills, and have something like a roadmap that they can put into action, rather than just expressing themselves.

I telephoned to book an appointment with the psychologist and remember being told by the receptionist that he

---

[7] https://www.beyondblue.org.au/media/statistics

was fully booked for the next month and I did not bother to make a booking. The following day, I was much worse and rang again, got the same story and broke down over the phone. The receptionist clearly had the training to realise the severity of my condition and got my phone number and rang back. Instead of going to the local office for the appointment, it was a thirty-minute drive to where the clinical psychologist was working that day, but he saw me that same afternoon. I think I had six intensive sessions in around three weeks and a special referral for additional visits.

While it is always easy to criticise a government, this is good policy in my opinion as it probably kept me out of hospital and circumstances that should never be contemplated.

It is amazing how much a person can be considered a psychosocial organism. Essentially, we each have our own psychological make-up, we need social interaction, we are a flesh and blood organism, and all three axes are interrelated and impact one another. One psychologist informed me he read a document which listed around 140 physical symptoms that can be caused by stress. The symptoms largely depend on you as an individual, but chest pains, headaches, stomach cramps (that I suffered every court case) and feeling like vomiting are familiar to many of us, and there are many others. It seems so many problems can be triggered by stress; that the old saying, "laughter is the best medicine", may have some basis.

I know I suffered a diagnosed medical conditions during this time which included the stress-related chest pains.

Common in therapy is the principle that:

One example is that if we feel depressed (think/feel) and don't get out of bed (act/behave), then it is unlikely we will find work (outcome). Some doctors will prescribe pills/anti-depressants to break the cycle, so you get out of bed and keep going, while psychologists will alter how you perceive a situation, but either of those approaches are working on just one of the three variables in the cycle. Fathers Support taught me that if I thought it was hopeless, as many men do when they are first faced with a custody issue, then I may not prepare and present the information to the court well and would get a bad result. Some may consider this a self-ful-filling prophecy. This helped push me forward to ensure I prepared for courts cases, and while I would probably be homeless or dead, if I didn't prepare, I was still trying to win the battle of reinstating my relationship with my daughter.

I had been to Fathers Support for a significant amount of time and it was just before returning to the Netherlands that I found I had to fill in as a group facilitator. The process is well structured, and it is really a matter of following the process and getting everyone to have their say and moderating, so despite of what I was going through, I was able to fill in.

The one thing I found running the occasional men's group, is that steering the conversation so that people learn from others experience and utilising some peer pressure can be very useful tools. When men come to the group, they are often very reluctant to see a clinical psychologist and with some encouragement, changing their perspective and often peer pressure, usually helps.

One of the main reasons that a parent in litigation is reluctant to see a psychologist is due to a fear that the "other parent" will say in court they are mentally unstable and need a psychologist. This is a scenario that as a facilitator you quickly learn to deal with, turn around their thinking and most importantly, not to tell them what to do but to give them options for possible actions.

The people that come are looking for answers and strategies to resolve their issues and I found it is rare that they are violent, drug-addicted or alcoholic. A direct question will normally give the answer if they are violent, drug-addicted or alcoholic or is revealed as they tell their story and complementary services are available if they are and willing to "own their shit." When they have been the subject to false allegations, the conversation then moves to:

Facilitator, "Yes, you have been accused of being violent, a drug addict, an alcoholic, or whatever other false allegation made to the police or in affidavits to the court. Have you ever been trained to deal with this scenario of being falsely accused?"

Participant, "No."

Facilitator, "Why wouldn't you be stressed?"

Participant, "I suppose it is normal to be stressed."

Facilitator, "One answer you could give the court if questioned, is that you were under extreme stress, never trained to deal with this situation and sought professional help to be the best parent you could. The chances are the judge will see your actions as positive!"

Facilitator, "When it was me, I would then often ask participants in the group who is seeing a psychologist and what you got out of it during the discussion phase when we get a reluctant new participant."

Once the participant realises there are benefits others have experienced and how to not only defend but turn seeing a psychologist into an advantage in court, they often make appointments quickly. The participants realise there is no shame, they were not equipped to handle their situation by their parents or at school, the stigma is removed, and their rate of improvement is greatly accelerated to quickly become a productive member of society and a better parent.

To demonstrate how everyone is different, one of the coping sessions I attended included the analogy of the five people at the intersection that witness a serious car accident:

- The First—Faints and falls to the ground—They later find the first person's sister had been killed in a car accident recently and was so traumatised by the situation.

- The Second—Looks at the car and sees the extent of the damage and relaxes. Turns out to be a panel beater and could see it was a minor damage to the front panel and the airbags had not gone off, so assessed it as not very serious.

- The Third—Who was trained in first aid looks and applies the DRSABCD (which is an acronym for: **D**anger, **R**esponse, **S**end for help, **A**irway, **B**reathing, **C**irculation, **D**efibrillation) in accordance with their training.

- The Fourth—Panics and screams uncontrolla-bly—Recognising the car, he fears the worst for his family or friend as he is not trained to act like the third person in this example.

- The Fifth—Immediately rings the emergency services, see the other heading toward the car and determines they are first aid trained, continues to assess the situation, ensure the first person is attended to and hasn't received a critical head injury from her fall and starts to co-ordinate and deal with the situation. The fifth person turns out to be an off-duty policeman.

We can see that the five people each have completely different backgrounds, training and life experience, which means they react differently. The same goes for so many situations in life. Such is the case with everyone that comes to the Fathers Support. They all have differing levels of family support, slightly different accusations (however false claims of domestic violence are probably the most common), different upbringings that impact their perceptions and so on.

Unfortunately, very few people have training to deal with Post Traumatic Stress Disorder (abbreviated into PTSD) such as those that lived through a disaster, or high trauma situations such as had a bullet pass them in an armed robbery. The lesser known variation is cPTSD being Complex PTSD that can occur as a result of repetitive, prolonged trauma involving sustained abuse. The physical symptoms of the chest pains caused by the stress of the situation and also signs of cognitive dysfunction that I experienced and still do, are likely to be cPTSD related.

Walking out of an appointment one day, I questioned myself, *Did I hear that right? Cognitive dysfunction?* It is amazing how you can mishear something and jump to conclusions about what you thought you have heard. Taking things, a step at a time, calming down and checking facts is something we all need to practice and is something that I learned to become more vigilant in carrying out.

Cognitive dysfunction is as common as forgetting where you put your keys when you got home. Some have this dysfunction as typical, it is part of their lives. I doubt anyone reading this has not forgotten where they parked their car or left their keys. There were several occasions when this happened to me during the trauma of those years in litigation. I have always had problems remembering names, but this was made far worse during the trauma of the separation process.

10

The heart-attack, more avoidance, threats and the high court

The first Australian case was held in the days after I arrived back from the Netherlands although the Australian decision was not handed down for some time. The court decided many of the facts of the case based upon the evidence, which was compelling. The differences in our two versions of history were extraordinary including where we lived, that Jasmine was the result of a one-night stand and that we rarely saw each other in Australia. Apart from the massive reconciliation of bank accounts, that proved our lives were intertwined, that we did things like dancing lesson together, that I did contribute to the household income, and there was also subpoena's which included one on Nellie's psychiatrist.

The first subpoena was on the psychiatrist notes and while I did not view the notes myself, there was three things that I was informed that were very relevant and shook me to my core:

- The first was that the diagrams of the family

structure proved without doubt that Nellie had lied in her affidavits and we were a family in Australia which supported all the other evidence that was collated.

- The second was that she had said I was her second husband. Being told previously that he was a bank teller that she had a relationship, in a way that led me to believe it was an affair that she became pregnant to, I could not reconcile what I was told. I could only conclude that she lied to her psychiatrist or to me. I actually think she lied to her psychiatrist, and that was the reason she was so defensive when I asked if she would like me to attend the therapy sessions, with what I thought was a counsellor, as her lies to the psychiatrist would have been exposed. I still do not know who she lied to.

- The third was that Nellie was jealous of the relationship I had with Jasmine and that she wanted to destroy it.

My entire life with Nellie was exposed as a lie and I had been manipulated all that time. The seventeen years together and now going onto another two years in court. I only knew I had no choice and that I could no longer allow Nellie to control me, that she wanted to destroy me and I had to defend myself.

Another subpoena was for all the documents that Nellie and Joe had removed from the Netherlands property that had resulted in the altercation between Joe and myself with the police being called. Those receipts showed some of the work that had been done on the Australian family home before we moved, but it was far from being a complete file that she had removed. I had personally collated that file as it showed the improvements to the house which would impact on the capital gains tax calculations. Knowing this file would be important from my postgraduate studies, I knew most of its contents.

One of the receipts made out to me proved that the house was repointed (which is basically cementing up the capping tiles on the top of the roof and those in the valleys), and many tiles were replaced. Building an access hatch under the house and removing the old heating systems so an electrician had access was an early task that I had carried out which had no receipts. We did recover the drawing of the house and where ceiling fans and power points were to be placed which I had done for the electrician, and there was a receipt made out to me showing that I had paid for the work. Similarly, other activities had no receipts such as removing the old rubber tree that was probably planted in the 1960s that had lifted the concrete slab inside the garage and the back access to the laneway such that the garage door would not even open. The receipts for the concrete works and new roller doors did exist and were made out to me. Some receipts such as replacement of water and gas pipes were able to be accessed and an affidavit was submitted by the tradesman that I had known for decades. I even managed to get the local government to provide the building renovations plans and the town planning application (which had my name on them) for the carport. Government registration documents for voting, Medicare card which was for Jasmine and myself, were registered to that address also proved where we lived.

I had raised Joe all those years, going to the parent-teacher nights, funded his education and even pocket money, not to mention taking him to all medical appointments, doctors and emergency call outs. I not only felt that I had been lied to about our relationship, but lied to about the income from the property that I had made habitable and about the increase in the rent, but that Nellie had also misled Joe about his parentage and how he was supported!

One other piece of evidence that we included was a statement Nellie had made to the Dutch police in April 2009 which put the date of separation as late March 2009. In fact, even that was a lie as it was early March, but I suspect Nellie made it late March to give the impression she wasted no time in notifying the police and that this report was instigated after advice from Bella (Nellie's Dutch lawyer). The same police statement had a supplementary statement in February 2010, nearly a year later, which asked the police to amend the report as she must have made a mistake and the separation was much earlier. This was done nearly a year after the original police report, possibly realising the revised dates would be to her advantage in the Australian cases. Her credibility in tatters, the judge ruled, to paraphrase, "That I believe the applicant in all aspects where the two versions differ unless stated otherwise," and, "That it should proceed to settling the matter in the second case."

The claim in the court affidavits, that we had never lived together and when we separated was seen for what it was, a complete fabrication and perjury, however it took enormous effort to assist the court in coming to that conclusion. All I could think of was that if this was to be finalised, then things may settle down and I could restore a relationship with Jasmine and hopefully, everyone can move forward.

The courts' primary duty in our adversarial system is to make decisions based upon the law and the evidence presented to them. The ability of the court to achieve an outcome that equates to justice: rests with the applicant and the respondent, with their lawyers to present good information; the skill of the lawyer to ensure the right questions are asked at the right time, and everything that is relevant is available to the judge. The court fails miserably when:

- One party is so traumatised that they cannot answer an affidavit/questions or issue instructions to their representatives, and

- The judge is not presented with the information they require, and that

- The parties fail to make the right requests of the court.

One thing I have learned is that it is difficult to prove an untruth never happened, however with massive effort, I was able to prove Nellie had lied to the court. At the end of all the litigation in Australia, I calculated that I had been before the family court on some sixty different individual days. Some were a ten-minute mention which involved the judge assessing if all required documents had been, or will be lodged; setting the court date; or handing down the orders where I was not required to attend; while others where a full day saga. The reason for the sixty days, and years of cases can be somewhat explained.

In order to delay one case and I believe wear me down, both financially and emotionally, Nellie hired a barrister that objected and delayed proceedings at every turn so that it could not be completed in the four days allocated by the judge. She later admitted that this barrister was selected to delay the proceedings knowing that it may be several months until there may be a space in the judge's calendar for the case to be completed. It was a week before the resumption of that case that more delays were orchestrated. We received a message that Nellie had been at the *Schiphol* (Amsterdam) Airport to fly back to Australia for a Family Court case when she had collapsed with severe chest pains, difficulty breathing, and been rushed by ambulance to the Amsterdam Medical Centre Cardiac Unit (accompanied by her son, Joe, in the back of the ambulance) and she was admitted. The message was that she intended to request a stay in proceedings while she recovered and couldn't get there next week as she would also need to rebook flights.

Upon hearing the news, the delays she had orchestrated to date, meant that my legal representatives believed it was just another act to delay and extend the case. My attitude was possibly the most sympathetic in that I knew the relationship between stress and chest pains from personal experience and believed she had suffered a severe panic attack and that it was normal to test and eliminate a heart issue as the cause. I still believe the chest pains leading up to the hospital admittance were real, although others thought it was all an act. As I had travelled back to Australia for my uncle's funeral years earlier at very short notice, and with the number of airlines on that route, I was fairly sure that flights could easily be organised.

In the coming days, I looked up the internet and verified my suspicions that there were many flights she could get on in the following days and I saved the flight availability to file as a record. We finally received the formal affidavit of the events and included a request for a six-month delay while she recovered.

The affidavit Nellie eventually lodged contained a medical document (in Dutch of course) that purportedly admitted her into the Amsterdam Medical Centre Cardiac ward. That was all that could be reasonably ascertained, as the attachment to the affidavit appeared to have been faxed and copied so many times, it was illegible in any language, apart from the letterhead and clearly it was the Amsterdam Medical Centre (which is a major hospital, or in Dutch, a *Ziekenhuis*).

Further details apart from the affidavit were not available as her legal representatives conveyed their client's wishes for a six-month stay while their client recovers to the judge. The motion was strenuously opposed as there was no evidence as to why six months was required or appropriate and we formally requested a legible copy of the medical certificate and the medical records. In short, we alleged it was a sham and if it was not, then the medical records would reveal the truth.

The judge stood the case down for one month and rescheduled. In the month that followed, we did not receive the medical file, but did receive a clear copy of the certificate from the Amsterdam Medical Centre. The diagnosis was clear in the areas that had been obscured through the faxing and copying. There was nothing wrong with her physically and the recommendation from the Cardiac ward was that she should see a psychiatrist.

Sir Walter Scott wrote in a poem, "Oh what a tangled web we weave, when we practice to deceive," was never more appropriate.

Here was a woman that may have had a severe panic attack. While other people said to me that they thought she should be forced to pay membership to the Actors Union. A woman, that was causing everyone to be sick (including herself), and wasting court time and costs. I will never know if Nellie had done an internet search into how to fake a medical condition, before she packed her bags to go to the airport, or, as I suspect, it really was a panic attack. I am guessing and prefer to believe that after she left the *Ziekenhuis*, Nellie sought to take maximum advantage of the event by trying to delay the case another six months and to provide her more time to alienate my daughter from me by putting off facing the reality of the situation and justice.

Nellie inferred that she had a heart attack, but the following day typed up a full affidavit, ensured the medical certificate was largely illegible, then travelled the several kilometres (probably by bicycle I suspect) to get her signature witnessed by the consular staff on the document, and liaise with her legal representatives.

I would hope that she had taken the advice that, "She should see a psychiatrist," but I am unlikely to ever know. As it turned out, this was not the first time a recommendation had been made that she should see a psychiatrist as was discovered in the referral documents left behind in the house. This was not the end of her deception. She sank to even greater levels in poor behaviour as time dragged on.

The timing of the objection and asking the court that the evidence be presented was the key to preventing the matter from being extended another six months. I am sure at the end of that period, if granted, she would have claimed she was still not right to travel!

The total inability to control oneself brings people down in astonishing ways. While some people may have an acquired brain injury that impacts the frontal lobe, removing their ability to consider others and is clinically diagnosable, others do not. I had read in one psychology magazine article, that it was found that people raised in war-torn areas had a less developed frontal lobe which impacted on their ability to show empathy and love and proposed that it was an environmental adaptation. Certainly, the inability to control oneself or total lack of judgement as to one's actions can have far-reaching consequences.

I recall that I tried to get mediation around seven occasions. One was before I left the Netherlands and Nellie, after the mediation attacked me which saw me depart to Australia. Another was where the two Dutch lawyers, that were also registered mediators, tried to get some agreement.

This time Nellie wanted to get a mediator in Australia. The proposal was that a retired judge and both our lawyers and barristers attend. What I discovered when I investigated the background of the proposed retired judge, was that she had retired early after it was discovered that she had copy-and-pasted her judgements and got caught out as she left the wrong peoples' names in decisions and had made the national papers. Quite frankly it made no sense as it would be all the expenses of a normal court case but our response was diplomatic. The response was something along the lines of we would consider if it was in Melbourne, that the person overseeing the matter be agreed upon by both parties and that Nellie would act with decorum in that she would not:

- Threaten to ring my employer and try to have me sacked.

- Not raise her fist to the mediators.

- Not yell obscenities.

- Not revert to standing, shaking and yelling, "I don't want him to have anything."

Nellie's response was immediate, with a threat to sue me, as "that was done in a meeting where I had signed a confidentiality agreement". The fact was, that I had never said those events had ever occurred in the past. There was never an attempt to sue me but that was the end of that attempt at mediation.

The time in court is nothing compared to the time one spends worrying and preparing for a court case. This will vary based upon your personality. With a salesperson that likes to think on their feet, being totally different from mine, which is one of planning and preparation. "Poor preparation leads to piss poor performance," is what Lawry from Fathers Support use to say.

Nellie would tend to leave things as late as possible, which was typical for her. In this case, it was more likely a tactic so that it was difficult to prepare a proper defence and therefore create more issues and delays. The first case in Australia, I had lodged, as there was stalling in sorting out valuation and I suspected the lodgement would speed things up. Her lawyer turned up late for the hearing and dropped the affidavit saying the case had already been listed in the Netherlands.

A few weeks before each Australian case, I would make a formal offer to settle which was also in the form of a Calderbank offer. Basically, a Calderbank offer is a genuine offer to settle, that their case has little merit or will result in a much worse outcome for them. In other words, they will benefit by not going to trial if it proceeds. In addition, should I get a better financial outcome than the offer made then, I will then request costs (for wasting the courts time, my time and all that money).

The week before one case, attempts to have the Dutch witnesses give evidence electronically were lodged by Nellie and this would be opposed. It would be opposed for various reasons such as:

- How can a witness be cross-examined when English is not their native language and only a fraction of communication is by words? Body language is even more important in this case.

- There was no information as to how the witnesses would be sworn in, and how it would be done such as in a Dutch courtroom.

- What were we to do if some "smart arse" comments are made, and how can we deal with contempt? Will they be locked up? And who will lock them up if the judge deems that should be done?

My greatest disappointment was that Nellie then flew Joe over to testify. I pleaded with Nellie not to put him on the stand and commit perjury, but she was unrelenting and took the pleading as a threat that I would have them both jailed as the penalty at the time was ten years for perjury and fifteen years for subornation (having someone lie for your benefit) of perjury. I was so concerned that Joe may be impacted by what Nellie was doing to him. I wondered what support I could put in place and being that he was being mistreated by his mother, wondered if he would search for answers in terms of his biological father or even reach out to me.

I actually succeeded in tracking down Joe's father through old phone books on a 1990's CD, talked to the neighbours, and eventually acquired his phone number which was unlisted. The conversation with Joe's father was difficult. He clearly knew that Nellie had moved overseas and upon hearing from me he went into panic, "You mean she is back in the country?" He understood that Joe was being made to testify in court to support his mother, and may be very distressed, but insisted that I do not pass on his details and that he did not want to see Joe. Maybe he had a new family and did not want them to know of his past. I sensed genuine fear of Nellie, but perhaps there was a level of apprehension of either meeting his adult son or telling people that he has an adult son. Perhaps what I sensed from Nellie was that he was in a relationship at the time may have come into play. Whatever the circumstances, Joe was to not be told. Joe never seemed to react to what his mother had him do and while he was very courteous to myself and my brother Graham over the subsequent years, he ceased acknowledging the birthday and Christmas wishes.

Joe was a great asset to Nellie and stuck to the script that Nellie had given him as to the history of the relationship. Again, he had not stayed out of the battle between his parents, and his allegiance was clear. Just as he was, when he helped Nellie take all the documents and the altercation in the street in the Netherlands. Nellie, however, buckled under the cross-examination and the two stories were now at odds. I was later informed that he missed his end of semester examinations and had to repeat half a year of his University course. Nellie had put him at risk (although perjury is never prosecuted in the Family Court) and cost him six months of his life.

Before the second case, we issued a series of affidavits to the banks which forced Nellie to make her financial declarations complete. Nellie revealed she had transferred money across to a third country (a well-known tax haven). While Nellie and I had raised Joe through our joint income, including the international school fees, she had lied that the income from child support from Joe's father was minimal and never increased from when Joe was born. She also had lied and that there was no net income statement from the rental of our former Australian family home that I had invested in to make livable and rentable. The court subpoena was in hindsight, the only way to get to the facts of the seventeen-year deception and its continuation through the court cases that followed.

Nellie entered the court with an apparent air of confidence and in this case, was accompanied by her new female solicitor/barrister. The Australian barrister Nellie had chosen this time had recently written an article for a magazine and I suspect that this is where Nellie had found her, and then recruited her. She was young, and physically attractive. This was the person that Nellie stated before we entered a mediation session in the Netherlands that, "She had visited and hired her after the last Australian court case." Nellie also stated that, "She is really good, and she is going to fix you." Little wonder why mediation failed when Nellie entered with that attitude.

I suspect that Nellie simply thought it must have been her previous legal team for not having the skill to present her case or that the judges were incompetent for "not getting it" and the next judge would. In her mind she was right, and all her actions justified. The perspective of other people was that this level of righteousness, based upon the facts and her demands, appeared to border on delusional. Some people envy such confidence while others consider it as a personality disorder associated with narcissism. How could she think like this after the recent setbacks in both countries?

The preliminaries are about how the full hearing was to be conducted, it started with the witness list and electronic submission was discussed in a very formal manner. Our position was made clear as was Nellie's, so we were all sent away by the judge to work it out, or he would rule in a couple of days' time. We could not agree, and the ruling was then made that witnesses have to attend, and the hearing would proceed with or without those witnesses.

I had just been on the stand under examination (some say interrogated), by Nellie's new lawyer and my barrister had just started the cross-examination when court went into a 15-minute recess. I was sitting with my brother in the foyer and Nellie goose-stepped up to us with a finger under her nose as if to portray Hitler. The hatred was seething. Then she blurted out:

"Are you and your brother still sponging off us?" I managed to respond, "Can we discuss Jasmine seeing a psychologist?" to which there was an immediate response, "You are the one that needs to see a psychologist!" "I should have put a bullet through you, I would have claimed domestic violence and only got five years maximum!"

My lawyer could see something was going on from a distance and approached. Nellie scurried away like a cockroach that had been exposed by the light and the footsteps of someone's approach.

"Is it all okay?" my clearly concerned lawyer asked. My response was, "Yes, Nellie just threatened to kill me," which was possibly surprising to him, but I did not regard this as out of character.

The barrister was not far behind, hearing as I responded to my lawyer, he separated myself and my brother and instructed us both to write down what had just happened.

After looking at the written responses from my brother and I, the barrister came back with the statement that, "I will be asking you about this when you are back on the stand."

In hindsight, I now realise the barrister separating us was just like what the police would do, to see if we told the same story rather than questioning us together or having time to concoct a story over an event, that had happened less than half a minute previously. It was a simple method to verify that what we said was correct.

What followed in court was a quick question as to what happened out in the foyer, my response and an immediate objection from Nellie's barrister. Nellie's barrister asked, "Did you go and report it to the court security?" to which my response was, "I thought lawyers were firstly officers of the court and therefore, yes I reported it." Nellie's barrister was clearly uncomfortable with what Nellie had done, but continued to follow Nellie's direction. The statement Nellie's barrister then made was, "The matter does not relate to the case and therefore the incident should be regarded as irrelevant to the court."

The facts of what occurred that day in that judge's foyer were never disputed and it was not until much later that I realised why it was so important to raise the event. That threat, more than anything else, revealed more about Nellie and the toxic, abusive relationship we had. The threat, also put many of the affidavits and other actions into context, including why I left the Netherlands. It was an event that was real, challenged the court to act to prevent what was clearly a case of domestic violence even though, this was meant to be a property settlement.

My affidavit included Nellie's Dutch affidavits, Dutch court decisions, all with translations certified by a court-approved translation service. What that meant was that all Nellie's statements were on record for this case. Nellie had looked at each of her cases in isolation and had crafted each story to get the maximum benefit for that specific case, be it Dutch property, Dutch custody, Dutch child support or the Australian affidavits.

As Nellie sat in the witness box, my barrister skillfully jumped from one affidavit to the other. "So, you said in the Dutch affidavit ... And in the Australian affidavit ... Which judge did you lie to, was it in your Dutch and Australian sworn affidavits?" Nellie's answer was strange and stated, "The Dutch affidavits are not sworn."

"So, you submitted documents to a court of law knowing the judge would make a decision on them and you lied. You even lodged the notification of the court case to my client's former address knowing he would not receive it!" Still no verbal response, just a shrug of the shoulders. "The Dutch court has ruled in their decision that you are to sign the documents to sell the Dutch family home and after all this time you still haven't followed that order!" There was no response to this statement but another shrug of the shoulders.

This was too much for the Australian judge, who stopped my barrister in his tracks. It was that intense, and not knowing much about the law and what was occurring, I had expected something like badgering the witness and ordering a court recess. He didn't call a recess but took over not so much asking but yelling, "Why haven't you signed the document?" "What is stopping you signing it here and now?" Nellie shrugged her shoulders again. It was reminiscent of the children's court where the judge got nasty weeks earlier and demanded documents be handed over immediately! I suspect that the incident earlier that day in his foyer with the goose-stepping, threats to kill, lying in court (perjury), contempt for his international (Dutch) colleagues and failure to follow those court orders, meant that he realised what he was dealing with and that she had no respect for his authority and that of the courts.

The hearing continued shortly after with more facts being revealed. Nellie had claimed to have contributed twice what I had financially in the relationship, and this was disputed. A document containing all my annual group certificates (earning statements) and my tax returns showed I had actually earned and contributed around 10% more. It also showed her inheritance was small and the purchase of the family home was largely mortgaged, so our initial contribution at the start of the relationship was similar.

The ruling by the Dutch court allowed the Australian court to rule without much concern as to any international ramifications as it was clear that the Dutch assets would be covered by Dutch law and the Australian assets by Australian law, which meant that the majority of the property assets would be decided by Australian law.

With these additional facts being evident, the judge called a recess and asked the parties to meet and discuss the matters outside to see if an agreement can be reached. The Family court has what they call consulting rooms where lawyers can meet with their clients and discuss their cases privately. They are also known in the trade as the "roll over rooms" where lawyers will spell out some home truths to their clients, the position they are in, and encourage them to agree to negotiate a settlement. A settlement was negotiated.

The settlement was, percentage-wise in Nellie's favour, even though I had done the major part of raising Jasmine and Joe during those seventeen years together and had contributed around 10% more financially during the relationship. I was to sell the former family home, that I had made habitable in those early years in Australia and we both kept our superannuation. In addition, there was a sum to be paid (after the percentage split) of $100,000.00 that included around half of my Australian legal costs that were incurred exposing the lies and manipulation. It did not cover the short or long-term impact on the kids or myself from the sheer terror that Nellie had inflicted. That terror resulted in lost job opportunities, the massive amount of preparation for court cases and the emotional trauma. It did not even consider the criminal acts of filing false police reports in the Netherlands, perjury, the cost to the taxpayer of tying up resources for the many false reports lodged, the sheriff's office, court staff, judiciary and the overall costs. From my perspective, Nellie got off very lightly.

It was over and hopefully, Nellie would stop the fighting and release Jasmine to again have two parents. It was so close to Christmas that it would be exceptionally difficult for this year, but there was finally hope that Jasmine could move between the two of us.

The threats and intimidation that occurred that day however, turned out to be a very mild and distant memory that paled into insignificance after the newest of the new hired guns appeared on the scene.

The session exchange in the foyer of the Court where people could see what was going on, even if they could not hear, showed me that it would never be safe for me to be in the vicinity of my former spouse again. This was later reinforced by the many incidents that led up to this court decision and the many more that were to follow. I can only hope that this will not be the case and that one day I will be safe in the vicinity or my former spouse, so that the kids can one day enjoy both our company at significant occasions.

Nellie informed me that she told the kids, "There would be no inheritance. Every cent would be spent on destroying Trevor." Such was her hatred that I now recognised was most likely driven by a mental health issue that stemmed from a need for control. A close friend also stated that the courts worldwide (and in this case, the Australian courts), were negligent for not protecting Nellie from herself. The courts, he asserted, had failed in a basic duty of care. Unfortunately, it should have been Nellie herself, her children, as well as me, that they protected, but seemed more interested in filling those deep pockets of lawyers within the legal fraternity.

The Dutch High Court was the most ridiculous experience to date. Not happy with the result of the appeals court, experiencing the various judges verbally berating her for her actions and reading the various reasons for the judgements, Nellie instructed her lawyer to lodge a *Hoog Raad* (High Court) challenge. The application according to some opinions was flawed as you can only appeal to the *Hoog Raad,* by claiming the Appeals court erred in law or process. The *Hoog Raad* will not consider the facts of the case which are established in lower courts.

It was one of the first times I went against legal advice (in this case, not to waste money defending it) and organised to lodge a submission. My logic was clear to me. Should I not lodge something, then there would be questions to Nellie from the *Hoog Raad.* If Nellie changed tact in her response (she could be asked for supplementary information), then I would have no right to respond if I did not make a submission. As such, my lawyer lodged a document.

Nellie's application did not submit arguments on either of the criteria the court could consider and contained the same old rhetoric, essentially that "Trevor is a ... (we will dispense with the obscenities) and want you to ...." What her legal counsel (Bella) advised, or whether Nellie did not follow Bella's advice is something only they would know. The submission was simply something the *Hoog Raad* couldn't consider.

In any case, there was no landmark case law made, and after a very long delay, the decision was made and issued that there are no grounds for the *Hoog Raad* to hear the case and the appeals court decision stood.

It is amazing how far someone will go. I subscribe to various groups and one of them frequently posts from psychology journals and psychology blogs, such as published in Psychology Today[8] and I read that for some personalities their attitude is "these lower level judges just don't get it and I have to appeal to a higher level. Those judges who will get it". Maybe that was Nellie or maybe it was tactical. The case being appealed to the *Hoog Raad* in the Netherlands, may have impacted cases in Australia (stalling and Australian cases should wait until a decision was made before being heard) or it could have been just to inflict suffering on other people. I believe the stalling also impacted Nellie enormously. If Nellie saw this as needing to take it as far as she could, I hope it gave her a sense of relief that she had exhausted all avenues. I believe that the money would have been better spent with a psychology/psychiatric service rather than the legal fraternity and everyone would have been better off (except the lawyers).

I thought with all those cases concluded, and a judgement in Australia settled by consent, that it was now just a matter of process and only several months remained of the family court process. I could not have been more wrong.

---

[8] https://www.psychologytoday.com/

11

My mother's illness and enter the "crazies"

It was only two weeks after the second Australian case had been settled by consent, which means the parties had agreed and the judge signs off on the agreement as fair and reasonable to both parties. It was also more than two years since I left the Netherlands and temperatures were increasing in the Southern Hemisphere with summer and Christmas being imminent. I went to visit my father who lived around two hours' drive away in the nursing home and returned that night to go to a Fathers Support meeting, when my mother asked if I felt okay? My mother was not feeling well, and thought we may have eaten something that gave her a stomach upset and maybe I was also not well. The following morning Mum was not up. It was past 8:00 a.m. and that never happens. I knocked on the door and she was very unwell. While I did not lose my temper, I assertively insisted she gets to the doctor.

Mum: "No, my doctor doesn't work on Thursdays."

Trevor: "Well, I do not care, there will be a doctor there," was my response.

Mum: "But you have to book in and you will have problems getting an appointment."

Trevor: "Don't worry I will get one."

A quick phone call with a bit of assertiveness got her a doctor's appointment. Then I helped her get dressed and into the car. I can still recall her wanting me to watch the bumps in the road as we proceeded to the doctors. She got in to see a male doctor, not her usual doctor, who gave her the referral to the Emergency Department of the local hospital for full examination of possible appendicitis.

"I don't think it will be appendicitis and will go home and rest," my mother instructed. It was her eightieth birthday in a few weeks and if it was her appendix it would have gone by now, I think was her logic. How could the doctor know more than my mother? In order to convince my mother, I spoke to the doctor's receptionist and in front of my mother questioned them in a way that they told my mother that she had better let me take her to hospital. Whether it was coming from a lady or more likely a third person convincing her to go to hospital, she agreed. We drove the short distance to the hospital and pulled up by the door and I walked her in. She was not presenting that badly, so they seemed to take their time. Déjà vu with the appendix of Jasmine, with the texts and phone calls, in this case to my brothers and other people to tell them what was going on, that she would need some nighties and toiletries, and if they can go around to her house and organise this and bring them to the hospital, that would be helpful.

Finally, the surgeon was called in and they started the preparation for surgery. Strangely enough, I was never concerned; after all, it was straight forward appendectomy. Mum insisted I go home, and she would be right, and she would probably not wake up from the surgery for a while and there was little I could do. This request, unlike the request to not go to the doctor, or to take her home, I could comply with.

The surgeon called me that night after the operation and between that call and the subsequent discussion, the situation was revealed. He had opened her with a small incision to take out the appendix and saw what he was dealing with and opened her up to a much greater extent. It was significant surgery, as the appendix had burst and half the colon had to be removed as it was damaged. It was one of the worst cases he had ever seen, and I was quizzed as to how she was leading up to the event. He was trying to work out what happened as he stated, "The intake assessment was that she did not present that badly when she arrived at hospital."

The next call was to confirm she had private health insurance and they could transfer her to the Epworth Hospital which was done in the early hours of the morning and she was immediately put into their Intensive Care Unit (ICU). The Epworth ICU from what I saw had very high staff ratio's, cables everywhere monitoring her every heartbeat on the screens with alarms and defibrillator at the ready. The smaller suburban hospital had good facilities, but I did not see that level of care and they were scaling down for the Christmas break, so Epworth was the best place for her to be. She was in a bad way, but strangely, I never believed that she would possibly die. She pulled through, but they did find an atrial fibrilla-

tion. Basically, an irregular heartbeat, so that was investigated.

She was in the Epworth hospital for two weeks, so she
missed the Christmas dinner and we celebrated her 80th
birthday while in the rehabilitation centre. Mind you, she
had lots of friends from the senior's activity group visit that
day but with no special dinner, it did not seem right.

Two weeks after admittance to the rehabilitation
centre, she could still not control her bowels, however
the hospital administrators claimed she was becoming
dependent upon them and had convinced us that she
had to be discharged. The nursing staff organised the
Royal District Nursing Service (RDNS) to drop in at
her home on her first day to do an assessment for her
abilities with taking drugs and organise the very regular
blood tests, to get the blood-thinning medication right. My
brother organised special bedding while I organised the
pharmacist to pre-package all her drugs into blister packs,
so everyone could easily monitor that she was taking the
drugs as and when she should and that there was no
chance of doubling up.

It was some time later, watching her lose weight, when
I requested the doctor for a referral to a dietician and found
a dietician that said she could help. The dietician agreed
to see me even if my mother could not be in attendance.
The solution was incredibly simple, the spices, sugar and
fibre that she was served in the hospital is broken down
in the first half of the colon, that part had been removed,
so we removed foods containing these from her diet! Just
over 24 hours, I was not washing sheets 3 times a day,

and she began to improve. Without a doubt, it was that dietician that turned things around from my mother losing over 1kg a week and not absorbing nutrition, to stabilisation and was gaining weight.

As with anyone looking after a sick parent, it can be a very worrying time. After my meeting with the dietician, I was given a list of foods to buy for Mum that would help her. Reeling and broken from the years of litigation, and unsure of any decision I made and the actions I undertook, unless they were standard work, I was suffering. Mind you, for me, standard work would still include what many would consider complex project management be it analysing faults on a state-wide information technology network, or programming hundreds of millions of dollars in expenditure that many people could not perform when at their best, but this was different. I recall one day being at supermarket trying to locate the lactose-free milk and other foods that the dietician instructed that my mother needed. Before I knew it, I was sitting on the floor of the supermarket sobbing. Sweat running down my face and back, my heart beating so fast that I wanted to throw up.

Unable to locate the milk had suddenly escalated into a full blown Post Traumatic Stress Disorder (PTSD) trigger. As I sat on the floor sobbing, thinking that, *I couldn't even look after my own dying mother*, with the thought that *perhaps I was better off dead?* I was so broken, it felt like walls were always closing in on me, just that bit more each time.

In retrospect, one of the hardest parts of a moment like this is afterwards, you feel completely drained and exhausted. You forget that the trauma just bubbles beneath the surface waiting to erupt with even a minor incident and when you least expect it.

Yet, somehow, life goes on under the unbearable weight of stress. Within a minute, that seemed like an eternity, I was back on my feet and continuing, fortunately without anyone noticing. The milk was eventually located by a helpful employee along with the other foods. Mum began to quickly improve and with the worry of Mum, the trauma I now lived with daily, I was still here.

I told a friend who worked as a senior nurse in a different area of the rehabilitation hospital where my mother attended. She had been keeping track of me and I explained to her what I had done to get my mother back to reasonable health with pride. I really had pushed the doctor to get the referral to the dietician who established that the diet of hospital food with pepper, and sugar crystals in the jelly, prevented her from getting better in the rehabilitation centre, so I was doing some things right. Maybe my decision making wasn't as bad as I thought, as my mum was improving. My friend did not comment and simply listened. The reaction of that friend, the following day was surprising, as she informed me that at a team meeting, she gave them some (apparently very blunt) feedback about my mother's case, what I did, and that if a patient needs a dietician, then that is the hospitals' duty. She mentioned other cases with special meal requirements and put the hospitals' performance as completely unsatisfactory and that improvements were needed. She now works at another organisation and is glad to be out of there. She told me they did not want experienced staff and hired less experienced (at a cheaper rate) people. Some of the senior doctors were quite upset by the treatment that she had received as they relied upon her for difficult medical cases. I was informed by a person in the sector, that they discharge at two weeks because government funding decreased and that the hospital would have wanted a fully-funded patient. That rehabilitation hospital has since closed, but the company is still operating in many other locations, and I wonder if their focus on costs is just as paramount elsewhere.

Mum went on to driving to the shops and going out with friends, but she was never the same again. She was always nervous with what she ate.

The internet is an amazing thing really. Websites exist that attract people with similar issues and helped me a lot with my back injury, but there are others that become negative, with predators looking for their next target. Some people search for others that confirm whatever bias they want to hear, and alliances are forged. Nellie and I had an agreement made by consent, ratified and witnessed by the judge and my mother was recovering while the legal issues were being settled, so life was looking good. Unknown to me, Nellie had changed her mind and found other people on the internet to support her.

The series of court cases and events that followed, one lawyer described as having more twists and turns than a snake in full motion, and no-one could predict what was to follow. They were the stuff that thrillers are made of, with the recruitment of people that were not only declared vexatious litigants, something that is not easily or often achieved, including one that appeared to be at times delusional, requesting for donations to recruit mercenaries and they aligned with Nellie to usurp the court-endorsed agreement.

In the lead up to the previous court cases, I was told that Nellie had to be getting advice from somewhere on how to create delays and stuff the system up. She was simply too good at stuffing up the system. I decided to search around some of the legal help chat rooms and made a search which identified some of her posts and her handle, or pseudonym that she used. I must admit it was a very appropriate pseudonym. There were questions posted such as, "How do you change your story during a court case?" With the more proper responses being, "What were the circumstances that led to you putting the wrong story to the court?" and that, "You should tell the truth and it will show what type of person you are." I downloaded them all and printed them off in case they were ever needed, but they were never required. It just went to show that Nellie knew what she was doing, there were more lies to cover the previous lies and she did not care about the truth from what I could see in the posts and what I experienced in court.

By the time Nellie had agreed to settle by consent, she had dismissed and replaced two legal teams for not getting the results she wanted and there appeared to be a revolving door of barristers. She had admitted that she had told the children, "There would be no inheritance as every cent would be used to destroy Trevor." All I could think was, that no child deserves to be exposed to so much hatred, indifference to their future, the absence of love, but when Nellie started her attacks both inside and outside the court again, I simply had no choice but to continue. Back then, and even now, I believe that if I did not defend myself, Nellie would have continued attacking me relentlessly. At one stage she put a caveat on the house in the Keys Estate and stated she was going to "take that as well for child support" leaving me with nothing, homeless and destitute.

Someone that was following the case dubbed those that collectively came forward to assist Nellie as, "Nellie and her cast of Crazies", and the name stuck. I was attending group sessions for displaced parents, and my life had become so bizarre, that one participant even admitted that he came each week to find out about the latest twists and turns in my life.

Each week it seemed a new event that was beyond normality would be orchestrated. One friend would ring me regularly and ask, "What has the Wicked Witch of the North done this week?" It was surreal enough that another friend extended it to, "The Wicked Witch of the North and the flying monkeys." That expression hails from "The Wonderful Wizard of Oz" where the evil witch has her team of flying monkeys carry out her attacks. How Nellie ever convinced them to believe her and do her bidding is beyond me, but then again, she fooled me for many years.

The people that she recruited to help her and collectively known as "the cast of crazies" consisted of Seth, Spike and Samael.

Seth, he called himself a constitutionalist in the letterhead of various documents and his blogs. He was well known in the courts as subsequent events revealed. He was a declared vexatious litigant that required a litigation guardian for his own case and had spent time in prison according to some documents. In one document he stated he was proud of that fact. He would write lengthy documents that he would submit to my lawyers and the court and at one stage my lawyer said he couldn't continue to read more than a few pages as he, "Couldn't in good conscience continue and then charge me." The judiciary in one judgement specifically stated to paraphrase, "That he had wasted the judges time, making him read the incomprehensible gibberish."

Spike, had a long history with one ruling against him where he could "never" see his children again, had overlaid his comments on the judgement and published it on the internet, which is a criminal offence that can result in up to 12 months' imprisonment under the Family Law Act. According to records, he was also a vexatious litigant in his own case. On one of his websites, he had supplied his bank details and was asking for donations to "hire mercenaries, to march up the East coast and kill all the women that wouldn't do a man's bidding!" At one stage he bragged in one email, that was widely distributed, how he would be vindicated and given credibility with the latest information he supplied police, so that all of his accusations against people would then be proven true. He stated how he was, "Assured by the police they would let the lead detective know and expected the lead detective would reopen the case and he could now go home." The case he was reporting to the police was the Azaria Chamberlain case (that had three Royal Commissions; and for international readers, this case was about the dingo that took the baby at Ayers Rock/Uluru), and he was apparently referring to a blog on the internet that he had found which was several years old and discredited. I could go on as to what else was discovered, but what I have outlined should give you some idea about Spike.

Samael was a country solicitor from interstate. He had represented a children's book author to litigate for plagiarism in two countries, against another author that had made hundreds of millions of dollars in movie royalties. In the US, the judge would not permit the case to proceed stating something like, "You would have to have a better imagination than either of the authors, to see the similarity in the books." In Wales, the judge ruled that the famous author would likely be awarded costs, so if he wanted to proceed a £500,000 surety deposit would be needed to be made before the case would continue. The case made him infamous in a regional paper that gave him the pseudonym of the township and a mythical creature that formed part of the litigation.

Samael did present several cases against me, all of which resulted in cost awards, as by now I had learned how to ensure the facts got to my lawyer and the judiciary. One of the requirements to have costs awarded, is that the case was wholly unsuccessful. His actions caused significant costs to Nellie, (regardless if she paid for his services or not), as well as the property purchaser. His actions delayed everyone from moving on and bringing about a level of peace, civility and closure. He was included in the group mainly because he continued to associate with Seth.

At the end of Samael's interlude into my case, I did write to the Legal Services Commission. Samael had officially engaged Seth for specified duties, however, Seth was openly purporting to be his agent, with business cards and letterhead, and Seth was a declared vexatious litigant with no legal qualifications. He had not supervised his agent and in one judgement against Nellie, it stated that Nellie's behaviour and that of her legal representative was appalling. He also refused to follow court instructions in providing evidence, and the court did not follow through. The Legal Services Commission (LSC) had him respond to the various matters which may have taken him a short time to construct his response. The LSC response then stated they had not been paid by the client and that they were not prepared to take action and included one brochure that stated, "The lawyer is considered an extension of his client and following their instruction."

I must say, that the brochure they sent me, and the explanation left me aghast, and still believe it contradicts the basic premise of a lawyer, being an officer of the court. Maybe those old-fashioned values are history in our world, but I can say I am disappointed by the values he demonstrated and can see why the many jokes about lawyers continue to exist.

What "Nellie and her cast of crazies" did in the next few months meant that my life had been reduced to one of a soap opera, or a thriller, full of strange characters and incredulous events. I have learned that sometimes you simply cannot control who enters your life and what they may bring to it however, like the ancient Chinese curse "May your life be interesting," mine became interesting to the many observers. Some of the events impacted the children along with my mother in ways, that they may never realise.

The settlement allowed a couple of variations regarding the implementation of the property split. Should Nellie desire not to sell the Australian family home by the real estate agent that she nominated in court to whom I had no reason to object to, she could borrow funds and settle. I even offered that if she agreed to settle world-wide in accordance with both the Dutch and Australian court orders, we could ensure there would be a transfer of properties with her keeping all the Dutch properties. We would not have had to sell anything and would delay the sale of the Australian property as per the decision, if she agreed. Nellie rejected all efforts to stop the madness, she still wanted everything, and was even frustrating the Dutch court decisions, trashing the family home to which the Dutch Real Estate agent notified the Dutch court that they could not sell the property with Nellie in there. The time limits passed and therefore the Australian property sale was to proceed.

I sought a quote from the real estate agent having him believe it was a competitive quote to get a reasonable deal and, proceeded with him to do the sale. I then presented to the court authority the other documents, and they negotiated with the tenants to sort out the open days and to make the sale occur. It was then that the "crazies" started their various actions.

It was around a week before the auction that the flurry of activity commenced as "the cast of crazies" activated their plan, the irony of which, was not lost by the real estate agent. He could see from the court orders that they were made by agreement between Nellie and I (which in legal lingo was "made by consent") and witnessed by the judiciary which specifically appointed their real estate agency to sell the house.

Seth started to campaign against the real estate agent, claiming that the sale was illegal and had no basis and would be challenged in court, asking for the names of those who had expressed interest so he could warn them. He asserted to the real estate agent that they would be held liable for any costs if the sale went ahead and the sale would be later challenged. This led the real estate company to waste time and money consulting with their legal advisors.

Nellie also owned a flat in Smith Street that was nearly fully mortgaged when we first met and had rented it out via that real estate agency to pay it off after we moved into the family home and later to the Netherlands. She also had a friend that owned one of the other apartments (a retired civil servant that should have known better) and it was this lady that approach the real estate agent on Nellie's behalf. She pleaded with the Real-Estate agent not to sell the property and withdraw from their involvement of the sales process. She even threatened that should the real estate agent not do as she and Nellie wanted, they would stop using their services for the management of the two rented apartments (one owned by her and one by Nellie). I will never know if Nellie had concocted this in the "roll over room" during the settlement negotiation when she insisted on this real estate agent. It made no difference when this plan was hatched as the real estate agent's ethics remained strong and served the courts and justice well, not to mention they were paid the commission from the sale.

The night before the auction, the real estate agent was with his father who was about to pass away. He received another call from Seth to stop that auction and repeated a request to supply information about those who had expressed an interest. Seth also demanded that the auctioneer makes all those aware at the auction, that this property sale will be subject to a legal challenge and that he intended to distribute leaflets to that effect. In spite of it all, the real estate agent being in his own personal grieving process, stood firm.

The day of the auction had finally arrived. I had organised some of the people from Fathers Support and friends to attend and watch the process, in case witnesses were needed. One of them, on his own initiative, even sat next to those who we believed may disrupt the auction. Seth was seen with a package that appeared to be a bunch of leaflets and I believed it had the same content as was sent to the real estate agent before the auction (which was later confirmed by Seth in an email but also that he had not distributed them). The auctioneer quickly spotted and approached Seth, personally informed him of the Real Estate Act/law and would sue him if he distributed the brochures or disrupted the auction, so the lines were drawn.

Spike was also in attendance, although I did not recognise him at that stage. It was explained in a subsequent letter from Seth that Nellie had paid Spike's airfare directly (from Sydney to Melbourne). The payment by Nellie of the airfare allowed Spike to attend the auction to film and take pictures. According to the letter from Seth, Samael did not know about the sponsorship by Nellie, which may have been stated to protect Samael.

My lawyer, knowing what was going on, also attended, and I was relieved as my nerves were quite heightened with all the going on and the relentless onslaught of the past years. The auction proceeded, however there was only one bidder. While there were expected to be five bidders, including developers, it was never properly investigated nor determined if Seth had somehow got to some of the other bidders. The real estate agent would be unlikely to tell me regardless as they would want to make everyone satisfied with the result.

The property was negotiated above the final bid and sold that day. I must admit that I was disappoint- ed, as the property market was going down after we advertised and was very much at the lower end of what we had expected. If Seth did get to the developers, then it is possible that the price was driven down by well over $100,000.00 I estimated. On the flip side, the property sold above the reserve imposed by the court, so it could proceed and another chapter in this long-running saga could be concluded. There were some conditions agreed to, such as vacant possession and a long settlement (which the bidders wanted based upon the date of settlement for the property they had just sold) but that should not have represented any issues, or so we thought.

Immediately following the auction, Seth approached the real estate agent demanding a copy of the sale notice giving the purchasers details which was discussed with my lawyer. He was not a legally appointed representative and therefore had no rights to the information and the request was refused. After all, I had been appointed by the court to sell the property.

I cannot recollect how they got hold of the sales information and the details of the purchaser so quickly and no one outside "the cast of crazies" could have envisaged what was to follow.

Shortly after the auction the threats to remove them from managing the two properties in Smith Street was carried out, and even removed them as the managing agent for the property that was sold, such that the rental was managed directly by Nellie. I dare say however, the real estate agent showed the highest ethics and were probably happy not to manage the properties of that type of person. While I did not realise at the time, in hindsight, this too was possibly part of a plan to thwart the sale that had just been entered into.

It was remarkable how "the cast of crazies" worked to raise the tensions and waste resources as the weeks proceeded. What I found disappointing was that there appeared to be no ramifications for the series of related events that followed for the perpetrators and intimidation became part of their tactics and a weapon of choice.

The First Tactic—False Police Reports

A report to the fraud squad of the Victorian police was made by Spike, that the property had been sold by me without Nellie's knowledge or consent, so I quite rightly became the subject of a police investigation. If my property was sold while on holidays overseas without my knowledge, I would expect a thorough investigation. Regardless of whether you have done anything wrong or not, an investigation on you personally can cause enormous stress. It seems disappointing that both lawyers and police carry on, as if legal conflict and investigations have no impact on people's lives, stress levels or health, and therefore appears to not factor into any consideration of urgency.

The fraud squad quite correctly went into investigative mode and called the lawyers responsible for the transfer. After some communication, they were issued a copy of the sealed court orders that had been signed by Nellie and witnessed by the Federal Court judge. Here was irrefutable proof that Nellie had agreed, witnessed by an impeccable source that she not only knew, but had authorised the sale. While the case had concluded, it probably took some time to go through the police command to review. Police policy, I was told, is that cases are never closed and they do not normally tell people their findings. The best we could get was that the investigation had been conducted and that no further action was to be taken. It was just one more stressor that continued to bubble deep within me.

Around two weeks later, due to subsequent actions of Spike, there was additional communications with the police. I was informed that they had not only concluded their investigation but that the file was marked "no crime detected." That information was well received and my underlying stress reduced and questioned why I could not have been told that weeks earlier. We were never told if a case was lodged against Spike for making a false statement or if his actions could be regarded as more than just mischievous but criminal. It possibly would have been a waste of time as well but we will never know what Nellie had told Spike and he had possibly been misled.

The Second tactic—Intimidate the purchaser

Emails were also sent to the company run by the purchaser, advising them that the owner had no knowledge of the auction, and that they had purchased the property through fraud and should pull out of the purchase immediately. I never found out how Seth and Spike determined the purchaser's details but never-the-less, they had.

A flurry of questions and answers followed, and the real estate agent eventually asked if he could supply the court orders to the purchaser to convince them that not only did Nellie know, but had consented to the sale and this was witnessed by a federal court judge. That would show Nellie was either oblivious to what was happening by the "crazies" or that she was acting in a totally immoral way in that she had agreed to the sale and was now trying to stop it using Spike.

Phone calls and a series of text messages from Spike were also made to the purchaser and while I was unaware what was stated, I was advised by the real estate agent that the purchaser was scared out of her house that night and stayed somewhere else where she felt safe. I often wonder if Nellie realised the type of person that Spike was, and if she knew what I knew, such as his blog site where he had posted his bank account for donations to "raise an army of mercenaries to kill all the women that would not do a man's bidding". As the fraud squad had already been involved, phone calls were made to them and a formal request was made by the law firm doing the transfer to seek police intervention. The request for police intervention asserted possible breaches in numerous laws including stalking and using a telecommunications device to menace that warranted police action. The sergeant in the fraud squad complied with the request and issued a verbal warning and the purchaser was not contacted again by Spike for several months. Spike, after all, lived interstate so a face-to-face warning would have been difficult, and the phone warning resulted in the outcome that the police sought.

The third tactic—Intimidate me

I received a phone call from a blocked phone number one Sunday night from whom I believed to be Spike. There was little said apart from, "I just want to tell you I have killed someone." I sat there in front of the computer and wrote down everything I could immediately. I had already been in contact with the fraud squad as they had investigated me, then done the right thing by the purchaser, so who better to report this event to and an email was sent with a copy to my lawyer.

I recall having a job interview the following day, and while I was walking into the building was discussing the veiled death threat with my brother, the report to the police, that was considering a request for a restraining order, how to ensure that my mother was not overly alarmed along with what and how much we should tell my mother. I found that I was constantly focused on security and in this case mentally taking notes of the security system of the potential employer to work out if it would be safe to work there, rather than focusing on the interview. With Nellie's driven personality all the threats such as, "I will make sure you never see your daughter again; I will tell the police you have been abusing me for ten years and they will believe me; I should have put a bullet through you;" then her actions that included the perjury; the police reports in the Netherlands; pretending to negotiate while covertly lodging a Dutch court case without telling me; stringing out the court cases, and now the funding of airfares for a person that was advertising for donations to recruit mercenaries, all those actions showed to me that I was in danger.

I missed out on the job, but it reminded me of a government-funded organisation, that suggested I should not be applying for work until the situation had been sorted out. I would be taking my tension wherever I went, and people will know something is wrong and possibly suspect I was lying or concealing something in any interview I attended.

I have since met one person through Fathers Support that dismissed ten staff as he could not concentrate on his business and organise their work while under similar attacks. He had around forty police interviews due to malicious and blatant lies to the police which saw him constantly picked up and questioned for Intervention Order Breaches. I also know the cost personally of such malicious activities to be incalculable with lies to police of the events; date of separation in the Netherlands; that we never had a relationship; that it was a one-night stand that produced Jasmine; that I did practically nothing raising the children and was all her. I believe that one day the government will be forced to act on false allegations and for those who have, spend time in prison based upon these false allegations, some of which have featured in the national press. Such a time cannot come quickly enough. It is not my desire to see people in prison but I personally believe, based upon many cases, it would be an effective deterrent to the individual and community at large, which is one of the main reasons for sentencing in our justice system.

After a couple of days without a response from the fraud squad officer, a call was made. The sergeant I had sent the request to was away on training and after a short time advised by his colleague that the matter needed to be handled by the local police and a formal report made.

The complaint was made at my local police station as directed by the fraud squad and gave them permission to request the phone operator to trace the source of the call. Even if this was not a threat of intimidation, there was a confession received, that the caller had killed someone and surely the police would investigate, or so I thought. After some consideration, the police decided not to investigate. They even went so far as to claim the Australian Federal

Police have greater powers under the Telecommunications Act but I knew that was rubbish and an attempt to simply get rid of me as all police forces can prosecute the law.

This was a disappointment. It festered for a day before I lodged a formal complaint being made, that the police review their procedures and conduct the investigation. Excuses related to priorities such as, "We had a woman in here that was hysterical that her spouse may come to get her and children." To me, at that time, it reflected the government focus on the "women and their children" rhetoric embedded into the police actions.

I had walked into the police station calmly, handed over a file that I had collated on the person that I believe to have made the call which contained:

- the correspondence showing Spike's original false police report;

- his alias's showing how they were easily matched through contact information;

- that he had done a series of criminal actions (i.e. against legislation including the publication of his Family Court orders clearly identifying all concerned in his case which is punishable by jail time, and

- possibly terrorism insofar as trying to "recruit an army of mercenaries to march up the east coast");

- along with several other documents and requested help.

Apart from priorities, another explanation as to why the police would not act was that they did not have the budget to do the telecom look up. Part of my work history was as a telecommunications tools expert which meant I had some knowledge and I had put in systems to monitor the health and performance of the telecommunications network of my employer. I knew firsthand how the signalling systems worked and how easily it is to trace the phone number and rough location of where a call is made from. These systems are standard across the world or the international phone system would not work. This was simply another farce from my perspective. I knew how long it takes to do the lookup of the caller ID (even when blocked) as having done it, I know it is only a few minutes after logging into a signalling system database. The only way costs could be high is procedural overheads of the police and poorly negotiated prices with the telecom providers by the public service which would be highly counterproductive to the justice system.

Apologies were made after the complaint went through the internal police review process. The sergeant liaising with me simply stated that it had gone right up the chain of command and they would not investigate. I was given stalking brochures and other leaflets which outlined when they would act for those offences.

I will never know why the police refused to investigate:

- It could be a patriarchal culture within the police, in that I am a man and therefore should be able to look after myself. In contrast, the property purchaser who was a woman and therefore, they made the phone call and the request came from a lawyer.

- It could be the squeaky wheel principle as I appeared calm when making the report and not hysterical in the police foyer, like the woman that "they had to assist."

- It could be due to the convoluted administration system and therefore an expensive processes to trace the call.

- It could be that if I was right, and the call originated from interstate, then the liaison would be all too cumbersome for a state police force.

- It could be that if he was drunk or with a mental health condition, the prosecution would uncover these mitigating factors, and there would be no appropriate sentence given and a conviction would not be achieved.

- It could be a combination of some or all of the above.

The reason was not given, just that it had been referred up the ladder and they couldn't investigate.

Unhappy with the response, I did write and went to meet with my local state MP. His advisor and I agreed that jail may not be the right place for Spike, but some action should be taken, and they promptly wrote on my behalf to the State Police Minister. The usual public service response came back that this is a police operational matter and it would be inappropriate for the minister to intervene. To this day I question why we have a police minister or Parliament for that matter if it is not up to the Government to oversee the police and review their performance?

I also wrote to the Federal Attorney General and asked similar questions. I specifically queried if using a "Telecommunications device to harass or threaten" contained within the Telecommunications Act had implementation shortcomings in so far as the police being unable to take action easily under the Act in the tracing of calls? This was especially when there may be a serious mental health issue along with some issues within the Family court. The response was another public service manifesto of excuses and non-intervention.

I do not regret writing to the relevant ministers as I have kept a file on Spike who subsequently slandered me with comments on Facebook years later and these were added to my file. The posts themselves were quickly deleted by the administrators of those pages who also contacted me and suggested I call the police. All I know, is that when I needed the police and provided them evidence, they would not act and my trust in the police has been diminished. Why would I call the police when I am only going to be ignored again?

The fourth Tactic—Telephone harassment

There was never any proof that this was orchestrated by this group. Whether it was part of a campaign to destabilise me or simply something that could happen to anyone and it was just a coincidence is something that I will leave it to you to decide.

A protracted series of text messages originating from a poker promotion group were constantly received. These grew in number and as I was always waiting for that call from my daughter, the rubbish texts were an annoyance, to say the least. I am not sure who was responsible, however Nellie knew I had a dislike for gambling as I believe it causes too many problems in Australia and elsewhere in the world. There was a return code to remove oneself from the text issuing system however, it had no effect. It was simply costing me the price of an SMS (if I went over my monthly limit of free SMS), along with some time, each occasion I responded to try to remove myself from their system.

I finally rang up the legal officer of the poker promotion group and the texts seemed to reduce for some time and then grew to even greater numbers again. From the initial enquiries, I had found out that their text generation machine had twenty-three phone line numbers that sent the texts. As I had not wiped the messages from my cell phone, I could take some action.

I set to work and collated the:

- List of dates,

- The times which the text (which was promoting poker tournaments at various specified venues they promoted) was received,

- The phone number that was shown as the originating source of the text, and

- The message.

Next, I crafted a letter to the State Ombudsman. The letter stated that the poker promotion group was promoting gambling to someone that had specifically requested not to receive the promotion and should be stripped of their license due to the irresponsible promotion of gambling.

A copy of the complaint was naturally sent to the poker promotion group concerned. A call was received within hours by the Chief Executive Officer of the poker promotion organisation and a statement that clearly the calls are coming from them, but they were not going to me, according to their software system. Again, I stood firm that maybe they are not aware how their software system works, and that they must get someone in that knows how their application works to rectify the situation.

Within hours, their database expert analysed all the calls I had received and found around seventeen people that had all submitted requests to receive promotional texts from those various establishments. All seventeen people were removed from the promotional system. The promoter believed that one of the seventeen had installed a device that specifically recorded the source phone number, forwarded the call to me and put on my display the original source phone number. While such devices are probably illegal, the calls immediately stopped. I do not think I even received a contact from the Ombudsman and as for the other sixteen that were taken off the system and wanted to receive the promotion, well maybe they have re-registered or hopefully given up gambling. Perhaps it was coincidence that the venues were based around the area of Sydney where Spike resided. Was it Spike? I will never know.

The whole situation was reminiscent and a con-tinuation of trying to undermine my ability to work and socialise with anyone and isolate me. When first getting back to Australia, Nellie tried to contact close friends on Facebook, however they had the sense to respond that, "you did not want to be my friend when living here and see no point, now that you are not with Trevor." Unsuccessful at destroying the relationships with close friends, Nellie then sent scathing emails to the Lions Club, essentially telling them they should not have such a disreputable person that has done various things to her, as a member and would damage their image. I had been reasonably open about my situation with the Lions Club and was given copies of the correspondence. That correspondence was eventually presented to court, demonstrated the situation I faced and why I had to get out of the Netherlands. This time however she had not acted directly or through lawyers but had recruited other people to do her bidding.

Nellie had recruited other people and was relentless and uncompromising. Whether Nellie commanded the actions, or her recruits were acting like an independent terrorist cell, only they would know. Apart from the legal court procedures, there were the false police reports; intimidation of people associated with the property purchase; a veiled death threat and possibly the phone harassment. The aim possibly was to destroy me and having me suicide.

The police offered little or no assistance and their poor ability or willingness to uphold both the law and common sense was at best appalling, and at worst, a gross breach of the reason that they exist from my perspective. While this sounds somewhat critical, I have dealt with the police that have both issued and enforced Intervention Orders on people as well as having false Intervention Orders served on them as Fathers Support members by their spouses and seen their predicament. While I can respect every individual police officer, there is a limit to how much I can respect the system in which they operate and question their personal integrity for not prosecuting the perjury and remaining in the system when they become aware of the facts.

12

Was this corruption?

It was following the auction, that the efforts of "the cast of crazies" continued to escalate and the enlistment of additional people they could align to their cause. What transpired was the tribunal hearings; the subpoena of a policeman's records; the subpoena of Seth and Samael records (which was ordered by the court but never complied with), and a series of court cases that stressed the purchaser, as if they did not get the property would have nowhere to live. As for me, I was already at high-stress levels and rode the wave of high anxiety.

The conditions of the sale were such that vacant possession was agreed to, so it was our duty to issue the notice to vacate and have the tenants move out. The tenant was a senior detective constable, and when visiting the house for an inspection as part of the sale process, his wife showed us the front room, where they employed staff and ran a security company and model/event management business. This was the type of business that will have the ladies and gents walk the catwalk in the latest fashions or serve refreshments at a high-class event. The notice to vacate had been served and the tenants had been very co-operative during the open days and realised they would be asked to leave. Even before the auction, they appeared to see the sixty-day notice period as reasonable and everyone seemed happy at the time. The settlement terms were much longer than sixty days as the purchaser had requested to match the sale of their other property so they would not require bridging finance (to cover the time between when the proceeds of the sale of their current home were received and the settlement for the Vautner street property).

What we did not know was revealed through a subpoena on the senior detective constable files and court testimony. Seth had been meeting with the tenant, that he later described as "a friend and had the right to visit" and provided legal advice that came from Samael as to how to object to the vacate notice.

It was some time after the notice to vacate was issued that something seemed not quite right. Neither the real estate agent or the law firm that issued the notice to vacate was getting any answers as to when the tenant was preparing to move.

There was no legal requirement for the senior constable to advise of the moving date and he stood firm that there is no obligation to inform us. The notice to vacate the premises date passed and I still had some time before settlement so took action. A hearing date in the Administrative Appeals Tribunal (AAT) to force the evacuation was made. It was then that the legal firm doing the conveyancing that had issued the notice to vacate realised that it had been served on an employee and not the principle tenant when they were preparing for the AAT hearing. The tenant asserted that he had not been legally issued the notice, although it was clear he knew about it, the day it was issued from emails and had read it. Requests to make it effective from when the constable had read the document were refused and the AAT officer ruled that the notice had to be reissued.

This would mean we would be in default of the transfer date as set out in the sales contract and was clearly treated as a victory by the "crazies." Within no time, Spike had texted the purchaser (in spite of the warning by the fraud squad to not make further contact), saying that she had missed out on getting her property. The anxiety of the purchaser and myself escalated.

I must confess it was one of those rare times I raised my voice and let fly at the lawyers. "How could your law firm, with your reputation, have made such a fucking mistake?" The junior lawyer that was there to observe, clearly contacted the legal partner that I had been dealing with and while walking down the street got the call from the partner to please come in and see them. An apology was made and there would be no further costs charged to me for removing the tenant. New notices were issued, and this time properly served.

It was at this point that the senior detective constable requested a financial incentive to leave the property before the contract settlement date. Questions were asked within the law firm if this would be illegal and if the request should be entertained. The tenant had already organised a new property to rent when the agreement was reached to pay him an incentive to move out. The agreement stipulated that he would vacate the property and provide the keys to us as the court-appointed party responsible for selling the house for the sum of $2,000.00.

I recall going to the bank and having the cheque made out to the tenant and in casual conversation was asked what the $2,000.00 bank cheque was for. The answer was quick as I was furious and responded, "It is to pay off a corrupt police officer," to which the shock on the teller's face was evident and there was silence.

The bank cheque was never delivered as the senior constable probably realised that I would have lodged a complaint with the police integrity and ethical standards department if he took it. As Nellie was now in charge of the tenancy management, it is also possible that Nellie said they had to give the keys back to the tenancy managers representative being Seth and would not get the bond back if they did not comply. The truth is, why he handed the keys to Seth is speculation. The handing of the keys to Seth however, led to yet another whole new experience.

In terms of the property purchaser, her lawyers eventually lodged a claim of around forty thousand dollars for their client's extra costs and legal fees incurred to the conveyancing service, which was rejected. There was a clause in the conveyancing document that allowed for delays and while they argued the clause was not there for when the vendor frustrates the sale, this was not accepted as I was the court-appointed vendor, not Nellie, and they were told if there is any legal claim, it is against Nellie and they should deal with her directly.

It was mid-July and around six months after my mother had the ruptured appendix and her health was improving. She had missed Christmas celebrations the previous year as she was in Intensive Care. As with her 80th birthday in mid-January, we could not properly celebrate that either, but did in a small way while she was in the rehabilitation hospital. We had therefore planned a special Christmas in July, belated birthday and getting better celebration at my brother's place which had been planned for several weeks.

The celebration was organised and was about to start when I got the call. The law firm handling the property transfer had been advised by the tenant (the Detective Senior Constable with the state police force) that he had moved out. We had believed it was happening the day before, however this was official. I had already lined up a locksmith, which I immediately rang and arranged to meet and took along a copy of the court orders. The locksmith quickly looked at the court orders and proceeded to open the door. While his efforts initially failed as the front door lock was defective, he managed to open another door and we entered the house. He promptly re-keyed all locks including the one with a defective cylinder and during that time we noticed something was wrong. The back-terrace door had been screwed shut as were the windows from the inside. Some tools were in the front foyer as if left behind and although there was no furniture, there was a suitcase and some women's apparel in the main bedroom.

I frantically contacted the law firm handling the conveyancing and they recited out a notice to leave on the front door. It was then off to the St. Kilda police station to report the strange happenings in the house and that it was possible that squatters had attempted to seize the property. I left a copy of the court orders with the police who suggested I simply put the suitcase and tools onto the nature strip, however that did not seem right to me.

I quickly returned from the police station to the property and there was now a car in the driveway. What was happening? As I approached, a lady appeared and I asked who are you and what are you doing here? Seth then appeared out of the dark, intervening and issuing instructions, "Do not tell him anything." Seth then went into a rant that the family court was not properly constituted and therefore has no rights to issue the orders it did and that he does not recognise the orders.

"You have no rights to change the locks," Seth asserted and demanded I open the house. All the young girl wanted was for me to open the door, so she could get her clothes out of the house and I never knew if she was aware of the trouble that she was in. Frantically, she consulted her boyfriend on her mobile phone and then claimed, "My boyfriend is a policeman in Sydney and he is really pissed!" I actually had no idea where her boyfriend was at that moment, but it did not matter and had to see this through.

There was no way known that I was opening the door for Seth or the young girl, and I had given up fearing police regardless of whether I considered them corrupt or not. That was enough confrontation for me, and I withdrew across the road. I called the local police station phone number as they recommended in the meeting fifteen minutes earlier where I had given them the court orders.

It was some time before a divisional van with two young police arrived. I greeted one on the road and was instructed, quite correctly, to wait on the footpath where it was safe in the event of any other traffic. They spoke briefly with Seth and I separately and made the decision to call in a senior officer. A police Sergeant eventually arrived and tried to assess the situation, asking me for the court orders to which the response was, that they were left at the local (to this property) police station.

I was quite happy to open the door and remove the young ladies' belongings but wanted her name as that would be required for the court hearing that was bound to follow. I stood firm, I wanted everyone's names and had already recorded the police names and simply wanted the young ladies name. After some coaxing from Seth, the sergeant refused to provide the name of the young lady and issued the instruction that Seth could break into the house to retrieve the young ladies' clothes. After advice from my lawyer on my mobile phone, I opened the door and the police helped Seth and the lady remove their goods. They refused to let Seth go further into the house than his tools and then ordered Seth not to return to the property without court orders, to which Seth agreed to comply.

I rang my brother who was still in the midst of the celebration that I had so looked forward to and missed. Seth had messed up my mother's belated eightieth birthday, Christmas and return to health celebration and added in more turmoil and stress. I asked that a foam mattress and other objects be brought around, thinking I should spend the night the Vautner Street property but Graham convinced me to return and have something to eat. I had missed most of the festivities but managed some food and I was clearly shaken by the ordeal and my mother missed the full family get together that we had planned.

I went back to the house the next morning and pho-tographed the windows that had been screwed shut and some of the other odd things that Seth had performed to fortify the property. An affidavit was drafted and submitted that afternoon to the court which was clearly anticipated, and a court date set for the coming Friday. Apparently, the news of the incident had permeated through the court and it was suggested by the Registrar that the young girl may have been the daughter of Seth.

The court hearing proceeded on the Friday and in the legal representative's seat was Samael. There was some toing and froing between the lawyers and the judge and eventually, Samael admitted that they had not lodged documents to the Attorney General or the Australian High court to challenge their assertion that "the court was not a legally constituted entity and therefore they did not have to follow the terms of the previous judgement," (that ironically was made by consent). It was confirmed the young lady was Seth's daughter, and why any responsible parent would put their child in the middle of this mess was beyond me. Nellie, in her absence, and Seth were reprimanded for their actions. They were also issued restraining orders from going anywhere near the property and indemnity costs were awarded. These would cover all my legal costs which were to be taken out of Nellie's share of the property settlement. I should point out that "costs" are a schedule approved by the court, whereas "indemnity costs" are usually higher and are the rates negotiated between a lawyer and their client. It was a decisive legal victory to a situation that Nellie should never have allowed to occur. Even with indemnity cost, the stress, anxiety and the time I had spent are never recovered, so I was not compensated but my lawyers were.

"The cast of crazies" seemed to be expanding. I now had to contend with Seth and his daughter, Spike (and any mercenaries he had recruited), Samael (the lawyer), a police senior detective constable that I had evicted and another interstate policeman that allegedly issued threats through Seth's daughter, not to mention Nellie (the Wicked Witch of the North). Clearly much had been achieved in recent months. Where to from here? Many more court cases with no clear end in sight.

I was reminded of what occurs when you take a journey. Although you do not know where or how much further the journey is, that if you are heading in the right direction, every step, is one step closer, even though you may not know how many steps are left. Similarly, when climbing a hill, you may constantly think this is the last section but then find the real peak is still further away. You are however closer to the real peak, although you may be frequently disappointed. The end of the relationship with Nellie was littered with frustration and disappointments, and there were still more to come.

There were several more court cases including the appeal court to the original Australian court cases, each time thinking it was going to be all over and had reached that final peak, only to have those hopes dashed and continuing the strange and sometimes bizarre journey. The first case in Australia revolved around when the relationship started and that the history of that relationship. The second in Australia featured the death threats in the foyer. There was also a recent restraining order issued to the "crazies" about the sale of the property.

It was around this time my barrister decided he was not needed in the actual courtroom but was still available. I believe he reviewed the solicitors' work and mentored the solicitor who performed both roles effectively. I was effectively broke, and the law firm had said they would not issue invoices until it was over and they were confident that would occur soon.

Nellie and I had been in a de facto relationship for around seventeen years which was legally seen the same as marriage in Australia. But was it? During the ensuing court battles, there was an article that made front page of the Australian newspapers. The government's public service had not properly processed a parliamentary decision on the legislation, and it became known as the "de facto relationship bungle". It was a huge scandal and impacting possibly tens of thousands of court decisions and the Attorney General, The Hon Nicola Roxon MP apologised for the error made years before her appointment. Both major political parties agreed to support the backdated ratification of the legislation, and it was seen as a *fait accompli* and would be passed through the houses of parliament quickly. It just had to be slotted into a given day to be passed through the system. In one news report, the Attorney General stated it would be "stupid" (or something like that) to try to appeal. Nellie, aided by Samael and Seth decided to appeal anyway. I pushed my MP hard stating this government bungle was going to cost me personally in more delays and court costs, that his office should act and was informed that they had advised the attorney general of the pending court case. I do not know if the lobbying helped to push forward the time slot through parliament, but the retrospective legislation was passed on a Thursday. Nellie was given the option to withdraw from the case, but proceeded with the hearing on the Monday. Essentially the judge stated, "It is well known the retrospective legislation was approved last week," and awarded me indemnity costs. Was Nellie stupid? Was Nellie driven by Seth and possibly Samael to proceed anyway, only they would know.

One of the more unusual cases featured the argument that the International Convention for the right to self-determination had not been considered and that Nellie had determined, in her mind, that there was no relationship. This meant that the courts had overridden her basic international right in spite of all our years together, joint bank account, life insurance policies where we were each beneficiary if the other died from the joint purchase of the home in the Netherlands, lots of other documentation including the birth certificate and the existence of Jasmine. As such, a paragraph in one of Nellie's affidavits, stated that the family court had made an error by not considering the International Convention. As such, by imposing the legal relationship on Nellie, that myself and the four judges, that had been involved in Australian cases to date, had committed an act of slavery.

I sometimes joke with people that they are in the presence of someone that has been to court for slavery! The application was clearly written by Seth and even talked about Abraham Lincoln freeing the slaves in a form of gibberish that no one could see logic and why that was brought up, along with most of the other rantings. The solicitor of record was Samael who presented the case.

The appeals case was more telling. They had got an exemption for not filing within the required time period. Again, Samael was the solicitor of record. He was made aware some of the things Seth had been up to but suspect he knew all along. These included using Samael's business card format to print his own cards, the use of Samael's logo, stating on his letterhead that he was the representative of the Samael's law firm and all the documents he had lodged under that guise. The hearing proceeded and during the lunch recess, Samael was hunched over, pacing back and forth in front of the judicial bench taking what appeared to be indigestion tablets. It was near the end of this hearing that it became clear that things were going very bad for Nellie, who was in the Netherlands and not even in the court. Samael was summarising the day to the judge and deciding when the hearing would resume when a bell from Seth's computer sounded. Seth got the attention of Samael, interrupting him while addressing the judge nonetheless, issuing the advice that his services had been terminated. Samael, not having anything himself in writing agreed to the resumption a week later as the judge had decided, and Samael would contact Nellie directly and notify the court that he was no longer the solicitor of record once confirmed. Samael was gone and never seen again.

The appeal continued the following week. Nellie was present and asked for Seth to speak on her behalf or to sit beside her as a "McKenzie friend" to which we objected on the grounds that Seth was a declared a "vexatious litigant". A "McKenzie friend" is someone that sits beside the litigant to take notes and give advice, but is not a lawyer. A "vexatious litigant" requires a litigation guardian for themselves to lodge and submit documents and it was revealed that he had spent time in prison for contempt of court, so was unsuitable. It was ridiculous that someone that may be called to give evidence, required a litigation guardian for his own legal case should take on the role proposed. The judge agreed that Seth could not represent Nellie, and later wrote the determination accordingly. The hearing continued, and after one lunch recess, the Applicant (Nellie accompanied by Seth) were absent when the judge entered the Chamber. I believe the judge muttered, "Well we are not waiting for them, we are going to end this farce." But I couldn't be sure.

The following day was interesting, in that I was walking along the road to the family court and pressed the traffic light pedestrian button. Whilst waiting, a lady approached and asked me how the case went yesterday and what did the judge think? My response was, "I don't think he was happy." Her reaction was like she had just been halfway through a glass of water and had to cough and exploded with, "Well that's an understatement!" I became more guarded about the case and asked who she was, to which the response was, "I'm the Registrar." We then began to cross the road and moved onto the subject of Seth and she said, "Yes. He is a regular problem for the court." My response being, "The problem is he has probably cost my kids over $100,000.00 with this appeal." She paused mid-stride in the middle of the busy road, thinking. After what seemed like an eternity she replied, "That would probably be about right." In any case, it was months until the decision was handed down with the verdict here paraphrased, "where the actions or the applicant and her legal team has been appalling and the actions of the respondent and his legal team has been impeccable," and I was awarded indemnity costs to cover all legal expenses.

Other cases involved securing the property title to complete the conveyancing where the judge used a little-known power. As this was a Commonwealth court, there is a constitutional issue of a Commonwealth authority ordering a state authority to do anything. He could only order a State Government Authority to act if it was a subsidiary part of a Commonwealth case, and so he acted under that power. He ordered the State Titles office to cancel the existing title and issued a new property title to be delivered to the lawyers responsible for the property conveyancing.

The final case was that I had not followed procedure and had to be punished. Nellie was unable to show how the process had not been followed, nor any consequence of the alleged breach if there was one, and then did not submit how the court should remedy the alleged breach. Costs were awarded again.

Possibly, Nellie's most bizarre action was after all the court cases and the property settlement. She was sent several letters asking her to provide bank accounts and simply would not claim the money owed to her, in the property settlement. I waited for months, as wanted everyone to be paid at once but eventually gave up. I found a house that I wanted to purchase and took out my share. Thinking of the children, I ensured Nellie's share was earning interest in case she never claimed it. If Nellie died without claiming the money, especially if it was decades away, the money would still be worth something to the children. It was nearly 2 years later that she requested her share from the legal firm. She did this while the lawyer was on six weeks leave, so then sent an abusive follow-up letter. When the lawyer got back from holidays he asked me, what to do, to which I responded, "It's nothing to do with me as it is her money but I would in your response, send her the various letters over the last 2 years asking her to supply an address or bank details."

13

Death, near death and meeting Jasmine

Lazarus was referred to in the Bible as the man that had died four days earlier and Jesus asked the stone to be removed from his tomb, prayed to God, and then Lazarus came out of the tomb. The ability to not give up is something that is within all of us and varies in strength and occasionally fails. The combination of factors that will see people cling onto life or awake from a coma after many years is unknown, but shows itself, often when its least expected.

My father had Alzheimer's for the last five years of his life and while I attended his eightieth birthday, the day after I returned to Australia, he did not know what was going on. Denise, his new wife, was not well as she was also a very heavy smoker, suffering emphysema and was required to go into a nursing home for recuperation. My elder brother spoke to Dad who did not want to go into a nursing home and leave Denise, but when he understood that Denise needed to go into hospital for recuperation, he said, "I will do it for Denise." Even with the Alzheimer's, he probably would not have remembered me, not realising it was his eightieth birthday, the love for Denise was still there. Dad went into the facility but never came out, although we did transfer him to another facility after Denise had to move.

I would visit Dad occasionally and recall picking up Denise up in Torquay on my way to visit Dad at the nursing home which was an additional thirty minutes drive for me and a minor diversion. Denise moved from Torquay back to Melbourne and at first visited Dad each week and as her health failed, then became every second week. I would occasionally take Denise from her retirement village in greater Melbourne, but that was not as often as either of us would have liked. It was good to sit in the car with her for the couple of hours and we would find out what was going on in each other's lives.

The drive to see Dad eventually got too much and Denise had a car accident. It was at that time a nursing home right next door to Denise's retirement village changed its rules so that Dad could be moved and the decision was made to move him even though he seemed happy where he was. Denise and I brought him to the new nursing home and they were together again geographical-ly and she would see him most days.

I got the call one morning from Denise that she could not get hold of Graham (my older brother) and tell him that Dad had been taken to hospital and that she needed help to get to the hospital as there were forms to fill in. My response was immediate and that I would let Graham know and one of us would be there shortly to take her. I quickly got hold of my brother (who was in the shower when Denise rang) and we decided that I would go.

I picked up Denise and we got to the hospital in less than thirty minutes. Dad had been examined but was still in the emergency area. The prognosis was not good, in that he had a severe lung infection and they had administered some antibiotics intravenously into him. He had suffered severe Alzheimer's for the last five years and rarely recognised the people around him and lost the ability to communicate, which must have made the diagnosis more difficult. We had all agreed on a "no resuscitation instruction" and the doctors did what they could. He would walk around the nursing home, sort of singing, and we all liked to think he was in a good place in his mind and we all wanted him to live without pain and be happy.

Denise signed the forms and within a short space of time, it was diagnosed that he was not expected to survive much longer. As my nephew put it, he was having the death throes and the regular medication was substituted for some pain medication to make his last hours comfortable.

A vigil was set up as the best estimate was that he would pass away within six hours, so my brother and I wanted to be there. Many of his relatives from his second marriage also attended. As the hours dragged on it was decided that I would go home and get some sleep, get back early in the morning to take over and then my brother could sleep. We were worn out as this had gone on much longer than anyone anticipated and on the third night neither of us were present.

He woke up on the fourth morning after being admitted and somehow managed to communicate with the treating doctor that he was hungry, thirsty and wanted to go home.

The doctor admitted that he was very hard to understand and work out what he wanted but there he was, talking (in a fashion) and was shipped back to the Alzheimer's ward in the nursing home. The hospital staff said that they expected him to regress, that if he lasted four days, they would be surprised and that they would send someone to the nursing home if required, rather than bringing him back to the hospital and prepared us accordingly.

Upon his return to the nursing home, he appeared more lucid than he had been for the previous six months. The staff reported that, "gee, he ate and drank a lot when he got back," and with no food or fluids during for those four days, no one should have been surprised. He lasted a lot more than the six hours that he was given shortly after being admitted, more than the four days was he was given when sent home from hospital, in fact, he lasted around two years.

It was in August 2013, my mother had been stable since the burst appendix for so long, driving to the shopping, out to see friends and as with many elderly people, her health began to fail. Her body was again, no longer absorbing nutrients and after I took her to the specialist, she was given powders that would remedy the situation. Unfortunately, it did not remedy the situation and days later it was off to hospital, legs weeping with slippers full of liquid. After some deliberation, they admitted her for a series of tests as that would be more efficient and only take days, rather than possibly weeks with outpatient services and she was transferred to another hospital.

My mother did not want people fussing over her and few people knew of her decline on this occasion, but in late September she asked me to contact her sister which I tried to do by phone and email. I recall visiting her one day as she came out of the toilet with the assistance of a nurse who promptly left the room carrying a bag. She explained how they "tested everything that came out of her," to which I responded, "So you are giving them the shits, Mum." The response was laughter down the hall at the nursing station, so they were clearly attentive and could hear what was happening.

In spite of weeks in hospital, she continued to deteriorate. The battery of tests, never figured out what was wrong in her gut and why she was not digesting food. I entered the hospital ward on one of my regular visits and was sent to the waiting room down the end of the corridor and watched the crash team with all the defibrillation equipment enter her room. While I never knew if that was precaution, she survived.

I had a series of contracted, project-based roles since I had returned to Australia and it was typical to end those once the projects finished and was looking for my next role. The following morning, I had some Intelligence Quotient and Emotional Quotient (IQ and EQ) testing as part of the intake assessment for a consulting role. Needless to say, I did not follow the instructions to not proceed if I recently had been stressed as I wanted, and felt that I needed the role. At the end of the employment testing, I naturally went back to the hospital.

It was several days later when they inserted a feeding tube directly into my mother's stomach and I was told this would solve the issue, however, logically I thought, it could not work, as the problem was below her stomach. I actually went and saw a psychologist that afternoon, was given some sage advice and saw Mum again that night. It was a Friday, the last day of the working week, early October and a glorious spring morning in Australia. The sun was bright, birds chirping and as I went for a walk, I thought it was a lovely day to die. I had resigned myself and accepted what was to be, and spent a short time chasing up some work prospects and went to the hospital that afternoon, to spend what I believed would be the last afternoon with Mum.

The events that evening were chaotic. It was around 7:35 p.m. when I received a call and realising it was from my cousin Sue, and I proceeded out of my mother's room. Her mother, my aunt, my mother's sister, had died that afternoon and she had rung to give me the news. She had just been to her mother's place to hear the message I had left weeks earlier and asked, "How is aunty Deborah?" to which I responded, "I believe they will both die today," which was met with a long silence. I could hear the reaction through the phone and whether it was the breathing or something else, the shock was evident, and that shock was confirmed as the conversation resumed. I agreed to keep her informed of my mother's status and we both agreed to keep our common relatives informed about both our mothers as we contacted them.

Partly in shock, I went back to the nurse's station and told them, "Mums' sister just died." They clearly had not heard me, or perhaps I was not speaking clearly, and they replied, "No, she is not dead yet, but you had better call anyone that should be here, as it will not be long." This time I said what just happened in more detail, "No, Mums' sister just died, around 2pm in Albury. I cannot tell Mum as she is not conscious," as we both took in what had been said, in that short but important message.

A flurry of phone calls followed, first to my brothers' daughter who told me her older brother was already on the way, my younger brother that lived interstate and I even made a mistake ringing my brother that I knew was on the way anyway. I told them nothing of the death of Mums' sister on the phone and had been going in and out of Mums' room, as I did not want her to hear all the phone calls. My mother died twenty minutes after I told the nurses of my aunts death, Mums' sister. While I did not tell Mum, I wonder to this day if she had heard me tell the nurses and knew of her sisters passing, just as the nurses had laughed when I joked with Mum, "You're giving them the shits." Some people say that hearing is the last of the senses that you lose.

The first to arrive at the hospital was my nephew Sean, and I can still picture him rushing down the corridor, his facial expression on seeing me, realising his grandmother had passed and taking him to the waiting room and telling him as he collapsed in the doorway. While still collapsed in the doorway he told me Erica, his sister, was on her way and that her daughter was being minded by their mother, so I did not need to ring her again. He eventually asked if my mum's sister knew and if I thought she would be able to attend the funeral. It was then that he was given that news of that passing earlier in the day, and while I did not think someone sitting on the floor could collapse further, he did. Erica then arrived to also be given the news of her grandmothers passing, visited the room to say goodbye and then given the news of the sisters' death. The word clearly went through the hospital and even doctors when speaking to us, expressed their condolences for both my mother and her sister. I was not meant to go back to Mums' place that night but changed my mind halfway home as wanted to get her list of friends.

With the ten hours difference, I stayed up and called Jasmine early the next morning, which was evening her time. She had avoided talking to me on earlier occasions, so I dispensed with pleasantries and upon her answering the phone, the first words I said was, "I have some bad news for you." It wasn't "Hello, Jasmine. I have some bad news for you," or "Hello, Jasmine. How are you?" in case she hung up. Cautiously, she answered, "Yes," and I believe she recognised who was calling. I do not know if she got the "get well card" that I had posted to her and requested that she and Joe to sign and post it to back to their grandmother at the hospital, or the other messages over the past month, but it didn't matter now. I told her of the death of her nana, (her grandmother), and suggested she talk to her older brother Joe and consider coming across for the funeral service. It would be just as I did some years earlier for my Uncle, (my mother's brother), and it may assist to process the loss. I also told her that I would pay for airfares if they decided to attend. I remembered the times when she insisted on sleeping in the same room as her nana, both when nana visited the Netherlands or when we visited Australia and thought *how much she used to love her nana.*

The following day I spent ringing my close relatives, my mother's friends and some relatives that I could barely remember. She had not told people she was sick and therefore the shock of the news was evident. She was an office bearer for one organisation and active with a walking group and so two calls to the names I recognised meant that many of her friends were notified. Her cousin was another difficult call, and everyone asked if I thought her sister would be able to attend the funeral, and then that news was also given. In each case, the shock was felt with the silence as if I had winded them again, just like what happened when I told my nephew. My cousins were notified, and the message permeated through the families. There were many callbacks, such as can you give me Sue's number and address so I can give her my condolences? Several of my relatives that got the message through their spouse (as that was who was home at the time) and others as the word spread also called. I was completely drained by the end of the day and while it was all very serious at the time, I now joke that I have never made so many women cry in one day.

I went out that night and told no one of the events that day and enjoyed the usual superficial discussions with friends. I particularly remember the banter with the two daughters of friends as they attempted to impart their knowledge and experience when it came to "pick-up lines." It was a long day by the time I got home.

The years in between leaving the Netherlands until now, felt like an eternity. I had not seen Jasmine and although I called regularly, emailed weekly and thought of her daily, I had not seen her. I wondered how she was coping with all this madness as we once had a great relationship but had withdrawn, communicating less and less but how had it impacted her? I knew that Nellie had inflicted a great deal of psychological trauma on her simply through what was said at the custody hearing, the presents being returned and the McDonald's meeting. It seemed parental alienation was targeted at me and also the extended family. Alienation had been thorough and took no prisoners. The process of the grief of the alienation, now combined with my mother's death, was a heavy burden to carry.

Part of a funeral is grieving, supporting others and saying goodbye. As many people say, it is not about the person who dies as they are not conscious to take it in but may on another plane be watching over us, if you believe that sort of thing. The funeral is often essential for everyone's wellbeing and that included my daughters'. After all, she had been removed from her grandmother, taken overseas and may need to grieve for the loss of the relationship she should have enjoyed. What happens however, when you are focused upon something else, rather than grieving the loss of your mother, I was about to find out.

Days later, my daughter confirmed that she and Joe would like to attend the funeral and we had a three-way conversation. Relatives had been told from the outset that the date of the funeral would be set after we consider the necessity for travel arrangements. The weekend had passed, and I had not set the date yet as Monday was a public holiday and I needed to check various funeral homes to ensure there was no prepaid plan somewhere. I was organising the funeral and asked Jasmine and Joe if they would prefer the coming Friday or the next. Jasmine wanted the immediate coming Friday as suited her better, which I took at the time as being related to her university studies. The horrible part of the three-way discussion with the kids was that they would not stay at my place. I conceded, as I believed they would simply not come to Australia for the funeral if I continued to push and felt it was important for them to say goodbye.

Frantically I was ringing a friend that was also with the Lions Club to find out if he could arrange flights and prices as he ran an Australian Flight Agency with a price guarantee but he could not match what Joe found, through his searches on European websites. My friend suggested they must either bulk purchase blocks of tickets or Europe are subsidising. We went with the tickets Joe had put a hold on and I paid for the fares.

The kids, well adults really, flew out the next day. I offered to pick them up at the airport but again that was refused, and they had organised to stay at a youth hostel and already booked and paid for the bus from the airport. After years of not seeing them, this restriction was not palatable, but I accepted it, as part of what happens to the children suffering from parental alienation. I had known the antics that their mother had played over the last few years which were many and varied. While many of the games and tactics were illegal under the Australian Family Law Act, there seemed little recourse and continued relentlessly.

Messages upon their arrival included that they had indeed arrived and required the directions to get to the funeral. The arrangements made were that as they did not want me or any of the other relatives to pick them up, they would come to the train station near my house and would be there two hours beforehand, have some lunch and then go with me to the afternoon funeral. I must say they did not turn up at the station until the last minute, too late to go to my place, so they did not eat the prepared lunch.

I was quite nervous and remember wondering if they were actually in Australia or just being used by their mother to make me late to the funeral. It is surprising what goes through your head when anxiety takes control. It was quite surreal seeing them on the station, they looked the same and yet so completely changed. Jasmine was now nineteen and being my daughter, possibly combined with her short stature, meant that in my eyes, she was my little girl.

She was dressed in a vintage overcoat which had one button missing and a mishmash of positives and negative thoughts flew through my mind. That was the fashion nowadays and she is being fashionable, that her mother had always liked shopping in opportunity shops for clothes which she described the clothes as "having character" and it is possibly her mother's influence, or, was it that she could not afford new clothes and struggling, but I said nothing and contained those random thoughts. Anything I said would be taken as a criticism and had little confidence that it would come out right, whatever I said. Her face was puffed as if she had been crying or close to crying, but apart from that she looked good. I greeted Jasmine with open arms to which she seemed to shrink away but gave her a hug anyway and certainly, the hug was not reciprocated as she stood there rigidly.

Joe was smartly dressed and tall. I had seen him at one of the Australian court cases and put that behind me. I do not believe he had a choice when he was dragged to Australia to lie under oath in the witness box which is perjury and at the time, up to a 10-year jail sentence that is never prosecuted in Family Law cases in Australia. All he had done was to support his mother, but remember being so upset with Nellie when I found out that he missed his final exams and had to repeat a semester as he deserved to be treated better than that. He was smiling and seemed happy to see me again and we greeted each other with a firm handshake and a hug which, unlike Jasmine, was well received.

We walked to the car and I asked how the trip went. "Good," said Jasmine. "How are you going at University?" I asked, and again the single word response came from Jasmine, "Good." It was just like at McDonald's all that time ago with one-word responses to anything I asked. We got into the car and Jasmine made sure she got in the back seat while Joe was comfortable in the front. I tried asking Jasmine open questions that she could not answer with a single word like, "why did you leave the arts course?" and "Are you enjoying the law course now?" to which Jasmine replied, "I didn't like it, and I'm not sure." Attempting to communicate with Jasmine was proving difficult and I could feel the tension as she shrank, surly, into the corner of the back seat where she was difficult to see. I began asking Joe questions about what he was doing, and the conversation flowed as he asked how everyone was in Australia and it was great to hear his voice and the tension seemed to dissipate. I did ask Jasmine another question when the tension had eased which was, "are you sure you don't want to say anything at the service?" to which she replied, "No," and while it was not as surly as earlier, it was still expressed with a level of animosity. We stopped at the shop just next to where the funeral home was, to pick up the flowers and then onto the funeral home.

There was, of course, a poster consisting of a collage of photos, a smaller photo and the flowers to place up the front next to her ashes. Joe and Jasmine helped bring the items in and we were all greeted by the staff and I began to position everything, aided by the staff just ahead of the arrival of my brothers and everyone else.

Jasmine burst into tears shortly after arriving at the funeral home and while being handed a box of tissues, she raced into the ladies' restroom and away from everyone just like at McDonald's. This time, no one was able to follow her, cousins and other guests had not yet arrived. I never knew if those tears were just for my mother, the relationship that she was denied and should have enjoyed with my mother when she whisked off to the Netherlands, or partly from seeing me. It was difficult for both of us.

Guests started to arrive and while Joe consoled Jasmine when she reappeared from the restroom. I greeted the guests with my younger brother that had flown in from interstate and older brother that both arrived shortly after Jasmine, Joe and I. The guests included many friends from the Lions Club, friends that

I had known for decades, the nurse that had been very outspoken about my mother's treatment at the rehabilitation hospital, my cousins that I had spoken to the day after my mother's passing and my remaining aunt, the widow of my mother's brother, my uncle that I had made a special trip back for his funeral and the last of her generation, with many of them wanting to meet Jasmine. It was actually my aunt that said days before the funeral when confirming her attendance that she hoped that Jasmine would come to her senses and something good came out of the funeral.

The funeral proceeded and was conducted by the childhood friend of my older brother that had become a priest and as it finished, everyone moved to the area where refreshments were served. Everyone thought it was a lovely service and years later when one of the Lions Club members father died, he immediately rang me to ensure he organised the same funeral home.

It seemed that many people did introduce themselves to Jasmine, but unsure what was said as so many people wanted to express their condolences and Joe and Jasmine seemed to move to their cousins and away from me. When the funeral was over, I took them to the local hotel for a quick drink with the immediate family being my brothers and the other grandchildren and Jasmine was largely silent. Jasmine and Joe asked to be driven to the local train station and insisted that I not drive them back to the hostel which again filled my heart with sorrow. At the train station, I managed to give Jasmine a huge hug which lasted a long time and believe she expressed a tear at the time and much more receptive than when I picked her up before the funeral. I had again failed to break through but maybe I moved forward just a little.

I was able to see Jasmine and Joe two more times before they left. My nephew, Sean and I picked them up from the train station near Grahams' as they would still not let me collect them from the Youth Hostel. They were very late again. At least this time I was sure they were in Australia, but was it being rude and inconsiderate being so late? Was that now their norm and late everywhere? Or was it the apprehension of seeing myself and relatives that they were encouraged to reject? Sean and Joe were a similar age and that helped break down the tensions with the way they spoke. We were on our way to my brother's house for the social gathering when Jasmine asked in a soft tone, almost with hesitation, "Does Graham still have the cats?" To which I quipped, "No, but there is a baby, so you'll be fine." Knowing how much Jasmine loved to play with cats and other creatures, a baby would be a natural I thought.

They were so late that we had all eaten, but Jasmine and Joe sat at the dining table, ate and joined in the conversation, although Jasmine was very reserved and quiet and didn't want to interact at all, Joe was fine. After they had eaten, I gave Jasmine some of the things I wanted her to have, and particularly remember Erica, my niece and brother's daughter, sitting on the floor with the baby, watching intensely. The first was a DVD of the funeral and also all the photographs used in the service. I also gave copies to everyone else as had spent many hours producing and copying them so they could take them with them. The second was a diamond ring that my mother had asked me to find at her place and pass onto her granddaughters in her final days. There were two rings of which Erica, the other granddaughter, had already received one, in accordance with my mother's last wishes. I remember going out to get the small ring boxes from a shop so that I could properly present it to them and told Jasmine that it that her nana wanted her to have it and that it was her nana's grandmother making it her great, great grandmothers ring. The third item was oval glass photo frame which contained a picture of a "baby Jasmine" being held in the arms of her Nana, which used to sit by my mother's bedside table, virtually since just after Jasmine was born and asked if she wanted it. She had it electronically as I had sent so many photos over one Christmas, but this was special, and she teared up and said she wanted it. After I gave her the gifts and explained their meaning the tears rolled down her cheeks and both Erica and I reached for the box of tissues. Erica sitting on the floor close by, had also teared up seeing what unfolded.

Jasmine had been taught to hate me, mistrust me, that I abandoned her, and that was revealed when Nellie spoke to the judge in the Dutch children's court with the statement like "I tried to explain to her why her father abandoned her and she wouldn't do that to her cats", "I tried to explain to her why there is no money for toilet paper," when the truth was very different and exposed in the court case but never to Jasmine. I had regularly offered to give Jasmine a holiday and meet up anywhere in the world and there was always a place for her. Perhaps not telling her the day I departed as I had planned in person,

I had left her wondering and the subsequent communications did not have the same effect. Nellie had taken Joe's father to court and got child support and at times said she was proud of that court battle. Perhaps Jasmine had been told her father didn't want to support you and I had to take Trevor to court which is what Nellie always told me about Joe's father. I will never know. The fact was, Jasmine had been told only one side of the story and I had been advised never to put down the other parent, something which every alienated parent initially has difficulty managing, and to just show unconditional love which is something I tried to do. As far as I knew, Jasmine still knew nothing of the threats made by Nellie and the attack six days before I left the Netherlands; the lies and tactics used in the court; the veiled death threats; the actions of "the cast of crazies" and telling her would simply put a greater canyon between us. I am certain that Nellie would not have told her the truth. Even with all that emotion in the room, I was unable to break through and could not bring myself to tell her what happened, and it seemed like I was in the fight of my life, but without limbs to defend myself.

A short time later there was a bit of joy for seeing each other and Jasmine settled down. Jasmine asked if she and Joe could see their grandfather and was pleased as that request gave me another chance to interact. Jasmine and Joe were warned that he was not in a good way in an effort to prepare them for what they would see. Jasmine did play with Erica's baby and had the hugest grin on her face as she helped a little one around who was just learning to take her first steps and was a sight I will treasure forever and captured it on my phone's camera. Not long after, I dropped Joe and Jasmine back at the train station, they would still not let me take them to the hostel and gave Jasmine a huge hug that may have even been longer in duration than after the funeral and saw them off.

The next time I saw the children was to take them to see my father, they again insisted on catching a train to the station near my place and so I agreed to pick them both up again. We needed to go back to my house as it was on the way to pick up a photo for Jasmine and could stop there for a quick sandwich before going to see her grandfather (my dad). Jasmine refused to get out of the car, sat in the car in my driveway but was looking around at the house and garden as I went inside to collect a few things. One of the things was a photo of Jasmine and her Grandad taken at the Country Golf Club where her Grandad had played golf regularly and there were kangaroos in the background. As I handed her the photo is was clear that she remembered it being taken and could almost see the memories being relived in her head as she gazed at it. As she looked on the photo I said, "Remember grandad like this, not what you are about to see." As I prepared them for what they would see.

As Jasmine and therefore Joe would not get out of the car for lunch at my place, we arrived at the Alzheimer's ward of the nursing home earlier than I had planned and it was their lunchtime. Grandad was having lunch and the kids sat down with him. My father was in his very final stages of Alzheimer's. He couldn't string a sentence together, couldn't recognise me or the kids, he was devoid of anything that made him resemble being human, and was in fact, more like a gentle zombie. It would have been a huge shock for the kids seeing anyone like that for the first time in their lives, let alone someone they once knew well. As they looked on their grandfather, I actually wondered why I brought them and maybe I should have protected them from this. But then, growing old, illness, even dying is part of life and who was I to deny them access to their grandfather and that part of life.

I left the kids with my father for a few minutes, telling them I would go to the nurse's station to check and see if there was anything he needed. When I returned, Joe asked, "Where have you been?" Joe and Jasmine mustn't have heard me, possibly reeling from the reality of what had become of their grandfather. It was a sudden shock rather than the agonisingly slow progression of Alzheimer's that I had seen develop over the years. I explained to Joe, who was sitting next to Jasmine, that I come weekly, check in with the nurses on what he needs and that is what I had just done. That I walk around the home and courtyard as he sings and talks in an incomprehensible manner even though I am sure he has no idea who I am but am equally sure he likes someone with him. Joe's remark, "Gee, that's really good," showed enormous insight and the response surprised me and I only hoped Jasmine thought the same.

The two of them asked to be dropped at the station on the way home. They wouldn't come back for a late lunch and pressuring them, I thought would be counterproductive. Saying goodbye was difficult. This could be the last time I would see them both and particularly Jasmine for who knows how long, if ever. I went to hug her goodbye as I had done on the previous two occasions and she yelled, "Don't you touch me!" then she burst into tears. As

I walked away, my heart felt heavy. I turned back to see Joe comforting her and trying to distract her by pointing out the funny safety posters on the station platform. I yelled out to them, "Just remember I love you!" I am sure they would have heard me, and if they did, they did not move or acknowledge that they had. That was the last time I saw them both.

14

The passing of my stepmum, dad and seeking inner peace

My step-mother loved my father and I believe her children did as well and especially some of her grandchildren. Like all lives, we can focus on the pleasures or the tragedies and in my stepmothers' case, the tragedies included the passing of three of her four children due to cancer and a car accident. As a couple, they were integral in helping raise some of the grandchildren because of those tragedies. Alternatively, we can focus on the good times and the closeness that such circumstances bring.

My stepmother always wanted to ensure that we remained in contact with my father which was more possible now that I was back in Australia and especially that he was living locally, not halfway around the world or even two and a half hour drive away. I would no longer pick her up and take her from the complex where she lived as it was next door to the Alzheimer's ward of the total care facility where my father now resided.

As such I would often see her while visiting Dad either as we passed each other going in and out of the complex or would stop past her place and say hello but must admit, not as often as I should have. I recall at one stage she was questioning if I had seen Dad and was concerned about my older brother and I. There was really nothing to be concerned about as we normally made sure one of us got there each week and she was reassured when I explained that I had the flu for several weeks and visiting him in his frail state may have been fatal. If you have been with someone with severe Alzheimer's, you may wonder why you bother visiting, they do not know who you are, and in some cases, would not remember that you were there once leaving their sight. He seemed to get pleasure with someone walking the corridors with him and putting up with his singing.

Denise had been a heavy smoker all her life and with Emphysema needed oxygen bottles and required greater care than what was able to be provided in her self-contained unit within the retirement complex. She moved into the same complex as my father but not in the Alzheimer's section, where she could put in some of her own furniture, all meals supplied and full-time nursing care was available. The other benefit was that she could simply get the lift downstairs, through a security door (to stop the Alzheimer's patients wandering out) and was there to visit her husband, my father.

I had visited her on the first week she moved into the facility and decided that I would visit her each time I visited Dad. It was only the second week after she moved in that

I dropped in to see Dad and spent a bit of time with him and then proceeded upstairs to see Denise and could not find her.

When I asked, I got told that she was taken away earlier to local a hospital (the same hospital where I took my mother for her burst appendix) as she had a serious fall. As I was not a blood relative, I was not on the contact list and I decided to proceed to the hospital, as it was only a small diversion on my way home, and of course, rang my brother to give him the news.

I got to the local hospital and asked where Denise was and informed that she had been transferred to the Alfred Hospital. This was sounding more serious and as I was not listed as a primary contact, the information was somewhat scarce.

I decided that night to go to the Alfred Hospital and see what was going on and found Denise there is significant pain with her grandson. The grandson was very close to Denise because of the tragic passing of his mother and it was then that I got the full prognosis. She had broken her hip/upper thigh, however they could not do anything as she is on blood-thinning drugs due to her other conditions. The surgeons would need to wait 10 days until those drugs were are out of her system before they could operate and attend to setting or pinning the fracture.

The hospital has their palliative care program which tries to ensure people are prepared for the passing and contacts you to ensure you are doing okay. It was interesting in that I had met the surgeon and after leaving the hospital, I received a call while driving down the highway from the palliative care team as the staff must have passed through my details as they could see I was a relative with the same surname and was treated as "one of the family."

I was working at the time with only a few weeks to go on that contract and was able to drop in and see her regularly as the Alfred hospital was on the way home. It was on the weekend after dropping in to see Dad first and then the hospital that I saw her lying in bed clearly in a lot of pain and went up to her, held her hand and informed her that I have seen Dad and he is normal. She smiled, rolled over and seemed to go to sleep. It was clear to me that she was happy in that I had been in to check up on Dad and someone was looking out for him. I thought she was going to die that night but it was not yet her time.

She had the operation a week later but never recovered and died in the hospital a week later. Denise died twelve months and three days after my mother. She was visited by many people on her last day with my older brother and I, being just two of the many. She had been a "clippie" in her earlier years which is an English term for someone that clipped the bits out of the printed paper bus or tram tickets that indicated which stop you got on and collected the fares. She could still tell how many stops and which tram routes to get to the hospital as her son tested her out. She was making jokes to the end, at least when I was there, several hours before she passed away, which was in stark contrast to my father.

We had consulted with the Nursing Staff that were looking after Dad to work out what to tell him. The advice was that it is best to not say anything as:

- If he remembered his wife, he would become distraught and could become unmanageable.

- If he did not remember his wife and was told, he would be terribly upset that he cannot remember his wife, and

- If he was told and actually did not understand, he may become frustrated with not being able to understand.

It was a no-win situation and the same advice we received years earlier, when we considered taking him to his stepson's funeral and just took Denise instead. There was no reason to tell him; was the best advice we had which again, we all followed.

I must confess I felt both strange and out of place at the funeral that was well organised by her remaining son and daughter-in-law. The reason I felt out of place was that I did not know my stepmother as well as I should and then meeting all the step-relatives, that knew Dad as part of their family and yet I did not know them.

It was several weeks after Denise's funeral that I got a call from the Alzheimer's ward of the nursing home. Dad had been walking a little stranger than normal and they had x-rays taken which showed he had broken his hip/

upper thigh, was being put in an ambulance while we were talking and would be taken to the Alfred hospital. I naturally consulted my older brother and as I was available, decided that I would attend.

Last time I was here in the Emergency Entrance, it was with Denise and the Lazarus' incident years before. This time, it was without Denise and wondered what the outcome would be?

I was directed from the Emergency Department to the orthopaedic admission area to see him in the hospital bed and the nurses approached me; "We are going to admit him, and the orthopaedic admissions doctor is on his way down," they stated in their compassionate and profession-al manner. I responded, "Will you be putting him in the same room as his wife was recently in?" and they looked at me a little stunned. I explained the recent incident with his wife being admitted and died in that ward and when they realised how recent, I could sense their reaction. I suspect they went away and checked the patient records and warned the doctor.

If there was a funny side to all of this was that either the pain or change in environment must have done something in his brain and he was able to communicate far better than normal. He knew he was in hospital and I explained that he had a broken hip and needed to stay in bed. The response was, "Let me get up and we can see if it is broken," or words to that effect as he tried to get out of bed and I gently persuaded him to stay in the bed.

The doctor came down and said, "I remember you. I admitted your mother and spoke to you about her condition." He went on to explain that this is completely different as he is not on any blood thinners and will be operated on in the morning. He even began to sketch both my mother's break and how my father's break was by comparison and explained the difference in the treatment.

I took charge even though my brother was the legal power of attorney. There were never any arguments about wanting what was best for Dad in the lead up to this but when Graham arrived we asked, "Should he be operated on considering his age and condition?" This is a major operation. It was explained to us that the bone had to be set or it would degrade internally, in other words, rot, and cause even greater pain and therefore was the best course of action and knowing that, we naturally agreed.

They moved him to the orthopaedic ward and somehow managed to put him on the opposite side of the ward that my stepmother was placed. Never the less it was quite a concern being the same admitting doctor and the same ward.

The next day he was operated on and we checked throughout the day. They had moved him to a private room for the benefit of the other patients. I was visiting the hospital the next day and was informed the operation was successful, however no one seemed to know how he would manage as he probably did not understand what was going on and broken bones take time to repair. I also learned that if you have Alzheimer's and they cannot stop you singing, then you are likely to get a private room even if your hospital plan does not cover it.

On the way home while in the car, I was again called by the hospital and it was again the same member of the palliative care team at roughly the same location on the highway. Didn't I have this call just over a month ago? It was all taken in, and we continued to monitor Dad through the hospital and very frequent visits, until he was discharged back to the Alzheimer's ward at the nursing home where he resided.

Dad died some weeks later and it was just outside the time required from the discharge from hospital where a coroner's report would have been mandatory. There was no negligence and it was his time. If you believe that sort of thing he was with his wife, Denise. Following the Lazarus incident, we had learned how difficult it was to predict his time of passing and was grateful, that I had been with him just 2 hours before he passed away and I received the phone call.

We knew exactly what to do and rang up the Funeral Directors that had performed my mother's service. The funeral was late in December and the same week as Christmas and like all funerals, the preparation was a rush. We could not get my brother's friend who was a priest, as it is the busy period for them, and the Funeral Director organised a Justice of the Peace to perform the ceremony.

I arrived home from my father's funeral and settling down, finally checked my email to discover our funding for Fathers Support, that I had only just been appointed Chairman, had been withdrawn along with the funding for around 4000 other community organisations. Before entering a proper grieving process, I launched straight into a political campaign against a government minister that would eventually become Prime Minister. There was no other organisation that dealt with men like we did. One MP did a speech in Parliament, a Senator encouraged all the crossbench to support us, around sixty organisations providing letters of their support and upon demonstrating that there was no one else supporting our client base, the funding was restored. It was an essential achievement as one of our large surveys showed over 6% of our clients would have died by suicide if we were not there to help. These days I am still a member of the board.

My feelings at the end of my father's funeral were again different to both my mothers' and step-mothers' as my father's mind and memories had long gone with Alzheimer's before he passed away. I had spent most of my life travelling for the construction industry or in Europe due to Nellie. While there was a sense of profound disappointment at the loss and his final years, this was put aside as I remembered what I was able to do which included walking him around the Alzheimer's ward (unless I was sick) on a weekly basis. I had notified Jasmine of his passing, however she never communicated back, such was the progression of the parental alienation. I also sent her a DVD of the service but do not know if she bothered to watch it or even received it.

I had now seemingly lost most of my immediate family in a short space of time. PTSD was apparent to those close to me (sleep, high anxiety, overly cautious at public events, cognitive dysfunction etc.) that I concealed, and the parental alienation continued at a constant and relentless rate. I had total intolerance of those I thought were trying to take advantage of me and the situation I was in. Still, I remained hopeful, despite the constant triggers in my life. I felt like I was to be stationed in that pinball machine for the rest of my life, no longer having any control over my life. It had been a tumultuous period for the better part of a decade.

I recall receiving a text from a service called 1800 686 323 (which displays as 1800 MUM DAD). I thought that one of the kids had texted and left a message so had to ring back. Naturally, I rang back immediately to hear how much it cost to listen to the message (around $5 taken from my account), only to discover that it was not one of my kids but what appeared to be a scam message nonetheless.

Investigating the service on a website, it was listed a scam to get $5 from fools that ring to get their message. Having had a child that I considered was kidnapped by stealth internationally and what had happened, then how could I put up with this injustice? I proceeded to lodge a police report with the particulars to be told it is a legitimate service in spite of the blogs on the internet.

When the police rang the 1800MUMDAD service, they were transferred through to a supervisor who checked the call records after my prompt. Someone had dialled and left a message to the wrong number (two digits reversed) compared with the number they normally dial to leave a message for their parents.

The same thing occurred a few more times and I just ignored it. I then thought if they were my kids, then they should know why their parents are not responding and eventually managed to get a message to the person that they are dialling the wrong number! I never got another message so assume I was successful and whoever it was they learned to type in the correct phone number.

There is of course, the constant hope and desperation that your child may come back and another event that triggered a disproportionate emotional reaction included fixing up my daughters' bedroom in April 2014.

I had been in my new house for a while but had only furnished the rooms I immediately needed. The spare bedroom, back room and study all remained empty. I was quite surprised at my reaction and the overwhelming sense of urgency I felt that my daughter's room must be made ready.

I had measured up the room and decided that a Queen size bed was too big for the room and would have interfered with the cupboard doors or would need to be against a wall, (which results in some difficulty when making the bed). For some unknown reason, I felt that I needed to get the bed and have it ready as a matter of urgency, as if I had not been looking after my daughter and what would occur if she showed up. I raced out to get a flat pack bed that would fit in the back of my car and the mattress could be delivered in the following days.

That night I worked quite methodically and managed to assemble the bed. I had assembled flat packs for years and having installed built in robes, kitchen cupboards had always been fairly handy. What surprised me was the relief (not satisfaction), that I had completed the rather simple and menial task.

In the following days, I picked out the doona cover and a small bedside table, upon which to place an alarm clock and later, the bottom shelf became the place for her twenty-first birthday present. That present, a Pandora bracelet with her name in letters was never collected from the postal service, returned and remains unopened, waiting for the day she returns.

When I look back the level of stress doing nothing or doing something or the procrastination that people suffer when subjected to parental alienation can be extreme. Putting the bed together so that the room was ready, even though it was never used for years was just another example of the stress from not doing that activity and relieved by me acting upon it. But ultimately, the stress and trauma are ever present.

Six years after leaving, believing Jasmine would be safe, the outcomes that if I did not leave could have been catastrophic, I awoke to find that I had missed a phone call at 22:58 p.m. on a Thursday night. Who was it? Was it my daughter? The feeling and thoughts raced through my head and emotions become so extreme that that stomach began to feel like it was tied up in knots and felt sick so quickly that I realised this is not normal. The background of difficult emotion-laden physical reactions is quickly replaced by logic and control restored within another ten seconds but what that ten seconds it is. The emotions are so intense that you can be easily drained for hours or even days. All this after six years is not only a surprise to me but an experience that one would prefer to avoid. Unfortunately, this is normal, at least for many parents that suffer parental alienation. Hope can be both a lifesaver to keep you going and a legacy that may need to be released through conscious acts of positivity.

The stresses of the court cases and hearings are immense. It doesn't matter if you are fighting for sole custody to protect children from the other parent's drug, alcohol, mental health, a perverse need for power and control, for full or shared custody from the unreasonable parent. The stresses of not being believed, ensuring evidence is made available and in my case, to simply survive and put an end to the attacks through the courts can be overwhelming.

Court case after court case, hearings, orchestrated delays, adjournments, enforcement hearings and with cases in two countries being run in parallel, I found that once it looked like I would have three decisions handed down the same day but were within forty-eight hours. Fighting to prove the facts and constantly defending myself was draining. It is so easy to make up something that did not happen, yet difficult, time consuming and expensive to prove something that did not happen, actually did not happen. Claims that we did not live together in Australia, that our relationship never happened was one of dozens of false claims and outright lies. With Nellie having taken all the paperwork, it was my word and that of my relatives, which could be considered unreliable and supporting me, until the subpoena for the psychiatric notes and other files that Nellie strenuously fought against, but finally granted, that proved the truth.

The images of the constant buffeting and exchanges of Nellie's lawyers, the veiled death threat, the personalities Nellie recruited to get her way and the real experience that police do nothing to protect some sectors of the community, is difficult to accept and remains with me. If someone wants either total control or to destroy you, driven to win at all costs, uncontrolled hatred, revenge or possibly an undiagnosed personality disorder that will stop at nothing including false statements to the police, perjury in the court and misuse of the court, the outcome will regularly be what I have experienced.

At the end of all the court cases, a national investigative news program filmed a piece on several of us and the problems in the family court. "Don't go to court," and "The problems when one party will not see reason." The program that night won its highest rating for the year and featured the impact on those noncustodial parents, the waste the system creates, the drop in living standards were featured which included my family's losses, estimated at over $700,000.00, involving two countries, and ten judges.

As I look back, the Australian judges had awarded me the right to claim costs in every case. They had stated in a judgement that the conduct and tactics used by Nellie and her legal team had been appalling. The appeals court in the Netherlands corrected, what I consider an illegally run case which I could not defend, and the highest court in that land agreed by not allowing the matter to waste their time. Legally and morally I was vindicated and had won ... but I had still lost everything and anyone who I'd ever cared for.

Jasmine emailed me during the height of the cases and asked for the photo albums that I had taken. I found that I appeared in very few photos as Nellie rarely took photos and that was something I did! After we split, I realised that I was barely featured. In any case, Jasmine asked for the return of the photo albums and I found I was reluctant as it was all I had of her. In addition, I did not know if it was her that was asking for her, or asking for her mother to strip me of yet another thing.

While all the Australian court appeals cases were on, I set about scanning all the photos (rather than order reprints) and tried with various scanning devices that a friend imported. I found those that stream fed frequently did not feed in properly, so reverted to a flat-bed scanner and one by one, scanned all the albums from the ultrasound scans of the pregnancy through to the various holidays and birthday parties right up until I left. The scanning was slow and not only did I cry, but felt sick through the whole process and it took significant time. I think it was several weeks and simply scanned whenever I was free and not answering court documents.

I found a very solid photo display in a leather wallet that looked a bit like a woman's wallet (around 200mmx120mm or 8" x 3") and could load it up in directories that matched the holidays and many special moments. It became a Christmas present that year and dispatched via Australia

Post to be signed for. I also wrote a card that it could be copied and was also for Joe as many featured him including when he was playing with his cousins and acting like a Ninja Turtle.

I had complied with Jasmine's request which I suspect was actually Nellie's, but not the way they expected, but in a way we could all share the photos. I was never thanked for all the effort or providing all the photos and perhaps that is not what Nellie wanted.

I got a call from Jasmine that Christmas as she got the present and my guess is it put Nellie into tears and Nellie was allegedly out in the backyard when Jasmine rang. The call revolved around if I could help her mum. It was very hard, and the response was that I tried and wanted to help her mum, but she won't accept help from me and really needs professional help, but she will not accept it. At one stage I also agreed to help if Nellie entered therapy and would do so via Skype. The children deserve a healthy parent but that was never taken up. I suppose compared to other years, at least I got to talk to Jasmine but it was a confusing time for all of us and remains so. Whether it was a genuine appeal for help or just another attempt to have me do what Nellie wanted I do not know. Either way, it was bittersweet.

Inner peace and acceptance are elusive and only time would tell if that is to change.

15

Ongoing incidents—daughter's 21st and the parallel journey

had been living in a bayside home for a number of years and while I tried to get the kids to stay with me during their visit for the funeral or even just lunch, Jasmine would not agree. The same cannot be said for a friend's cat, Barnaby, that I looked after several times and seemed to like staying with me.

It was the second time Barnaby stayed with me and he had just had a skin cancer on the nose removed but was otherwise considered very healthy. I took him to the veterinarian to have stitches removed in the first week but he was well settled. He was a lovely cat, and always pushing the laptop aside to be on my lap, when he suddenly changed. He stopped eating, was more lethargic than the last few weeks and I eventually took him to the veterinarian who detected a tumour in his abdomen. The cat was put on steroids but passed away one week after the owners returned. The contrast between the reactions of Nellie over the death of Smokey and my friends over the death of Barnaby still staggers me and just another example of how differently people react and see things. I was made to feel it was my fault for Smokey but thanked for being observant and looking after Barnaby and this contrast was just one more incident, that gave me insight into Nellie. I wonder to this day if such manipulation of how Nellie made me feel when Smokey died were really part of a broader personality issue. In aggregate, the many incidents of Nellie's behaviour and her reaction brought so much into question.

In Australia, like many other countries, the twenty-first birthday for some reason marks the passing into adulthood and a big party is normal.

I looked back at Joe's twenty-first birthday party and wonder about the similarities with that of Jasmine's. Did she even have a party? When Joe turned twenty-one, his cousin Kyle was staying with us and using our home as a base while travelling around Europe. I suggested to Nellie that we should arrange a celebratory dinner for Joe and go to a restaurant as a family and of course, include Kyle and invite some of Joe's friends. The conversation went nowhere with Nellie and the celebration was reduced to take away Thai food. Celebrating a big date and marking Joe's milestone seemed almost irrelevant to Nellie and I could not make sense of it and succumbed to her wishes. I would normally bake a Black Forest cake on such special occasions and followed through with this household tradition. Even when Jasmine was little that seemed to be my job and remember the caterpillar cake (as she was at the caterpillar room at the crèche), while still in Australia for her birthday.

For the many years after I left the Netherlands, I would often purchase jewellery for Jasmine as birthday presents. As a child, like many little girls, Jasmine loved being a princess and as she grew up while still in an intact family, many of her photos featured a lovely smile and a necklace and continued to love jewellery. Even when I returned from Australia for my uncle's funeral, I gave her a jewellery box that I had purchased on the flight and was something that she treasured. We hadn't allowed her to get her ears pierced until she was sixteen and then she could have pierced earrings which was something she was looking forward to. After we separated, I sent her a collection of earrings, bracelets, necklaces, lockets with photos and more over the years. I recall one bangle engraved with "Love Always", which is how I sign my emails, letters and cards to her and jewellery is usually small which meant it was easily posted. I would spend hours in shops procrastinating on the right gift. For her twenty-first birthday, the jewellery selected was a large bracelet with her name in letters from the popular shop, Pandora.

It was in one of her last emails when we were communicating that Jasmine told me she doesn't wear jewellery. Years of presents, never used. Her change from loving jewellery, I believe was just another tactic Nellie used in what is parental alienation, where the child is taught to reject and despise anything from the targeted parent, which in this case is jewellery as well as me, both of which she once loved.

One day, perhaps all those presents will be treasured if not for what they are, but the thought and love that went into their existence. Gone was my little princess who had once loved being adorned in a plastic tiara and then in her early teens, necklaces from her grandmother and wanted her ears pierced.

With the communication back to me non-existent and not knowing how Jasmine was, I felt something had to be done through a complete change in tack on the communication strategy. No longer writing to Jasmine was considered after some of the emails were used by Nellie in court, meant that they were monitored but that was years earlier. I felt that I needed to continue to write to Jasmine, just as I had for years, even without a response, as I had to do something to show her I loved her. Many experts in the parental alienation field also publish documents on when the children are reunited, they reveal that they always like the effort, even if their response is abusive or do not respond, such is the power of parental alienation and so, I did continue and continue to this day.

A week before her twenty-first birthday, I decided that not a cent would be paid to Nellie on behalf of Jasmine as I had been led to believe that child support continued to twenty-five if Jasmine was a full-time student. Some documents were drafted ready for translation for the Dutch court asking that payment of child support be paid directly to my daughter and into the bank account that I had set up for Jasmine very shortly after Nellie had left us.

The advice was that the law did not require child support after twenty-one unless she had a serious disability and was unable to contribute to her upkeep. I knew she had been working part-time in a supermarket and then a movie cinema, so it was clear she did not have a serious disability and therefore I was not legally obligated to help support her.

I simply wrote to Jasmine and told her that if she needed support, then she should communicate with me, which was an activity that Nellie clearly discouraged from her actions and statements in court. I had already paid two weeks beyond her twenty-first, so there was time for her to respond without causing a break in my support.

It was the 4th of July when I received a polite email from Nellie that the monthly child support had not been received and if I could investigate it. The email was the most civil I had received since the split, around six years (2009-2015) earlier. I discussed a possible response and several people said I should not answer it as she has asked for a response, then to answer only meant she was still controlling me. My perspective was by not answering, I would be contributing to escalating confrontation and not resolving the matter through adult communication. I responded around four days later with words to the effect, "That is correct and child support will only be paid directly to Jasmine from now on. She is twenty-one and I have already written to her to contact me if support is required."

Nothing happened for around two weeks and I have always suspected that Nellie had contacted lawyers as Nellie had clearly stated, and had me believe, that there was a requirement to support Jasmine until she was twenty-five if she was a student living at home. I suspect Nellie believed what she told me about the child support was correct however all the lies that were exposed in the court cases, showing I had been deceived since the day I met Nellie, means I remain suspicious and may never know. As expected, the money did create a resumption of communications between Jasmine and myself and I suspect this was prompted by Nellie.

The email from Jasmine was rather abrupt and to the point that "I am still in school and need support." This was the second communication from Jasmine since my mother's funeral. The first was a request for the death certificate and while I panicked at the time as to why she would want that, I eventually figured it was probably just to get her absence from university accepted.

The condition of communication, if she wanted me to support her as a parent seemed to be working and some communication proceeded with me asking questions like:

- Whether she had received her twenty-first present?

- What was your course and how was it going?

- How was she going?

- Could I see her marks?

- How much did her course cost?

I tried to keep it light and loving and on her.

In terms of the response, she allegedly went to the post office upon notification of the attempted delivery of her twenty-first present, and possibly followed up when I again sent the details of the international tracking system and its location. Whether she followed through or not I do not know, however the parcel was eventually returned as not received.

The communication continued, however, perhaps I was not a good communicator. I continued paying Jasmine the equivalent of child support directly into her bank account and made it clear that I was under no legal obligation to do so. I wondered if Nellie would force Jasmine to hand over some of the money under whatever guise, but if that happened, at least Jasmine would know I continued to fund her like I always intended (and maybe Jasmine would get upset with Nellie for taking money). It must have been very difficult for Jasmine and I often joke with people that I must be really messing with her head. Here is an alienated child who has been taught to despise me for what I have done to her mother (which was essentially stand up and remove myself from danger), who is paying her each month when I did not have to. What was Jasmine thinking? Perhaps, *"What is going on?"*, or, *"Is what I have been told for the last six years correct?"* Maybe as she matures, she will question what was going on.

Many parents would consider that such an email, that Jasmine does not wear jewellery after many years of sending her jewellery and her general attitude shown in the emails should not be tolerated, however those parents are not able to put their feet in the shoes of an alienated child. Since I left the Netherlands, and particu-larly in recent years, I have met many parents that are not seeing their dearly loved children due to a spouse for who vengeance, hatred, insecurity and an unhealthy need for control, a possible mental health condition such as a Narcissistic Personality or Borderline Personality Disorder (BPD) or often a combination of some or all of the above have impacted on the children. Which of the many causes that has driven Nellie to perpetrate parental alienation has never been properly answered.

The impact on the children of this form of child abuse can be significant, with the inability to form meaningful relations in the future, simply because they have been taught to reject and to not reciprocate the love of a parent. It is not the children's fault as they never asked to be put in the position they are in. The conditions that lead to parental alienation are often ignored, simplified or hijacked by groups as a gendered issue and results in the alignment with either feminist organisations or men's rights groups that remove the focus away from the suffering children. I have met many good people and professionals that are able to describe in detail the accusations against the alienated parent which prove the accusations are impossible, at times even proven in court and yet the alienation continues unabated. I still have hope that we can breach the gender divide to address the root cause of this evil.

In my correspondence to Jasmine I have tried to follow what I have been told by a psychologist, who is also a personal friend, that there are three things that a parent of divorce should do:

1. Never let the child feel that the separation was their fault. (You should also never say anything bad

against another parent as this places the children into the centre of the conflict).

2. Never give up on the child and make them feel that they are not worth a parent's love (despite all of what you are going through and some of us experience more violence, abuse and witness child abuse such as parental alienation more than others).

3. Always be available.

The children may be adults when they come to realise they have been deceived through their childhood and well into their adult years. I have a close friend that his children realised years after being abducted that reached out, only to find out that he was a grandfather when they made contact. Sometimes a parent may die before they are reunited with their child and this can be incredibly destructive for that child as they were never able to reconcile with the targeted parent and can be left with enormous guilt that overpowers them. These are just some of the problems that can transpire for the children that suffer as victims of parental alienation.

I have tried to follow this, however like any parent, I am not perfect.

I was brought up with respect for others, to accept that we are all different and that became part of my personality. I was not raised by my parents to deal with difficult personalities, mental health or even consider what healthy boundaries were in relationships and that had not changed before I met Nellie. Weeks after the separation, I wanted to formally sort matters out, Nellie asked if she could move back into the house and we could go back to how it was. My response was "No." I was not prepared to continue like it had been as Nellie's indifference to anyone's needs but her own became clear and I needed to set a healthy boundary or knew that it would lead to my demise. Perhaps that attacked Nellie's sense of control in that she thought she could always move back and realised she could not. Perhaps saying, she could not move back in and revert to how it was, directly challenged her sense of self-value. While it was acceptable for Nellie to reject me, the reverse may have been seen as an attack on her, as she quickly moved to destroy the person that challenged her very identity, and found people who would stoop to the lowest of levels to aid her in her quest.

I only have snippets of information what Nellie has done to Jasmine since my departure and that is heart-breaking for a parent.

Jasmine did go onto study Arts (mainly Animation) for one year, before changing her direction and moved to a Dutch course *notaris* which is essentially Law. Jasmine pulled out of Law Studies after one year and in one, of her "one or two sentence emails," said she did not like law and she was studying Literature and was considering doing an Honours year.

I recently found that Jasmine was travelling. I wonder if she is staying in the safer areas? Or going into high-risk areas where life is not so highly valued?

I hope we can compare our journeys as I suspect that we have so much in common. When she does question or realise what has occurred, will she seek me out? The healing for both of us will be able to be completed if she can find it in her heart to seek me out. Hopefully, we will both have a good life and while I will never have that little girl with me, a father-daughter relationship will flourish again, even if it remains geographically challenging.

Good parents only want the best for their children and to be happy, safe and healthy. As parents, we don't always get what we want and hopefully, this experience into parental alienation is a bump in the road. Jasmine will achieve what every good parent wants and I will find out and then have peace of mind.

16

Trauma now presents as cPTSD

I still find it amazing what will trigger a dream or a thought and how quickly the emotions can return. The constant thoughts are in the back of my mind, even when having an unrelated conversation which leads to careful management of my emotions, that most people may never understand. From the initial trauma of the separation, the assault and the canal episode, I recognise the immediate and ongoing trauma that was in my past. My trauma became elongated and drawn out through the years of court cases and presented itself when I collapsed on the supermarket floor trying to shop for my very ill mother and continues due to the long uphill battle of parental alienation. As close friends point out, my avoiding many situations and a level of social agoraphobia, always on guard are just some of the signs of cPTSD.

It was April 2016 and I recall vividly having had a dream the previous night and was probably caused by some stressors. I dreamt that I heard some kittens and went to the back door and found some baby kittens (one was nearly dead). I picked up the poor little one and my daughter appeared to help. The mother cat then stuck her nose and was looking through the fence. I woke up and quickly realised it was just a dream. I questioned what the poor little dead kitten represented, and I wondered why a cat wouldn't have been able to jump over a timber fence?

It had been seven years since I have spent any sensible time with my daughter, whereas in the past, I would have always been taking her swimming, the movies, shopping, be it for a game, something for school, clothes or the hairdresser. I am not sure whether there had been a squeak in the house that night to spark that particular dream but, either way, it stayed with me—I wondered if Jasmine or I or in fact Nellie was the nearly dead kitten.

Jasmine and I had enjoyed having kittens in our house. We had 2 cats that had a litter of kittens each, and we like to believe they all went to good homes. There was also the incident where after we gave away the 8-week-old kittens and one week later the children down the street, found a plastic bag full of kittens dumped by the canal, the same canal where the infamous canal incident occurred and while bringing them home, two escaped next to our house.

Our cat heard the two kittens and tried to get to them thinking they could be hers and escaped through the front door toward the busy road. Our daughter was hysterical as her cat was in danger and I regrettably yelled at her to "slow down," so I could understand what she was saying. Quickly we then both raced outside, down the quiet street toward the busy road only to find the two kittens scared and behind a garbage bin, her cat, had realised they were not her offspring and rejected them and was walking away from them, so we brought the kittens home.

While it was dark, our daughter went to tell her friend, around six doors down and found out the full story of how they had found the plastic bag of kittens, that two had gotten away outside our home and so we reunited the two we found with their siblings, all of which were to be taken to the animal shelter. We could not look after them as were heading to Australia for a vacation in the coming week. It was probably an amalgam of thoughts:

- when Jasmine's first cat gave birth initially abandoning the first kitten leaving it squeaking outside the bedroom door,
- another which which was stillborn;
- the kittens abandoned by the canal;
- the cat that got lost and I found at 3:00 a.m. searching the neighbourhood; and
- yet another cat that somehow got all the kittens over the fence and all those events that were mixed up, just like my head.

Many of those that have been through terrible separations will suffer similar symptoms. For those returning from a war zone, it is commonly known as "Post Traumatic Stress Disorder" (PTSD) and is similar to those that have had a gun pointed at them or bullet pass them in an armed robbery.

One form of PTSD is defined as cPTSD or Complex Post-Traumatic Stress Disorder, "is a psychological disorder that can develop in response to prolonged, repeated experience of interpersonal trauma in a context in which the individual has little or no chance of escape". The definition varies from the different sources but all are aligned with the prolonged nature of trauma such as stated on Wikipedia that seems to collate what you will find on the many government and psychology association websites such as Healthline[9]. If this sounds like a high conflict separation, followed by countless hours of preparation for court cases and appearing at those court cases, after the years of abuse that you have read in this book, then you may be right.

I re-live the experience repeatedly, sometimes at a popular local sporting club bar with my back to the wall, my breathing intense, feeling like I could be in danger from the person Nellie flew down from inter-state, the one trying to recruit mercenaries. At times, I manage to regain full control, while I recall one occasion when I had to leave, covered in sweat and breathing in a panic-stricken manner. For some years, I would always position myself so that people were not behind me, even at the gym I would be at the back corner, but those needs have largely subsided. In all that time, no-one noticed as I was able to conceal what was going on.

I saw Nellie's uncontrolled rage that resulted in me leaving the Netherlands. This was not a single event as it was repeated in the phone calls, in mediation, the court foyer and then the uncontrolled rage that escalated to the cold and calculated actions with a false police report made in the Netherlands, the funding of the "crazies" with veiled death threats, harassment of the property purchaser along with myself, and the extension of the court conflict which ran for many years.

---

[9] https://www.healthline.com/health/cptsd

Having run groups, I see firsthand the stories of child abduction and the pattern of this type of abuse on a spouse. When the displaced spouse's ability to protect the children is removed, the abuse often continues unabated on the children as was the case for my friend Lawry. One of his children contacted him twenty-four years after they were abducted to discover the now adult boy, was about to die from the abuse, and another was never sent to school and could not read. That was just one case.

Nellie's uncontrolled temper was such that I truly believe, would have resulted in one of us being hurt or dead and the other in jail should I have stayed. The subsequent abuse on Jasmine through parental alienation, what Nellie stated in court that she had been telling Jasmine continues to play on my mind and weighs heavily upon me to this day.

Especially after a period of lack of sleep, the mind plays tricks that become more difficult to control, and I may need to withdraw, but am quite adept at this. Ultimately, there is little escape, except by enjoying life that will hopefully create new neural pathways and positive memories.

One day, I was in the car heading towards an organised snorkel at a beach that the snorkelling group attends maybe once a year. Across the radio came the report that one man had died in an apartment fire in Smith Street Elsternwick. My blood ran cold as that was the Street where Nellie's property was. At this point in time, no one knew what my former spouse was capable of and I confess I panicked. Had she caused a fire that killed someone just to set me up or some other reason? Were the police looking for me?

I calmed down enough to decide that regardless of what has happened there is little that I could do, and I would go snorkelling. If they find me after the swim and want to talk to me or arrest me then so be it. There is nothing I can do in the interim. It was a good snorkel and saw an Eagle Ray along with a lot of fish.

As I came out of the water, no one was there. I later found out that it was an apartment fire in Smyth St, Elwood. I had misheard the name of the Street and suburb because I was always living in a heightened state of stress. Good thing I was calm enough to not panic and told virtually no-one of the incident before now. Such is the illogical nature of cPTSD at times.

I have found that in most cases, recognising the triggers and understanding them, or bringing them from the subconscious to the conscious, so that they can be managed to me is the key. When I do not know what is upsetting me, then that is a real problem. At one stage I was working at an airport and constantly seeing families depart for holidays and I was starting to get depressed. It was not until I realised that I was relating those departures to our family departure to the Netherlands subconsciously, that I could deal with it. Once in the conscious, the thoughts were brought under control and the depression stopped.

The careful management of one's stressors (which may be work or unemployment), or simply recognising the wisdom of the "Serenity Prayer – Grant to us the serenity of mind to accept that which cannot be changed; the courage to change that which can be changed; and the wisdom to know the one from the other;" and dismissing the things that we cannot control is the source of a positive path forward. Looking after ones' health both physically and mentally, doing things one enjoys whether that be a swim at the beach or helping another person, are all important. Those activities provide me with that balance in life and something that keeps me going.

Some of the most common symptoms of PTSD[10] and how I manage or have overcome them include:

Intense feelings of distress when reminded of a tragic event	This is managed, although every day the absence of Jasmine and the thoughts of losing her, has me thinking of her constantly and wondering if she is well and how she is coping.
Extreme physical reactions to reminders of trauma such as nausea	These are far less common nowadays. Occasionally, the stomach is tied up in knots which can still occur. One occasion was when, in a mini-bus to a conference on a similar subject and I simply cancelled the event. Chest pains are now rare.
Invasive, upsetting memories of a tragedy	These are not a distant memory. They stay with me but are controlled.

[10] https://theoakstreatment.com/ptsd/signs-and-symptoms/

Flashback (feeling like the trauma is happening again)	The separation from Nellie was easy. The possibility that the criminal actions of the "crazies" could start again weigh heavily as does the knowledge that there is no support through the state authorities should they resume.
Nightmares of either frightening things or of the event	When writing parts of this book they were nightly but for the final edit, only occasionally. They are controlled.
Loss of interest in life and daily activities	I do have trouble with things like job applications and find myself heavily involved in suicide prevention and system reforms. I have found several things that I enjoy such as snorkelling, teaching blind children to swim, gym and therefore have established a level of acceptance and a sense of normality. I am coping.
Feeling emotionally numb and detached from other people	I think of myself as a caring person, however I have removed myself from many people as they cannot relate and if they do, then sometimes it compounds my feelings. I do have trouble trusting others nowadays.

Sense of not leading a normal life (and not having a positive outlook for the future)	I could never describe my life as normal and the hope for a positive future varies.
Avoiding certain activities, feelings, thoughts or places that remind you of the tragedy	While at times I pull back from some activities, it is normally when tired and the mind becomes more difficult to control. During the editing phase of writing this book, I had to leave a music venue with anxiety related chest pains, however symptoms are now minimal and rare.
Difficult remembering important aspects of a tragic event	It was amazing when writing this book putting things in a chronological order and some of the details. Looking through correspondence, I realised that I had been repressing many memories that came flooding back. Hopefully, they will again be repressed and I keep remembering the good ones.

A conversation with a clinical psychologist I occasionally visit for treatment stated that in terms of cPTSD, "the diagnosis is precisely accurate and completely irrelevant" and continued to work with me in terms of the issues that arose while writing this book. I concluded that it is how you manage the reaction that matters and I am overcoming them all.

I will never go back into a toxic relationship where there is an emphasis on controlling me, to be what someone else wants, where I cannot be me. I know that a course of action where I cannot be me is a path to self-destruction. I also apologise to those that I cannot give the attention that they deserve, as there is only so much one can give.

PART 3:

Lessons learned,
the future and hope

17

The town hall speech 2015

In 2015, I was invited to speak at a town hall on behalf of Fathers Support which was attended by around 300 people. I recall sitting up late one night preparing my speech. I wanted to talk about the many examples of parents in distress right now, parents after separation, parental alienation along with the current landscape of the organisations and the court systems themselves which actively encourage this type of behaviour in parents.

When it came to the night, all the speakers ran over time, they also had so much to say on the dysfunctional family separation industry, so it was very late when it was my turn to speak. I moved to the front and nervously stood in front of the lectern. I began:

There are many people in the audience tonight that I hold in awe. For a few of you I have some insight into your story and what you have been through; are going through; or are about to go through.

Tonight, I would like to talk about our distressed parents as it relates to the landscape of organisations, and I will describe some of my heroes.

Many of you know that Fathers Support was informed on two days before Christmas in 2014 that it would no longer be funded. There was one lady who may be in the audience that worked for a Church based Counselling service who said to me, "I hope you do get your funding reinstated as there will be nowhere to send good men that are simply in trauma from the shock of separation. We received a lot of support from organisations and individuals that refer people to us and all letters were published on our website. Thanks to that support from those that refer people to us, from politicians of all parties, the error was substantially corrected with around 80% of our funding reinstated (our consultancy which provided surveys of clients perspective was not renewed). We will be running at a significant loss this year and will struggle to continue without support, so there is a donation tin near the exit. We run with four full-time equivalent staff and around 100 volunteers that range from business executives, psychologists, and those that run the 17 groups across the country on a weekly basis.

1. *The first hero is a man that came to Fathers Support one Wednesday. He told the story of the complaint against him for violence and could not believe how his former spouse could accuse him of such horrible things and prevent him from seeing his kids. This had challenged his belief system which is a person's essence, of telling the truth and what is "just" and right to such an extent he had*

attempted suicide four days earlier on the Sunday. He heard the stories in the Fathers Support Group and realised he was not alone. He realised it is not unusual but common to lay false complaints to the police (who will—by procedure—generally evict the man from his house to separate the two warring parents). He was asked one question, "Okay, your former wife has accused you of a horrible thing and turned on you, what will you do if she turns on your kids?" The answer was he would be there for them. The perceptions and actions that resulted from that conversation was such that he became incredibly strong, Not for himself but for his kids. This was verified by a psychologist that I asked to check on him the next day who advised I don't know what you did, but he is fine.

2. *A man that came to Fathers Support a bit shell shocked as his former spouse had asked him to leave—so he complied. She wanted to keep the kids and he was giving money for the rent, so his children had a roof over their head. Unfortunately, all the money was destined to the drug peddler. When eventually the first child came back to him (effectively thrown out and in trauma as she could not stay and look after her little brothers any longer – and we are talking about a child that was not even a teenager) within weeks the mother was evicted, and he had custody of all the kids. He was given the choice by his employer—work or the kids—so he went to Centrelink. They looked over the counter and said we have a document here saying*

the mother has the kids. "We don't think they are yours." The Fathers' Support coordinator made a call and the matter was quickly reviewed with some gender discrimination training given to the person that made the accusation. He was incredibly nervous going through the court system, but the court ensured common sense prevailed (especially when she told the judge that she was on drugs and that is why she refused to take drug screening, but that is irrelevant to any consideration as she is the mother and therefore should have the kids). He still has the kids and the mother visits occasionally but quickly dismisses them, does not act like the stereotypical mother we as a society picture in our minds. Discrimination is against the law and the law reflects that however in many organisations the culture and practices require improvement.

3. *We had one client that had raised his kids for over eight years when he discovered his daughter had been interfered with during a visitation to their mother. The threat was immediate and left on an answering machine that if he goes to the police, she would take the kids. As such the next two years of trauma was set. Suddenly he had an accusation made against him and DHS took the children. We must remember that when a complaint is made, DHS should act (and in this case did). Unfortunately, they put the kids with the person that made the complaint, where she had allegedly been interfered with, by the mother's boyfriend's child. The heroes in this story included not only the father that had*

the courage to lodge the complaint with the police but also a barrister that agreed to take on the case "regardless of how many times he had to go to court" for a fixed fee of $8,000. The barrister was so incensed by what he had seen and the evidence before him (even if some of that evidence could not be tendered in the family or children's court). It took years, but the children came back to the father that had raised them as the primary custodian after all the fuss. We often find that a case based upon lies that takes years to resolve, that it is during those years that the substantial damage is done.

4. *Another is a parent whose former spouse wanted to separate. An agreement was made for the parent to see the kids whenever he wanted to—which sounded fine until she disappeared. Tracked her down to Tasmania and a legal agreement was then reached as to the conditions upon which he could see the children again whenever desired with notice. They then disappeared again and 24 years later, received a call from one of the children. Upon reunification it was like a time warp and that the 24 years disappeared, and relationships renewed. Finding out that his biological children had lived under four different aliases and had not been sent to school, and one was unable to read. The boy that he knew from the age of 3 had been abandoned several times as an example to his children and had turned to self-harm and other practices so is not expected to live much longer. The alienator is now threatening suicide if the kids*

do not take the alienators side – more commonly known as emotional blackmail. If only the estranged parent (nowadays a social worker) had known, the outcome may have been very different particularly for the boy who was denied the opportunities that we as a society should ensure are available.

Fathers Support (and our lesser known counterparts, Mothers Support) are exposed to Heroes such as these on a daily basis with 100 people every week attending one of our 17 peer support groups across Australia each week—in addition, 5,000 people a year call our Helpline.

I ask you all here tonight if we deserve a system that produces some hero's, but with far more victims being the generation of children and the fundamentally good spouses that simply cannot cope or are estranged from their children through a series of lies and accusations.

I would like to quote Rosie Batty at this stage about why a woman will often stay in a house with an abusive spouse, "Why would you want to leave your home, your family, the dreams that you've built? Nobody wants to leave something [like that]."

While everyone here I am sure finds violence offensive, we need to address the violence perpetrated by people and also that by the systems our government manages. A simple unproven accusation of fear will result in police turning up at a man's work or home and having him pack a bag under supervision and never be allowed back to the home he has helped make—or even able to phone the children until the legal system resolves the issue. If he or she (and we have had a female client accused of sexual molestation) are then proven innocent, and have had the strength, patience and funds to get through the legal system, he or she, is then often faced with the argument that the children have a new life and it would not be in their best interest to disturb their lifestyle. In effect, the system encourages false allegations and delays—and often rewards the perpetrators due to them being financially incentivised along the way.

Anecdotally, we are seeing an increase of fathers making false accusations and I am disappointed with that trend as well. The police in their first encounter have effectively and unwittingly set in place a chain of events (due to the slow nature of the legal system) and can become judge and executioner. We deal with cases like this every day.

Why is this happening we need to ask in the high conflict cases?

1. *We see **greed for money** to procure drugs or other self-indulgence which is greater than the love and responsibility their children deserve.*

2. *We often see a **clinically obsessive need for control, delusional beliefs and other mental health issues**.*

3. *We see a **level of vengeance** that a partner has not lived up to the childhood dreams and expectation and are reduce to hatred. I hate you because you did not make my life ideal and will punish you by any means and as one judge stated, "will do or say anything".*

There are often other factors in play but forgetting that, let's look at why things go so horribly wrong and the incentives that cause the delays and conflict:

1. **The less time one parent spends with the children, the greater the child support** *the other receives. Time with the children is a major cause of conflict. As with an earlier example, we often see this play out with one spouse trying to alienate or deny access the other for financial gain and not necessarily for the love of the children. The Child Support Agency (CSA) assessment process is not aligned with the court processes—and the genuine desire of a good parent who makes themselves available.*

2. **A woman wants to leave her spouse and needs some help**. *She looks for help only to be faced with service providers that prioritise domestic violence so immediately people are going to (and referred to) police to fuel the claims of domestic violence. More than a year ago I was speaking to the CEO of one of the many organisations that provide emergency housing to be told that "we never admit to helping men or the feminist lobby would shut us down". We hear these stories regularly and let's face facts. The woman facing genuine domestic violence should get priority – but that sets up a motivation to get to the front of the queue. Should we give "unlimited resources to such agencies" and should agencies that discriminate based upon gender continue to receive funding are political questions to ponder.*

3. ***Incentives exist for the legal profession to keep a battle going***. *We have clients that the accusation of sexual abuse against them was known to be false by their accuser several months before the case appeared before a judge. When questioned and asked why he had not revised his statement to court to avoid or minimise the court case he replied his lawyer had told him not to change his statement against the mother. The mother got sole parental responsibility. There were no cost awards or actions taken against the person that kept up the perjury, or the lawyer (who is seen as an extension of their client).*

4. ***Financial resources are often used to force the other party to withdraw***. *While one can self-represent and in rare cases, pro-bono lawyers and barristers become engaged. The aim is to intimidate and deprive the spouse of all income so that they feel they cannot continue as a part of their children's lives as they do not have the resources to get into their own place with bedrooms for the kids.*

All these are fundamentally wrong on many levels, yet, encouraged by an adversarial system which pits one parent against the other and away from the focus which should be on the children.

Four years on, in 2019, and I find it depressing to think nothing has changed since the time of this speech. The only change is the migration of cases from the Family Court to the Domestic Violence Court and wear down the partners that way. It still feels completely disgusting.

According to the "Perfect Storm" definition of:

- no wife,
- cannot see your children,
- you are removed from your home so have nowhere to live,
- you are accused of domestic violence so your friends become wary of you,
- you get back to work and are dismissed particularly if you hold a job that requires you to bear arms such as the police, Armed Services or Security,
- even if allowed to work, are mentally overload and cannot focus at work and poorly viewed or dismissed,
- with no money to fight the court battle ahead,
- with no apparent hope, and
- you're unable to see the alternatives, why not suicide?

But we must remind ourselves that if nothing changes, then nothing changes. There are people fighting hard in this space for a fairer and decent system. There are children out there wanting to be reunited with their other, removed parent. There are also good examples of people parting harmoniously out there, more than we think because we hear about the terrible ones as that is all that is reported. Could there be a way for the media to portray the good examples also? A way to focus more on hope, rather than despair? I would like to think so. The hope of reuniting with your child is the most powerful motivation there is, to keep putting that one foot in front of the other, each day, every day. Can we in turn, then ask the question as a society, "What do we want?" as opposed to "What we get!" out of the family law industry and especially from the child's perspective.

18

The impact on children of parental alienation

The primary reason for my personal, ongoing trauma is knowing the impact parental alienation has on children. There are many leading experts around the world working on this issue and new practice standards are being developed. Countries and states are now recognising the issues and legislation is being introduced to make the conscious practice of parental alienation illegal.

While the situation has been described for decades, I was warned to not use the term and just describe what happened in the Dutch Children's court. As such the statement was something like, "I was talking to my daughter, my former spouse found out, and the conversations stopped and we do not know what is going on." But we knew exactly what was going on. The same occurs here in Australia, and rarely spoken of in the courts by name.

The fact is, the impact on kids is horrendous. One father came to Fathers Support after he went to pick up his son on a court-ordered access visit and left with the mother screaming abuse, telling him he couldn't see his son, who witnessed the spectacle. The house went quiet and hours later the mother curiously looked around and found the boy had died by suicide. I have also personally dealt with estranged fathers, that had daughters attempt suicide, one of which when he went to the hospital, was abused in the hospital by the vindictive mother and was forced away by the restraining order. I have also dealt with estranged mothers in similar circumstances.

The psychological damage is huge and often the child is forced to enter into a psychological splitting defence and will quote from one of Karen Woodall's blogs, from 21 Aug 2018 titled "Breaking Down the Walls of Heartache: Treating the Split State of Mind in Children and Young People Affected by Parental Alienation."[11]

"The split state of mind is a defence mechanism which is unconsciously deployed by the child who is in an intolerable position." …. "The point at which the child deploys the defence of psychological splitting – dividing their feelings into wholly good for one parent and wholly bad for the other is called at the Family Separation Clinic—the 'Tipping Point.' … "It is however, the state of psychological splitting which is of greatest concern in our work because it is that which leaves a lasting legacy, it is that which is so abusive to the child." … "Splitting is an infantile defence mechanism which is described by Object Relations Theory as being the separation of 'objects' in the

---

[11] https://karenwoodall.blog/2018/08/21/breaking-down-the-walls-of-heart-ache-treating-the-split-state-of-mind-in-children-and-young-people-affect-ed-by-parental-alienation/

psychological self into good and bad parts. The good parts remain conscious and the bad parts are pushed into the unconscious and as such are split off from the conscious awareness." Jasmine (my daughter) is past the tipping point (some would say over the cliff) and regardless of what I have done, by this construct, I am "all bad" to her which is exactly how she behaves.

When the child is forced to reject a loving parent that, like all good parents that have been regarded by the child as their protector and fundamental to their needs then the psychological impact can be devastating, when they are forced to reject and will refer to the EMMM.org.au website on the impacts:

- Disrupted social-emotional development.

- Insecure attachment style.

- Interpersonal problems.

- Paranoid thinking.

- Obsessive-compulsive tendencies.

- Low self-esteem.

- Resentment.

- Grief.

- Anger.

- Depression.

- Anxiety.

- Somatic symptoms.

- Substance-related problems.

- Suicide.

And as such lead to:

- Family violence and abuse.

- Trauma-related disorders.

- Persistent complex bereavement.

Is this the legacy of Nellie's vengeance? Yes, I have contributed by removing myself from imminent danger and even in hindsight, I firmly believe I would be dead if I had not. I knew practically nothing about mental health when Nellie walked out that night. The uncontrollable anger and the statement "don't care about Jasmine and her future" that ran through my mind at the canal that day, leading me to think the best solution for my daughter and the only one that I could think of at the time was to leave, believing the conflict would dissipate if I was not there.

I am not the only one that has walked away, hoping that by not continuing the fight, the children will get some love and peace and someday soon return. For one friend, the court battle would have gone on for years and his kids were like my Jasmine, alienated, and the courts unlikely to order them to do change residence. He negotiated hard and called the Independent Children's Lawyer, and his wife lawyer's bluff and managed to get himself unrestricted access to the school's parent-teacher nights, school reports, protocols for delivering birthday presents and a few other things that were initially refused. The children will know he cares enough to monitor them and may even receive those presents. Compared with his children being openly abused through years of litigation, presents being returned and many other alienating tactics they were suffering, hopefully they will see the signs of love. The loss of access to his children and inability to directly show his love to his children, is the very heavy cross that he bears.

For too many of us, the question is how long until the children realise and make contact if ever? How long will it be, until governments and child services realise the impact of what they are doing by failing to act? Only time will tell.

19

Parental alienation, mental health and personal revelation

I was recently asked, "Do you believe all Parental Alienators have an underlying mental health issue?" My answer was, "No, not all have mental health issues, but some do. There is a spectrum of behaviours, some of which are mental health related, that make up parental alienation." In my own situation, the analysis has been a revelation.

I find that it is important to separate the impact on the child which is also categorised into levels from that of the parent. In terms of the parent, there can be the subliminal messages where the alienators don't even know they are perpetrating parental alienation through to personality disorders, mental health issues, inter-parent hatred and there are three main types in my view:

- The alienating parent who doesn't know they are doing it. The parent that unknowingly sends signals that I don't like him/her and the child acts on these signals to please the alienating parent. For example, the child says, "I'm going to see the other parent this weekend," the alienating parent says, "Oh alright? Are you sure you want to do that?" The alienating parent showing the slightest sign of displeasure when the child wants to please that parent, particularly the custodial parent where the child lives with most of the time, can result in that child becoming alienated.

- The ones who are overtly doing it. They know they want the other parent out of their child's life as doing so removes the parent from their life. They may hate the other parent as they thought they had managed to get the perfect husband or wife, who has not lived up to expectations. There may be unresolved mental health pathology and may have frequent episodes of hysteria, regularly ignore visitation orders and little compassion for the targeted parent and child.

- Very overt most often have a personality disorder. They have limited or no empathy or compassion for the targeted parent or the child, constantly program the child, will repeatedly manipulate the state institutions and the court.

While some researchers and commentators may classify as mild, moderate and severe, there may also describe more or different groupings or subgroups. Without exception the researchers and commentators I have read, state that they all create damage and trauma.

In my personal case I have to look at what happened:

- Nellie once told me that she was on antidepressants as a teenager which would have therefore been in the 1970s.

- Nellie's upbringing where it appeared the men were cast out of the family to start again and the woman retaining nearly everything, may have been her benchmark of what should occur, but was not mine.

- Nellie's family background where one brother left without the parents even knowing if he was alive and appearing to hate or had very little to do with other siblings.

- There was deception throughout the relationship.

- The emotional manipulation was present at many levels shown from the contrast in reaction over the death of cats, the revelation that she did not like me taking the kids out on Sunday so she could study, the move to the Netherlands.

- Nellie made threats that she would lie to the police that could have seen me jailed, in a country where I could not speak the language.

- I did find a police report that she made around a month after separation that she was concerned that I held passports. The same report showed she requested it be amended nearly a year later, to change the dates of events to suit a new court case (her changes were noted as an addendum to the unchanged original report). Police reports meant nothing to her and just another tool to force her will.

- I made several offers via mediators and lawyers, but Nellie rejected them all and the court awarded me costs. A requirement to succeed in costs was that I made an offer that was reasonable and less than would be achieved if went to a full hearing, with the rights to claim costs being granted in all Australian cases. Nellie was incapable of being reasonable within normal standards.

- Nellie didn't want to agree to anything, she just wanted to punish me, she had no regard for the children when she told them, "There will be no inheritance as every cent will be spent on destroying Trevor."

- Nellie's statements in the children's court on what she had told Jasmine, showed highly destructive alienation was being perpetrated.

- That Nellie fought against our daughter getting any therapeutic support in court.

- There was parent/child role reversal between the children and Nellie. Nellie admitted the kids had told her to settle and there was another incident at the front door early in the separation. Jasmine witnessed her mother starting to get hysterical, and told her to, "Not do that or I will leave and you will never see me again," and Nellie stopped. I have read too many articles outlining that when the parent/child roles are reversed how unhealthy it can be.

- Nellie's recruitment of "the cast crazies" and the antics that followed.

- Nellie's use of her friend in the attempt to coercively control the real estate agent, not to sell the property or would lose the management of rental properties when they were following court orders made with Nellie's consent.

- Nellie's attempt to have a former judge who had quit, due to plagiarism accusations (the article in national newspapers was quite scathing) to do the mediation.

- The revelations in the psychiatric notes that were subpoenaed.

All these and many more incidents together showed that nothing was beneath Nellie. She would stop at nothing to bring about revenge and perhaps showed a significant underlying clinical pathology.

At one stage I was assisted in preparing for a job interview by a psychologist who listened to what was stressing me and wrote down on a piece of paper "BPD" and stated that is what your wife has, but I just dismissed it. Then I was discussing my situation with another clinical psychologist that stated the incident of "I should have put a bullet through you" in the court foyer in front of witnesses showed such an "extreme lack of judgement and personal control it most likely had an underlying pathology," possibly borderline personality disorder (BPD) that I took notice. When facilitating men's groups, one psychologist often sits in, and would watch me facilitate and would regularly deal with people in desperate need during breaks, so he was following my court cases and drama and I asked him what he thought? He bluntly stated, "If it looks like a duck, quacks like a duck, and walks like a duck, there is a good chance it is a duck. Your ex has borderline personality disorder." None of the professionals had ever diagnosed Nellie directly but the consistency concerns me to this day.

Since the separation, I have frequently questioned Nellie's mental state, her behaviours and hatred, her stubbornness, unreasonable constant arguing with the courts and the heavy debt she possibly acquired as a consequence from all of this. The truth is I will never know if she has borderline personality disorder or a narcissistic personality disorder as she would not see a psychologist after she left Australia. While in Australia she did tell me that she was seeing a therapist but would not allow me to attend to assist her therapy sessions and I suspect it would have impacted the diagnosis. Unfortunately, when she refused to let me see her therapist (that was a psychiatrist) that she was seeing when Jasmine was a baby in Australia, we lost the opportunity to assist me, in managing my reaction to her behaviours and thereby helping her.

Nellie was exceptionally calculated and planned separating at least 2 years prior to the breakup and although that is quite common, the secretly taking money from accounts and purchasing a new property is not. She was about revenge, not about fairness. French theologian, John Calvin summed it up best when he said, "The torture of a bad conscience is the hell of a living soul." Only I think when it comes to those perpetrating parental alienation, it is the displaced parent that suffers "the hell of a living soul" as the perpetrator often has no conscience.

Recently, I posted my thoughts on a social media private group relating to parental alienation. I feel somewhat that I may have lost my heart to pragmatism! Here is what I said:

"How many psychologists does it take to change a light bulb?"

"One; but only if the light bulb has to want to change!"

When dealing with others, either directly or in a group environment, both men and women, listening to their situation, I am often told that their former spouse has a clinically diagnosed mental health condition and at times had drug and alcohol problems. The use of the children to control them or prevent them protecting children with false police reports are exceptionally common and the prolonged battle they have caused by false allegations and orchestrated delays, has devastating consequences.

I have seen people change with the tough love of the courts (for alcohol), to which I credit the courts for giving them the incentive to change. I have personally seen one-person, that I suspect was Nellie, trawl through chat rooms asking about, "Penalties for perjury," (realising it was never prosecuted and was free to say whatever she wanted) with impunity for their actions. Other questions posted later "how to change a statement to the court," needless to say generated some interesting responses.

They know what they are doing and can be calculating in their controlled rage as vengeance pushes them forward and also experienced the "less-controlled" fits of rage as they threaten to kill in public spaces or manipulate others, (sometimes with payment), to do their bidding regardless of the consequence to them and those they once loved.

The law is a means of setting boundaries and acknowledging damage. When applied, then hopefully those perpetrators will request help to change and the judiciary can use their discretion when sentencing. When the law becomes an option, never enforced then problems will ensue.

The saying "Repeat a lie often enough and it becomes the truth", means that many perpetrators convince themselves over time of their new reality that they have made up. By the time they are on the stand in the Family Court, they are telling their truth and therefore would not be guilty of perjury. The lies however, in many cases, are told to the children and believed. When people believe what they are saying, they become convincing and are able to enlist support. In one case, the mother recruited a social worker and the questioning method by the social worker to the child meant that false memories were implanted into the child that she had been sexually abused by the targeted parent. It was proven in court that the memories were false and the abuse could not have happened, yet the child retains the memories which must be devastating, and will not see the father. The consequences for the real perpetrators of abuse, the mother and social worker, have not yet been realised.

I hope the research does progress in the mental health spaces as the lack of understanding of conditions, some claim as commonly related to parental alienation such as borderline personality disorder and narcissistic disorder[12] appears to be lacking. Certainly, there are organisations lobbying for borderline personality disorder and hope that the understanding is rapidly improving. In Australia, Medicare may fund six (which is easily extended to 10 and believe that with additional paperwork can be increased beyond that) mental health visits on a GP Mental Health Plan and there is a trial in one Primary Health Network (PHN) which extends that to unlimited visits. Hopefully, advances in the supports for the family members, particularly spouses, and research into the impact on children of being with a mentally ill parent will not lag far behind.

Right now, I would much prefer to focus the attention on the application of the existing laws and people be held to account for their actions. When I see the massive issues that false allegations cause through people I meet, I can only conclude that procedurally mandatory prosecutions for the first false police report would see many matters not escalate as they currently do. My very limited experience has shown that tilling of the rudder early, just as Jasmine stopped Nellie, when she was about to go hysterical, can keep people on track and in line with community expectations of proper behaviour. For those that do have genuine mental health issues that is preventing them from acting within the law, then a defence will require the identification of their condition, and hopefully, they will follow through with treatment and judicial leniency will be granted.

---

[12] The Attachment-Related Pathology of "Parental Alienation" C.A. Childress, Psy.D. (2016)

I believe that Nellie was the one that was trolling on the "Family Law Website" and this started when I was physically incapacitated. As a teenager, Nellie was treated with anti-depressants and was seeing a psychologist the year before I agreed to head over to the Netherlands. The psychiatrist that treated her in 1998 could not even remember her from his files when asked to attend the court in 2010. While only Nellie will know what she truly believes, her massive perjury in the early cases, the recruitment of Seth and Spike and their many activities may have never occurred with the application of existing laws. The outcomes may have been much better in terms of the mental health of all the family members. I can only hope that these lessons are learned by others for the sake of those that may follow.

20

Fathers Support – The Tsunami of Pain – The perfect storm

In a separated family setting, I see people that are despondent and sometimes angry. The cause is generally that their former spouse has decided that they do not want them in their life (remembering that some research shows those initiating the separation (usually women) will be considering the separation for up to two years before giving the news) and it will often be a shock to the recipient. In my case as terrible as it sounds it was more of a relief. When the news is exceptionally poorly delivered and presented in the form of a restraining order:

1. They may be totally despondent or angry at their former spouse for lodging a false report to the police (and I see accusations of bestiality, paedophilia, physical abuse and the list goes on, often encouraged by others to provide a tactical advantage in court),

2. They are totally despondent or angry at the police for removing them from their home.

3. They may be homeless or couch surfing at a relative's place (based upon lies and their governments' complicity through the actions of the police)

4. They are totally despondent or angry at the court for issuing a restraining order and not hearing their version of events or evidence. The median hearing time for each uncontested application is three minutes.[13] Cross-examination of the applicant is usually limited to confirming the content of written applications. Almost no exploration of the grounds for the application takes place.[14] Both figures were widely quoted in the press. Based upon the damage that I see from false allegations, to the children and the targeted parent, the use and abuse of the court system should be met with harsh penalties. This would not prevent genuine cases from being submitted and prosecution of a false allegation would need to follow a similar rigour to that of perjury.

5. They are faced with waiting lists for the Family court that can be years which is a long time for a parent but from a young child's perspective sometimes longer than their entire lifetime to date.

6. They have the false allegations against them permeate through their social network, become a pariah and are shunned, losing friends.

---

[13] Rosemary Hunter, Domestic Violence Law Reform and Women's Experience in Court: the Implementation of Feminist Reforms in Civil Proceedings (2008), at 77, 8 1–2.
[14] Rosemary Hunter ibid 84-8

7. They focus and struggle to cope with the unknowns of what this is doing to their children and there is so much literature out there on the impact of splitting, the defence mechanism associated with parental alienation where the child will sever the parent-child bond impacting their ability to form relationships later in life!

8. They are unable to concentrate at work and lose their job. For men being a plumber or whatever, their occupation often defines in their mind, part of who they are and they may feel they have lost a key part of their identity.

9. They have never been to court and suddenly enter a new system and are immediately delayed from being able to present facts and find it could take years.

Typically, from being a happy family member one day, they are suddenly suffering the impacts of the:

- Loss of Partner.

- Loss of child/children.

- Loss of housing.

- Social exclusion/shunned.

- Financial problems.

- Loss of career/job, identity and self-worth.

- Bullying by their former spouse through lawyers and "The System."

- A deep sense of hopelessness.

It is the tsunami of pain and the perfect storm for suicide. In my case, the group I saw taught me the things I can do and it wasn't to take pills to feel better, in this most disgusting of situations and deal with the situational distress.

If we reconsider the standard construct of how we think/feel to act/behave to outcome/results in the diagram below:

Think / Feel **Act / Behave**

Outcome / Results

If what we experience (our present outcomes/results) is an attack on ourselves, then we may think/feel in a very negative way and react poorly and there will be bad outcomes. An attack on persons integrity and identity as a parent, using false police allegations can be the trigger for a cascading, never-ending spiral downwards. While many professionals in the mental health sector work on "Think/ Feel", in some cases the cycle is best addressed through "how I can act/behave", encourage and help them identify good and constructive behaviour to influence the results they obtain. It is possibly why the facilitators and peers within a fathers' support group regularly encourage people to psychologists and vice versa. Fathers support are often not able to provide the clinical psychology perspectives that a one to one session can provide that can be beneficial. The psychologists however, rarely have the insight into the world of the family court processes and procedures, and they have difficulty normalising the experiences, whereas peers do that naturally. I therefore see the services offered by psychologists as complementary, working on two of the axes in the fairly standard psychology construct.

I tend to describe the model used by Fathers Support as being both psychotherapeutic, which is essentially "get your story out of your system," achieved by sharing your story in turn, without interruption. This is then followed by a break which leads into the psychoeducational part, whereby the group will workshop the alternatives to the problems that have been revealed in the first half. This may provide an insight as to what may be the likely outcome of actions to determine if those actions are likely to be good, not so good or bad through the experiences of others which helps them to make more informed choices. Sometimes we use the opportunity to read a restraining order and make sure the person understands it and how not to breach it! I have seen several cases of entrapment where the wife wants the night off and the father jumps at the opportunity to babysit, thinking that is being helpful and will assist in improving the situation as well as spending time with their child. The father has been at her house breaching the order (which is not between the two of them and can only be varied by the court) and is reported and arrested the next morning.

I recall one participant that was attending for his own personal reasons; he was a police officer and from him the group learned how police work. They get a complaint, they interview and if appropriate arrest. We get people that are upset because they are interviewed for sexually abusing their children or assaulting a family member. It is fairly easy to give them the scenario:

Facilitator, "If their neighbour's kids were being abused you would report it?"

Participant, "Hell yes!"

Facilitator, "And you would expect the authorities to investigate?"

Participant, "Of course."

Facilitator, "So if someone has made a complaint against you! Should they investigate?"

Participant, "But I didn't do it!"

Facilitator, "But they should investigate?"

Participant, "Yeah, okay then."

By changing how they think and act toward the police or child protection agencies when subjected to an investigation being conducted on them is important. Instead of being what was seen as a very personal attack on them, the investigation becomes not only tolerable but good, as the parent would be disappointed if the agency was not there to help protect their children. Their attitude toward the police or child agency can change immediately from being angry which has consequences if they don't resist but embrace the police or child agency inquiries and often matters are settled immediately with good outcomes. This however, does not work if the police or child protection personnel work in a manner that is not professional and their actions are based upon the:

- The discredited[15] gendered Duluth model[16] (a domestic violence against women model that ignores male victims and that violence is largely

---

[15] https://honest-ribbon.org/mega-featured/duluth-model-buries-key-facts-on-domestic-violence/

[16] https://en.wikipedia.org/wiki/Duluth_model

due to women's unequal social, economic and political status, ignoring many of the known factors such as mental health, drugs, alcohol that affect both genders) or

- Personal background of those conducting the investigation (they may have suffered DV and have a negative attitude that all men are violent or they had lies told against them and believe all women are liars or the much-quoted sexist saying "you have to believe the woman") prevents them from seeing the facts.

I had spent significant time in the Fathers Support, peer support group. I would usually arrive early, help open-up the room and participate and after one or two years I eventually became a facilitator of the group sometimes for months at a time.

My friend, Lawry, could see that with my background, education and how committed I was to helping others and hence, I was invited to run for election to the National board. My educational background, as a professional Engineer, had an MBA, worked in IT and had personal experience in this space—it was the perfect role for me to help others and assist and if required represent a "community of common circumstances."

The organisation, Fathers Support, was designed as a peer support model to help those most in need. I found that many front-line services, lawyers, psychologist and suicide prevention services for the separated parent referred people to us because of the peer environment. Our existence was built on the principle that every child should have the right to see both parents and have a great relationship with both parents, assuming the parents were safe, decent members of the community. It was our aim to ensure the groups helped them meet the personal and physical challenges of a family separation as seamless as could possibly be.

By working with each individual, we believed we could create a cultural and systemic change in a positive way and help many separated families to go on and live a fulfilling life. Through the means of helplines, peer support programs, awareness of the many issues surrounding a separated parent and family breakdown, we may eventually improve outcomes for all involved.

The results being, that separated parents get connected to a community of support that they need and in doing so, the parents can cope better at being separated from their children and find a better pathway to reconnect with them.

Over time I was encouraged to become Chairman of the Board and I did so for three years. This took its toll too, with politics, government consultations, presentations at parliamentary and senate hearings, new systems implemented and changes to key staff.

21

Where to from here?

I suspect that I will "live an interesting life" to quote the Chinese curse. I remember starting off in community service as the youngest committee member (that were otherwise all parents) for a youth club. I followed through when I helped out as a founding member of a branch of the State Emergency Services and was registered to drive the Ambulance while on a Queensland construction site. I normally, held first aid qualifications and now hold a Mental Health First Aid certificate as well.

I particularly love my work with Lions Club and have been president, teaching swimming (to the blind children as part of Lions Club and transport a young boy most weeks), active with a marine care group who so often help paraplegics with the snorkelling experience and for many years a guest lecturer in Universities.

I am considered by people as an honest and decent person (although, I am sure Nellie would go to great lengths to dispute that). I have learned to listen and show empathy which is probably why two other incidents have occurred in recent times:

- The first was a celebratory night out and some ladies asked me to help get a very intoxicated young lady (barely older than my daughter), to their car so they could get her home. The young lady however panicked as we approached the car thinking there may be a bomb under it, a few other events occurred and then she asked me to hit her in the temple (side of her head) and kill her. I was able to find out some of her interesting past and she had seen it done by soldiers in a village she came from. Out of control, an ambulance was called by security and when they arrived, I informed them of the strange request. To this day I am grateful that it was me, and not some equally intoxicated individual that may have complied with her request.

- The second was a request from a family "do you know anyone and help find a home for their 10-month-old grandchild." To say I was shocked was an understatement, but their predicament was clear—they weren't able to look after a baby as it would soon be a toddler. With all efforts to keep this little one out of the system which some in the sector call "Department of Human Sacrifices," the family managed to help find a good home for this baby to bring up the child so it could still be connected with the existing family. I found a home shortly after they did and learned a lot about the problems with child services being that children are often "kept in the system," bouncing from foster home to foster home, with little or any value being put on that child's quality of life in terms of a stable family environment and the fundamentals of attachment theory. I was also told of scandals in the UK where the foster child industry, actively worked against adoption as they were funded for monitoring foster children and wondered if it was happening here in Australia. On a bright note the child is doing very well, clearly loved, now runs up to hug her grandmother on very regular visits. Occasionally the grandmother tears up for letting her go but knows it was the best thing as the baby, the old family and new family are all winners.

I dare say there may be more shocks ahead in my life but like in the past, I will just work through them.

While my community service activities were suppressed for many years during the relationship with Nellie, it really is who I am and will probably continue in similar capacities. In more recent times, my time as a facilitator and chairman of a not-for-profit in suicide prevention, and then identifying that most of our participants have suffered actions that are defined as domestic violence, I am likely to stay involved in that area.

Have the experiences for the relationship and what has occurred left me with a permanent level of distrust? I think the distrust is more of myself and ability to trust my own judgement. I like to think it has not impacted my ability to trust others, but maybe it has made me more aware in what look for in a prospective partner and have barriers that are yet to be broken down. When looking for a new relationship, I have found that I wonder if there are alternate reasons for what people see in me. I wonder if they want someone they can manipulate? I know it must be a mutually beneficial, healthy relationship, we will have a something in common like a level of community service on a voluntary basis. Time will tell how and if, a new relationship, will eventuate.

From an advocacy perspective, I have been a part of Fathers Support, I have spoken at Parliament and been a part of a team that has lobbied to change the processes inside the court and around the court and some of what I have observed and learned is in this book.

Through my years of supporting so many through Fathers Support (and Mothers Support) firstly as a participant, then a facilitator, to Chairman of the Board and finally, as an active member on the Board, I have seen and learned so much. It is unfortunate that many issues are hijacked in what is best described as gender politics and like parental alienation the commonalities are greater than the perceived divide. Staying current with popular beliefs and government sensitivities in order to continue to do the good, life-saving work we do, is a constant challenge. When I meet a displaced, traumatised parent, or those suffering from a domestic violence situation, the confirmation that we all have far more in common than our own differences caused by gender or sexual orientation is reinforced.

Over time, what I have learned from being in this space, is a new direction that I want to tackle further and that is the term known as "Situational Distress" or "Situational Suicide." The fact that many people would not even be contemplating suicide but for the fact that they now find themselves under such extreme situational distress that I have seen in the separation and parental alienation areas. The extreme distress also applies in farming and other sectors subject to significant changes and some call it "Transitional Anxiety" and the inability to transition leads to suicide.

I recently put together a proposal for a new national organisation to be called, "Situational Suicide Prevention" to address this.

In our current environment, the bodies charged with suicide prevention are dominated by psychologists focused on the "think/feel" area and medical areas, and the suicide rates continue to grow. A new organisation may be needed to provide a new direction away from the proposed solutions which involve hiring hundreds or thousands of professionals and to prescribe more medication at excep-tionally high cost to the government. Many consider the current direction to be a failed or failing policy and model and it is continually subjected to criticism and review but without any meaningful insight or solution emerging. This proposal aims to ensure community ownership of the suicide epidemic and empower them to not only make the difference locally, but to take pride in their achievement as opposed to, "it's out of my hands and it can only be done by professionals."

When I see people, still in trauma after years of perscription drugs and traditional therapy that have simply not accepted or dealt with their situation, so they can transition to something new, I realised something is wrong for some people and a complementary approach is required. This proposal outlines a method which, if applied, will seek to coordinate and support practical "Situational Approaches" across one state initially, to address suicide prevention. Situational approaches are well known and proven, but lack any significant support. The existing mental health and medical orientated groups in place, are well-funded and good at political lobbying and like most organisms seek growth rather than industry disruption and new approaches. The proposal is for a new organisation that will be called "Situational Suicide Prevention" which would initially be established in one state. The aim of the organisation would be to show the benefits and the great work community groups involved in "Situational Suicide Prevention" across the state perform. To establish those organisations as having a proper place in the system as complementary and in many cases, pathways to traditional providers.

Much of the initial expertise will come from the lessons learned in recent years and systems developed by Parents After Separation in their Peer Support program. The organisation would require modest finance to bring together all community groups, share best practice and provide a central repository of expertise that they can access and apply, giving them the skills (including organisational, IT and training) that will be provided free of the normal costs. The aim is to allow members to focus on their community's needs and expand their service through their volunteers that directly support those in need.

The initial cost was estimated at $500,000.00 p.a. for a five-year program.

If you had asked me years ago, if I would be putting together another proposal for government funding to help support the men and women, currently facing the fight of their life related to situational distress and suicide prevention ... well, I would have looked at you like you were crazy. The result of being thrust into this path and trauma now means I have a responsibility to help those also walking the same journey with me.

22

What is the Truth? The courts

There is a saying in family separation circles:

"There is his story, there is her story, and somewhere in between is the truth."

Other philosophers and famous people talking about the truth say things like:

"Oh, what a tangled web we weave. When first we practice to deceive!" —Sir Walter Scott.

"If you tell the truth, you don't have to remember anything" — Albert Bigelow Paine (editor for Mark Twain).

"Three things cannot be long hidden: the sun, the moon, and the truth" — Buddha (quotation paraphrased).

I found the above quotes exceptionally useful whenever I needed to prepare an affidavit for court. When you are on the stand and under oath, being questioned by experienced barristers, that will jump from one statement in your affidavit to statements in others and expose the inconsistencies, the truth is far easier to tell.

The motivation for the conflict may be anger and vengeance which has consumed one party, a mental illness or personality issue, sometimes brought on by their own childhood trauma, that bubbles to the surface during the stress of a separation. This may result in false allegations and can be exacerbated by a third party such as a friend that had a bitter experience with their partner, or a lawyer.

All of these situations, I now believe, occurred in my case.

Nellie eventually told me that Bella (her Dutch lawyer) told her that, "You have to take everything, it is your duty as a mother for your children's future," which seemed to justify all Nellie's actions that followed. There was no concern that perjury is illegal as it is never punished but appeared that perjury is justified and the right thing to do. She appeared to be encouraged to pay so much of the family's asset base to the lawyers as it was both noble and responsible, to protect her children rather than wasteful and destructive. The truth, or more to the point; lies and perjury, meant that the truth had to be argued in the court and that is what makes money for lawyers.

What I soon learned was that when false accusations and anger is assisted by lawyers, their letters and statements often have incitement clauses. Your former spouse knows you intimately, including what upsets you the most. This may be your sense of truth, honesty and integrity, especially if you are a parent brought up in the Superman era or on cowboy movies where "my word is my honour." Letters are often carefully constructed so that the lies or insinuations strike at your core values, with accusations concluding you are a bad mother or father, and the conflict spirals into heights that are unimaginable. It is these reactions that can lead to a mental meltdown and sometimes behaviours that are counterproductive and result in the huge fees, as lawyers argue over the false allegations. The fact that you love your child, just as every good parent does, seems to be lost in the litigation that follows as an adversarial system takes control.

If you have the capacity to document and tell the truth, stay calm, then the legal process may serve you well. I ran men's groups (occasionally women also attended and once consisted of one third of the group) and when people are presented with an affidavit from someone that they possibly still love, full of lies, slander and unspeakable depravity (such as sexually abusing their own child), they sometimes become unable to mentally process anything let alone briefing a lawyer or addressing a court. Calming them down and getting them to work through the affidavit, paragraph by paragraph stating:

- Agree or disagree to the paragraph, (and even saw one affidavit where his wife's country of birth was wrong) and

- If disagree what is their version of events? and

- Any proof of their version of events?

This assists their lawyers who generally read quickly and also then have the facts at their fingertips.

Unfortunately, I have also seen people that are so traumatised by the lies, that they are unable to answer an affidavit which means that the legal system cannot help them. The legal system fails both them, their children, justice and the community rightly loses faith in the judicial process. Organisations that assist people through both the legal and emotional maze, while under a character assassination are in many cases integral to a successful outcome. Unfortunately, most organisations are often either legal or emotional without the bridge in between.

The other thing to consider is the legal definition of perjury and the legal tests. While this may vary across jurisdictions it is common that one needs to establish that:

1. The defendant was lawfully sworn as a witness in a judicial proceeding;

2. The defendant made a statement wilfully – that is to say, they made the statement deliberately and not inadvertently or by mistake or at cross purposes with the person questioning him/her;

3. The statement was false;

4. The defendant knew it was false;

5. The statement was material, that is, it was of such significance that it was capable of affecting the decision of the court. In this case, the statement was, as a matter of law, material.

Many consider that lying to the court is perjury, however the five tests show that if the facts show the person is wrong then far more needs to be considered. If we consider the test number four and its implications, then we can assume that if you truly believed that what you were telling was the truth, then perjury has not occurred even when the facts show what is stated could not have occurred. In some circumstances people that cannot accept the situation, a situation that challenges their beliefs and value system, have been known to reinvent their historical events to justify what they have stated, often referred to as cognitive dissonance. Some literature outlines this situation as a method to prevent the emotional overload in the brain, a sort of a short circuit. The fact is, they really believe what they have stated, and it is their truth. Prosecution for perjury in those cases would not succeed, however the investigation may highlight the signs of their possible condition and may assist in management of the person themselves, child safety and literally everyone involved.

There is one more quote that I like which is,

"Our lives are not determined by what happens to us but how we react to what happens, not by what life brings us but the attitude we bring to life" — Wade Boggs (American; former professional baseball player).

When facing the barrage of lies and often false testimony by a bitter and twisted former spouse, that may have mental health issues, there may be nothing you can do to help the one you loved or still love, but how you move forward is what you can manage.

One thing I have learned about the family court route is that mothers, fathers and children are all losers. I know that without escaping from the violence and control that I was under and the protection of the courts, I would not be alive today. I would not be alive today if I had of stayed in the Netherlands and therefore not alive for the day my daughter reflects on what she has been told, ponders what may have happened, looks into her heart and returns. I feel that this means I have lost a little less by staying alive and going down the court route although if processes were improved, Nellie, I and the children would all have been better off.

I like to think that people are not inherently evil, however when the person you once loved decides they are all right and you are all wrong, therefore you should have no rights and you must do as they dictate, then conflict is assured.

The correct attitude of focusing on the children's best interest and work out your path forward is often the only appropriate course of action.

23

The pinball players compounding conflict

Police

I remember when I started primary school. I would walk to primary school with my older brother which is unusual for a lot of kids nowadays and a policeman was sometimes at the crossing on the main road. One day our dog, a border collie which are bred to herd sheep, known to be really faithful and protective of their family would not listen to us and followed us to school. He was very protective and I was told that as a baby when I was crawling around in the backyard, he would herd me up, keeping me on the footpath and under control which really upset me, at least that was one story. We stopped numerous times, turning his head and pushing him towards home and telling him to go home but he wanted to be with us and protect us. We eventually got to the main road and the policemen yelled at our dog to make him go home and certainly followed those commands and probably knew we were now being looked after to cross that road. The police were part of the community, were well respected and protected all of us. The police were someone I could trust, a protector of all and deserved the enormous respect that they held. Nowadays, maybe they are more insulated from the community and my view of the police have also changed.

Those that initiate the family separation often contemplate for years without communication with their intimate partner, they have gone through a grieving process and prepare, often consulting others. The number of times I hear from men that find out their relationship was over from the police, in the form of a restraining order (called by various names), that they cannot go home, go within a certain distance of their former spouse and often also includes the kids, I could not count. These are men where the only interaction they have had with the police was maybe a traffic infringement, which are often done by camera technology, so the police are removed from that as well. Others, like me, called the police when things got out of hand to try to settle things down but unlike me, their situation is often made far worse and they are issued a restraining order and told to move out.

The police spend significant resources on domestic violence matters and in some states the police claim it is 30% of their work, 40% of all homicides. Based upon the Australian Institute of Criminology Report 2015[17], a quarter of all intimate partner homicides are toward the male which seems to go largely unnoticed in the press due to their societal focus. Regardless of the figures, domestic violence toward anyone is abhorrent and must be addressed without prejudice.

When I grew up, I thought it was a serious offence to lie to the police. The police, by not dealing with false allegations, appear to have made such practices acceptable and the

[17] https://aic.gov.au/sites/default/files/publications/annualreport/downloads/2015-annual_report_2015.pdf

impacts appear to be significant. Conspiracy theorists say it is to get their crime statistics up in a campaign for more government funding, but I will stay clear on commenting on that! I will demonstrate the problems this causes by example of a man that we will call "B –." B – was picked up and questioned by the police more than fifty times for breach of intervention orders and many of the complaints alleged that he was driving past his former wife's place and screeching his tyres. The police (acting very unprofessionally) would ring him up and abuse him for breaching an intervention/restraining order by driving past her residence and demand he drop what he was doing and report to the police immediately. He would remain calm and often respond, "I cannot get there now, I am not even in the country. I couldn't have done what is claimed as was not in the country at that date," and, "I will see you Tuesday and show you my passport when I return." The police would often respond that they did not believe him and will send a car to his home or work to arrest him. The response was, "Feel free to try and as I am not there. You will not get anywhere, and I will report when I arrive back on Tuesday night." On his fiftieth complaint, he was not responsive by phone and the police tracked his whereabouts to a hospital, where they arrived to be told by the charge nurse they could not see him as he was currently in an induced coma (from a plane accident) and had been for three days (which covered when the alleged breach had occurred).

The case of B – show that the police rarely look beyond a single incident and treat each event in isolation. In my opinion, they failed in this case and in their duty of care and should have arrested the woman for making the false allegations so that the facts could be presented. If she was really lying, then they could deal with it and bring an end to diversion of police resources away from those that are in danger. If it was paranoia or mental health issues, then this could be brought before professionals in this area with appropriate support and ensure the safety of the children. It should be recognised that when appropriately managed, mental health issues rarely preclude someone from being a parent. He was still having more complaints and police pickups when I saw him last. It should be noted that I have also dealt with a woman that has had 20 accusations filed with the police, all thrown out by the court, so this should not be considered a gender issue but poor police practices in terms of not following through when a false police report is submitted.

The police will act on an accusation of domestic violence and treat the claims as correct (i.e. guilty until proven innocent).

When you meet men and

- their first encounter with the police is at their door when arriving home,

- police supervising them to pack a single bag and dropping them at a hotel,

- they often find their credit cards maxed out,

- due in court next week to ratify the restraining order,

- then find out that they cannot even get to present what happened,

- if do not agree (generally without admission of guilt) it is put off for months with an interim order,

- in many cases they find out they had bad legal advice from printed brochures and lawyers, and the restraining order prevents them from working (particularly in professions needing firearms or working with children). That is months away from seeing their kids which they have never been separated (apart from going to work), you realise how bad the system really is.

Another friend's experience was that of his wife attempted to stab him, she then threw knives and saucepans and then he did the inexcusable, he retaliated, with a cake.

I asked him, "Was it a heavy Christmas cake?"

Friend, "No, it was a cream sponge cake."

Trevor, "Was it on a plate?"

Friend, "No, I took it off the plate."

You guessed it, the man was arrested! For those from my era or before, this is classic 3 Stooges (cream cake in the face) and Keystone Cops behaviour! While in this specific incident, I do not know her side of the story, I do know that years later she was arrested, and the children's custody was changed as she was considered dangerous to them.

Police entering a domestic violence situation, generally want to separate the warring parties so that matters do not escalate into the assault and murder statistics. Their documented procedures are generally well written and non-discriminatory. Command and the culture that overlays the procedure manual is however exceptionally biased. A friend while doing a mediator's class was able to talk to an assistant superintendent in the domestic violence area. While this is secondhand information, it is from someone I trust and the assistant commissioner allegedly stated, "The constables know that it is career limiting to arrest too many women in domestic violence situations." Similarly, one social worker I occasionally deal with, interviewed around twenty constables in another state to determine how they work and the consensus was overwhelmingly "the sergeants rewrite their reports before they go into the system to match the current perspective of gendered violence unless the situation is overwhelmingly clear."

The police are not trained in dual risk assessment in Australia. I only know of a couple of jurisdictions across the world where dual risk assessments are performed to work out which parent is the greatest risk to their children and spouse and therefore who should be removed. Statistically, mothers kill more children than fathers, according to the Australian Institute of Criminology (AIC).[18] Do the police even consider the AIC evidence in their culture when they decide as to whom to remove? In spite of the evidence they use a patriarchal construct of protecting the little woman, men are bigger and more powerful, and therefore pose the greater risk to each other, usually ignoring all other factors and the children.

When I called the police to attend the family home incident in Australian accordance with the court orders where Seth and his daughter appeared out of the dark, the police showed their true colours. While they refused to supply me the name of the unidentified trespasser (Seth's daughter), the police sergeant even stated, "You can do what you like and if you subpoena any of us we just won't turn up in court and will put them on essential police duties the night before and will keep avoiding the court." This sergeant was convincing and appeared to think he was above the court and therefore the law.

---

[18] Australian Institute of Criminology (AIC), Research In Practice No. 38, May 2015, Domestic/family homicide in Australia Tracy Cussen and Willow Bryant.

When I reported the death threat to a local police station and provided documents as to the sinister and probably mentally delusional nature of the suspected perpetrator, the treatment I got compared with the purchaser of the family home (a woman), or that of the woman that was hysterically screaming in the police station "so they had to deal with her," was a stark comparison.

The way the police are acting, means that perhaps some demographics do not have the same level of protection, the same level of access to government services and just perhaps *"there is no option, I cannot be heard, I am not valued,"* is causing some of the social problems that we see. A level playing field may decrease violence and suicide.

Recently in the news, the Australian Federal Police have arrested various people for running an organised child abduction ring. The claims that the fathers were not fit had been investigated, put through the court and the fathers awarded shared care. They have been found to be good and decent parents, devastated for the loss of their children and fearful for the children's safety both physically and mentally. The mothers contacted a group of what may be best described as vigilantes, taking the law into their own hands against court orders, that allegedly abducted the children and hid them and their mothers, evading police for sometimes years. Some involved have already been jailed, while others are on a very restricted bail (with tracking devices), yet others now charged with "Conspiracy to defeat justice." Many of us await the future developments on that case.

The evidence I submitted to the police, (the court orders) and what the subpoena's revealed, I am informed that they clearly showed an attempt to defeat justice in the Family Court. The defence of Seth was that the law was wrong, the court was not properly constituted and therefore he was not obligated to follow its rulings. You would have every right to wonder if cases like mine were prosecuted, along with perjury, if such deterrents would have served as a warning, stopping such vigilantes with the consequent damage to those children of being abducted, not going to school for years and the mental trauma caused.

Another case that remains in my mind was the man explaining to me that his wife was removed from the hospital, after, according to hospital staff, caught her strangling him while still on the gurney under anaesthetic, screaming, "Why didn't you die?" He was also told that the emergency surgery was to have his stomach removed due to poisoning over a period of weeks, representing two counts of attempted murder and yet there was no police action which is very concerning and may reflect the gendered police focus on domestic violence.

The statements to the mediator in training; the survey by the social worker; the police protecting the family home purchaser and protecting the hysterical women but not protecting me; the man arrested in the cake incident; the man that had been poisoned and strangled; and the literally thousands of stories I have heard are of such frequency must lead me to some conclusion. Are we all equal before the police and deserving of equal treatment?

Lawyers

We have all heard the jokes "What is a busload of lawyers that runs off the bridge and drown in the river: a good start." In my opinion, lawyers play an absolutely essential role in society as I pointed out with my opinion of the relationship between the welfare, medical treatment and law in the Netherlands and they do defend people.

Lawyers however are human, and unfortunately, some need to be prosecuted and struck off, which in Australia, from my perspective, is simply not occurring at the level it should. The majority of lawyers that I meet through social or the peer groups, seem to simply work within the system, are ethical, and work to ensure their clients get what is fair and reasonable so everyone can move on with their lives. From running peer support, one of the challenges I regularly see for lawyers, is that clients often expect lawyers to win when they don't provide information in time or at all. Some people I have dealt with were so traumatised, they could not string a sentence together when talking about their case and some lawyers are not skilful enough at getting the information out of such clients.

There is also a darker side too, which is often reported in the press and occasionally makes national front-page news, when a judge actually says what they see. I gained significant insight into those who misuse their position to drive conflict and billable hours, those who fuel outrageous cases that usually get paid, win or lose. One lawyer informed me of a dinner meeting with a barrister who stated, "We will carve up this estate," (largely to themselves as if carving up a Sunday roast or a side of beef). I have already talked about incitement clauses, and how lawyers are able to keep conflict going.

Through my connections, I learned of a term called "Burn Off." This is where two, less-than-honourable lawyers burn off, say 70% (sometimes up to 90%) of the assets and then pretend to be a hero, and mediate settlement of the remaining 30% (or 10%). The parties leave the room thinking, "Thank goodness, after all that, my lawyer managed to get him/her to settle." The client then actually thanks their lawyers, never realising what has occurred and their assets have been "burned off." One of the first questions that you get asked is, "What are the assets?" which may be used to advise on the likely split or, very often, determine if they want to get involved. If the assets are minimal, they may move straight to successful mediation, otherwise less ethical lawyers will use tactics to incite conflict, sometimes for years, regardless of the damage to the children.

Domestic violence has become major focus in the community concerns and so it should. It can come at a huge cost which is the misuse of accusations and gross over-exaggerations. A classic conversation I hear too often from females I speak to after their first meeting with their lawyer, is that the conversation goes:

Lawyer, "Has he ever hit you?"
Client, "No."
Lawyer, "Has he ever yelled at you?"
Client, "No."
Lawyer, "Has he ever withheld money?"
Client, "No."

Lawyer, "I would like you to go away and think about that more, as it would be better for you if you can think of something!"

Invariably, what they are doing is trying to ramp up conflict and move litigation into the domestic violence court. What this has led to is an enormous increase in cases before the domestic violence court, often the applicant of the restraining order includes the children, which removes the children from the targeted parent's life.

This disturbing trend away from the family court to crush the opposition in the domestic violence jurisdictions is best described by a law firm L.G Yves Michel & Co in their "RESPONSE TO PUBLIC CONSULTATION PAPER & EXPOSURE DRAFT FAMILY LAW AMENDMENT (FAMILY VIOLENCE AND OTHER MEASURES) BILL 2017[19]." Their submission on 20th January 2017, which I have taken from their submission to the Attorney Generals website, has the figures, showing the migration of cases in one Australian state from the Family Court to the Domestic Violence Court and the relationship to mediation in section 4 along with some conclusions.

The reason this may be occurring may be due to the complete lack of ethics of some lawyers and while I like to think they are a minority, other observers disagree. These lawyers are aided by the failure of their industry and government bodies to prosecute such damaging behaviour. Lawyer-client confidentiality in Australia is often used to hide their actions, the legislation that restricts publication of cases that identify persons (lawyers are normally named in

---

[19] https://www.trevorcooperauthor.com/book-referenced-material and https://www.ag.gov.au/Consultations/Documents/amendments-family-law-act-respond-to-family-violence/the-forgotten-victims-of-family-violence.pdf

decisions but were not in several of my cases) has aided such practices, where anonymity is ensured.

The advice I received from the first two lawyers, one in Australia and one in the Netherlands, proved to be correct in terms of final outcomes and that the advice, "It is better to sort out yourself if you can," proved to be both honourable and correct. One person I know, had even created a website where you could load in the critical factors such as how long together, financial situation, contribution, age of children and producing a normal range of the likely final settlement from litigation. If clients were given realistic expectations at the start, they would know they are only arguing about say five or ten per cent of the assets, rather than much more and may facilitate earlier compromise and settlement. It may help reduce the practice of "burning down."

Should we eliminate lawyers from the system? The law reflects society's values. It protects us from crime. Lawyers help judges keep police and others in check, by ensuring evidence is tested and as such, they are part of the glue that holds society together. Lawyers are specialists in interpreting the law and will always have a place in assisting their clients understand their legal obligation and the pursuit of legal entitlements. The real question however is, are these rogue lawyers a benefit or encumbrance to the good working of society, especially in their part of the family separation industry? Are the correct checks and balances in place to ensure they cannot turn rogue and be an encumbrance to maintaining the high ethical standards that the public have every right to expect?

How can we ensure that lawyers do what they are meant to do?

- Should we eliminate or reduce the adversarial system to assist separating parties (and I use the term parties as I remember in one case they were a gay couple and lesbian couple who had week-on and week-off shared arrangement of the upbringing a child for five years when the birth mother wanted full control)?

- Would an inquisitorial system be better? An inquisitorial system is where the court or part of the court is actively involved in the investigation of facts of the case, as opposed to the current adversarial system where the court is primarily that of an impartial referee between prosecution and defence.

- Would a collaborative law framework achieve better results? A collaborative law framework is where lawyers use skills similar to those in mediation enabling those that decide to separate to work with lawyers and may involve other professionals to reach a settlement that best needs the parties and their children without the threat of litigation.

- Should we limit lawyer's utility, (the income from a case)? Would a fixed fee 10% of the family assets turn the lawyers into the greatest of mediators (rather than utilising their skills to promote conflict and income) and the conflict finished in a couple of sessions rather than go on for years? Would a fixed fee stop the countless court appearances and ensure lawyers are ready in the first hearing as a second will not increase their utility and increase their effort? Note:

a fixed fee is completely different from a schedule of rates which may be so much per letter or so much per court appearance that can run on indefinitely.

- Should many of the cases be treated as a health issue? Some submissions show the devastating impact on the family, the children, the associated suicide and subsequent mental health issues and suggest that many of the high conflict cases are driven by mental health and personality issues.

The Australian Law Reform Commission (ALRC) is stacked with lawyers (according to the ALRC website the recently completed "review of the family law system", president and commissioners consist of four judges, two solicitor/lawyers and one representative from Relationships Australia (i.e. 6 out of 7 representing the legal profession) and by its very makeup has to represents the values of lawyers. The Australian Law Reform Commission, for example, forms committees of which according to their website, "Members of these committees are selected because of the expertise of each committee member in a particular area relevant to the area of law under consideration," and need to ask:

- Do these committees represent the values of the public and the consumer of the services?

- Has it been stacked to ensure the objectives of the lawyers, rather than the stated objectives of simpli-fication of the law and its accessibility and cost, is in accordance with community objectives?

- Has it been stacked in a way that the committees suffer cognitive rigidity; essentially the inability to thnk about things in a different way or "outside the box"?

- Are they able to override and disassociate their traditional loyalties for their colleagues which is in significant conflict with the community at large?

- Is the barrier to high to climb? I believe it is!

There have been many reports and inquiries over the decades, speeches by the attorney general that lawyers that are found to have escalated conflict will be prosecuted, however I have not seen any action. Powerful vested interests have ensured the terms of reference for many inquiries, suit their agenda of making the law more complex and expensive while vital reforms do not happen! Is it time to force the governments to do something?

In terms of the current system, from the consumer and societal perspective it was best described by Lord Chief Justice Coleridge in the United Kingdom who refers to it as, "An exercise in absolute futility and a carnival of despair."

The social workers

Social workers are generally idealistic, and the majority are acting in the best interests of the people they deal with.

I would like to go over a case of a man I will call "S – " which I followed as his peer for many years as I watched his matter progress.

S – had been removed from the house in which they lived as S – was accused of violence and child abuse and had not been allowed to see his child for around six months. "The Department" turned up where he lived one day, without notice with his son and said, "We know who the abuser is now, and you will need to look after the child." No apology for labelling him as abusive when it was now clear to them is was his spouse. While he had no infant formula, bottles, nappies and other items, he was told to organise them which he did, took care of the child as every loving parent would, even though the child was presented to him with a broken arm and ribs and needed significant care. The child stayed in that loving environment.

A new worker from "The Department" arrived on his doorstep around a year later and took the child, again, unannounced, stating, "A child that young must be with its mother under the tender year's doctrine." The tender years doctrine is that a child under five should be with the mother due to parent-child bonding and development but has been largely discredited. "But what about the child abuse?" the loving father asked. "That was never proven, and you can no longer see the child as the mother does not feel safe around you!" was the response.

The father, denied legal aid, and with insufficient resources, self-represented and fought "The Department" in court. The social workers had a disproportionate influence and with their lawyers won.

The child, again neglected and in need, was eventually again returned to the father. Hearings were eventually instigated by the mother, and the father who had become quite competent as a Self-Represented Litigant (SRL), found himself against the Independent Children's Lawyer

(ICL) and the mother's lawyer. The judge saw the progress of the child in school, extracurricular activities and the huge strides that the child had made in a loving and nurturing environment. The case was interesting in that the ICL represented the mother's interest, even though the mother did not even bother to turn up and the Judge seeing the bias asked the ICL to stand down. The judge saw the competency of the father from his latest submissions and was very critical that the father had not appealed the previous judge's decision that was clearly wrong. The child is now in a safe and loving environment.

"The Department" in so many cases, fail in its basic purpose of acting in the best interests of the child and history will judge the governments, its departments and the social workers who they fund. Unfortunately, it will be too late for many of our children and I foresee that yet another government apology will be issued to the victims of their poor policy and management.

Social workers are often the family report writers. They are of exceptionally poor quality and many family reports have been brought into question, most recently in the "Parliamentary inquiry into a better family law system to support and protect those affected by family violence." I sat in, listening to the part of the inquiry when the social workers' industry body was questioned and they agreed with the politicians that the problems were widespread. The inquiry clearly saw this and Recommendation 22 was: "The Committee recommends the Attorney-General pursues legislation and policy reform to abolish private family consultants, with family consultants to be only engaged and administered by the Court itself." We need to ask if this would fix the core issue? I doubt this will fix anything, unless the family consultants video record their interviews which are subject to supervisory review and then made available for experts to use in cross-examination. Failing to implement those controls will simply result in another professional opinion that is not subject to checks and balances.

I know first-hand of cases where social workers reports have been so steeped in ideology that the needs of the child were largely ignored. A professional psychologist and report writer that the courts consider beyond question due to their knowledge, understanding, and integrity had to be called in at significant cost to counter the ideology-based family report. I am, by background, a problem solver, who has worked across many areas and one of the main methods are what are called Cause–and–Effect Diagram or Ishikawa Diagram, Root Cause analysis (drill down at least three levels to find the real root cause as to why a certain outcome occurred). When I consider the case of S – and the many others I have witnessed over time, there are some root causes that are evident.

When I talk to social workers, they tell me that there may be two or three men in a class of fifty, i.e. more than 90% of social workers are women. I do not have the exact enrolment and completion statistics. It actually makes sense, as courses are filled through self-selection and as social work is considered a helping profession, I understand there would be a gender bias. Those attending the courses, both men and women tell me there is, unfortunately, elements of their education that have included feminist ideology including the discredited Duluth doctrine and have included the "tender years' doctrine" and therefore this bias finds itself in the workforce. Compounding the issue is the lack of male social workers, including and especially those in mediation, whereby they fail the many people who come to them for support due to perceived bias. The universities (in Australia) have approved through their ethics committees, research, and publication of documents such as the "tender years' doctrine". In the 2010 study led by Melbourne child psychologist Dr Jennifer McIntosh, produced many papers such as the "Australian Association for Infant Mental Health: Infants and overnight care – post separation and divorce," which influenced parliaments. A critique of that research can be found at Professor Warshak's[20] website which had the support of 110 academics and found the research to consist of academic misrepresentation and while the counter-arguments ensued for many years, good parents would leave the courtroom having been McIntosh'ed. Eventually, even the court started to overturn the doctrine but many of the social workers have not, and as such remains and permeates through the social workers' culture.

In the case of the of the child of S – , the root cause of the problem was the education system and young, inexperienced social workers who placed a high priority on a misguided, gender-biased, attachment theory. They ignored the physical abuse and lack of development that the child exhibited while with the mother.

---

[20] https://sharedparenting.wordpress.com/2014/05/22/45/ and https://www.trevorcooperauthor.com/book-referenced-material

I have met with men who have sole custody and hence "The Department" does not have a total gender bias, however, many men in society perceive a very strong bias that is due to the cases like S – . The perceived bias certainly, in my opinion, impairs "The Department" and their perceived right to morally operate. The bias however is not always present as I have seen loving mothers that have no access to their children, do not have a drug, alcohol or mental health issue and appear to be actively raising step-children well. The case I am thinking of, we will call "A – ", and the root cause, seems to be that "The Department's" social workers believed initial domestic violence claims that upset the mother to such an extent she appeared angry, and she possibly appeared irrational about the accusations. "The Department," years later, refuses to admit a mistake may have been made and delayed the case for the maximum time they legally could, which was two and a half years, and has asked her to admit to child abuse (that has never occurred), before they will consider reassessment and child access conditions. It is cases like A – that brings into question why "The Department" seems unable to change their position, when new evidence is presented to them? Is it because they do not want to consider they made an initial mistake as there could be repercussions?

I must confess. I often feel sorry for many of the mediators. I know one who told me one day, "It's so frustrating, some of those people need real help," and was referring to people with personality disorders that will defy logic and cannot be reasoned with. It did not reflect her skill as a mediator, but her inability to inform the court that in their opinion that there was an undiagnosed mental health issue. Should they have the right to outline their suspicions, so the court can enforce (on both parents), a proper mental health assessment to aid both the mediators and courts in their decisions?

The Judiciary

We need to appreciate what must be a difficult and emotionally draining job that the judiciary face. How they manage to oversee what was described by the English Lord Chief Justice Coleridge, as an "Exercise in absolute futility and a carnival of despair" on a daily basis and see the worst of dysfunctional families, is beyond me.

I disagree that more resources are needed, and that puts me at odds with the judiciary, but I do agree that they need help. The judiciary rely on the social workers and their reports are often the primary focus of decisions, when the parliamentary hearings have outlined their concern to how misleading these reports can be. Legal precedents within the court system, seems to mean that endless delays can be easily orchestrated by legal teams on the court. The judiciary generally works meticulously and with caution, so that if a legal team lodges an appeal, it is unlikely to be successful, and a retrial not granted.

I was dealing with one woman who was frantically preparing for court (she left her court response until the day before her appearance) and then couldn't attend to her preparation as she was called up by "The Department," who wanted to meet her that day in their own desperate attempt to get their evidence together the day before the case. The fact is, the woman was not complying with the court processes and submitting documents in the required number of days in advance. The matter showed me the difficulty the judiciary face with the government services that are also meant to supply information to the court in advance.

It reinforces the experience I had with a department when I was asked to review their IT systems as a consultant. Reports from users at some locations were that the printing systems could not even manage to print a page with two pictures on it that were required for court submissions. Caseworkers were leaving in frustration as could not present the evidence they collected, and cases were being thrown out of court when the investment to fix the issue worked out to be paid back in two weeks with the productivity gains. The core IT issues and estimates were confirmed by the government IT division. Unfortunately, there was a change in government and a policy that meant nothing would be spent on IT, all contractors will not have their contracts renewed and will employ more front-line child support staff. The government decision was exceptionally counterproductive. This seems to be reflected in many systems to which governments are involved in and letting off a government department for being busy should be no excuse.

The judiciary seem to not care about the mental health of those entering proceedings let alone the long-term impacts of protracted litigation such as cPTSD. Are one or both of the parties, suffering from a mental health or personality disorder that would impact their ability to compromise, focus and act in the best interest for their children and instruct their lawyers accordingly? There are always ethical issues in the restriction of access to the courts and the rights of those with mental health issues. While I would never advocate that the judiciary eliminate child access unless there are severe and dangerous mental health concerns, knowing personality disorders and mental health issues could assist the judges in managing the cases and the parents' personalities. In the case of S – ", the judge ordered a mental health assessment on the mother who returned to court three months later and simply said, "I didn't do it as did not have the finance." The judge seemed to progress the case regardless but this was clearly in no one's interest as three months were lost and no progress made. Was the government or court support also negligent in not ensuring services ordered by the judge were not made available and scheduled?

Do we expect the judiciary to act like public servants and process paper as and when it arrives? Or should we expect the judiciary to show a firm hand and leadership within their court?

A firm hand on the progress of court cases, not accepting the delaying tactics, and holding people accountable for their actions such as:

- If the government will not prosecute perjury, simply lock up the individuals for contempt.

- Awarding costs when perjury has been detected.

- Demanding government departments provide the reports as and when required (normally affidavits and evidence must be submitted several days before a hearing) and raising hell when they fail to do so! Sure, a government may get embarrassed, government department heads may change, and eventually government department budgets will be appropriately reconfigured to meet the courts' demands.

- Demanding lawyers and their clients submit documents on time. Judges should not accept submissions on the day. Proceed with the case based upon the evidence submitted on time, unless there are extraordinary circumstances. Those lawyers that don't notify their clients of the specific need for documentation and court demands immediately they are aware, (so the client has the maximum time to process) and ensure they submit documents for their clients, may get sued by their clients or action taken against them by legal services bodies.

- Demanding legal bodies (such as the Legal Services Commission) to issue leaflets to all litigants of the ethical requirements of lawyers, their duties to their clients to inform them of documentation schedules, and availability to prosecute lawyers who are non-compliant and welcome complaints.

- Demanding the police perform the risk assessment on both parties, what logic they used to select which party was to be removed, and body camera recordings as part of the evidence.

If this was done, then the system may be brought into line.

The Australian government

One of the most fundamental concepts in the environment is that an organism will maximise its utility. A fungus will multiply on rotting fruit until the environment will not support it and it dies off or is cast away to find somewhere else to survive. In the business world, we see the creation of a product and trying to manage the customer needs and perceptions. The business will try to manage its image as good, while keeping competitors in check and to maximise sales and profitability. The tobacco industry succeeded for decades suppressing information on the negatives of their product. The various components of the separation industry are no exception in their attempts to maximise their utility, promote their image and benefits, and suppress negative information. The things I learned from my journey and through that of peers, research, and the less reliable articles from the news services, confirm a system where the components are as toxic as the fungus on the rotting fruit.

While I cannot talk about other governments around the world, I can comment on the Australian Government, which has often followed both the best and worst practices from around the world, so this section may be of interest to those outside Australia.

117AB Costs where false allegation or statement made

    (1) This section applies if:

        (a) proceedings under this Act are brought before a court; and

        (b) the court is satisfied that a party to the proceedings knowingly made a false allegation or statement in the proceedings.

    (2) The court must order that party to pay some or all of the costs of another party, or other parties, to the proceedings.

This false allegation clause was repealed which means removed. At the same time a more modern definition for what is domestic violence, including the coercive and controlling behaviours and financial abuse added.

While many politicians have even recently stated that perjury is still illegal (i.e. this was just a clarification and costs can still be awarded in other parties), the so-called simplification and removal of S117AB was a signal that perjury was acceptable, and litigation exploded into the new forms of violence to which lawyers could argue and litigate over.

The successive governments since the instigation of no-fault divorce has never measured the impact and has never considered the number of children impacted by the family court as revealed in a Senate Estimates committee hearing by the then Senator John Madigan[21]. The court administration keeps statistics on the number of parties in litigation (parents), timeframe from lodgement to deter-

---

[21] https://www.trevorcooperauthor.com/book-referenced-material

mination, time from final hearing until judgement handed down, how many are in the family court process and passed through all of these statistics are easily recorded and managed. Unfortunately, in a dispute like mine that had ten court cases, each are recorded separately so they effectively reset the start date of any dispute with each new court case. One parliamentarian that stated in the "Parliamentary inquiry into a better family law system to support and protect those affected by family violence," said that "they were informed that the worst case length was two years." The family court administrators appear to not report in their statistics of litigation lasting a decade with the repeat business and some lawyers call the family court "the court of high returns". The name is so appropriate as if parents do not comply with court orders the aggrieved parent is forced back to request compliance, children grow and circumstances change and the chances are there are new things to disagree over. Not to mention high returns in terms of fees for lawyers.

The government has never set up systems that would see liaison between the siloed courts and the Child Support Agency (CSA), that does not even consider court orders when calculating benefits. The CSA was set up to force parents to support their children which is something no one disagrees with and has the power to garnishee wages and take money directly from bank accounts. I know of a case where they took funds from the father's bank account and could not purchase petrol to go to work and lost their employment. If one parent submits a statement to the CSA that they physically have the child full-time (or the majority), then the parent that does not have the child will be forced to pay the higher amount. This applies even when the court order is equal time and the child is being withheld, often against both the child and the other parent's wishes, even if contravention cases have been filed and the parent still refuses to comply. What this means is there is a financial incentive to not comply with court orders to maximise financial benefit. In one case, a drug-addicted mother kept the children simply to receive greater funds from father through the CSA to support her habit while the children were neglected. Such siloed practices undermine the law.

The government have NEVER measured if the best outcomes for the children was achieved, which is meant to be the primary focus of the system through the legislation. They have NEVER measured the number of suicides— attempts or deaths between parties in litigation or the children.

The successive governments have also failed to prosecute perjury. Justice Collier, in the film, *DAD*[22], a documentary made by independent filmmaker Karen Hodgkins in 2015, clearly stated that all the judges in the Australian family court had at one stage lodged cases to the attorney general for prosecution, however none were prosecuted. On the 29 June 2018, The Courier-Mail news service reported that that judges gave up and "'In the last three years we have received no referrals from the Family Court relating to perjury,' an AFP spokesman said." While

---

[22] https://www.youtube.com/watch?v=v5n9vUZYZhc&feature=player_embedded

some of the judiciary have called for additional funding for more judges and more legal aid, perhaps if the games were removed, the resources needed would not be so great. From my perspective, the government has failed to support our nation's judiciary through the lack of enforcement of perjury, so they can control the time wasted due to false claims that plague the courtroom.

I attended a presentation recently by a former chief justice of the Australian family court where he proposed that things have not changed much in 30 years as you still have one household trying to make two households and fighting for resources. Broadly speaking, he said the majority of cases can be categorised into:

1. Difficult issues relating to valuation of assets, e.g. what is a business worth especially after it is split up to give a proportion to a former spouse.

2. One of the parties is grossly unreasonable.

3. One of the parties has grossly unreasonable expectations given to them by advisors (mostly lawyers).

With all the inquiries and changes to the law, none seem to have addressed the issues associated with this former chief justice analysis of the situation and I have to ask why?

The successive governments have failed miserably in managing "the system," from the education system that trains various components, police, lawyers, social workers, and supporting the judiciary and the family court itself, which does not consider measuring its impact on children. The government regularly diverts attention to law reform rather than taking a systematic approach. Such law reform has proven ineffective when there is no support for the judiciary, no coordination of the various components upon which is essential for the judges, ensure compliance at each stage of the systems interaction with the family, and the best interests of the child is actually measured.

The relationship between a person's situation, their ability to cope, and that of suicide is unquestionable. A survey by one organisation dealing with separated fathers, found in a national survey that over 6% of clients would have died by suicide if they had not been there to assist. An analysis of the 10-year study of the Queensland Suicide Registry extrapolated across Australia, suggests that around 1 in 4 male suicides are related to relationship breakdown. At today's rates, that equates to around 10-11 men per week. Julian Lesser MP in his House of Representatives speech of 26 Nov 2018[23] talked about the link to suicide and the need for reform while discussing the amalgamation of two court systems.

I have already outlined the impact on the applicant or respondent's mental health and the possibility that the family separation industry is directly responsible for causing some mental health issues such as cPTSD. I have also outlined one example where 10 people lost their employment and the impact on the children where parental alienation is involved. The social and economic cost of failing to reform the system is enormous and the successive governments have, in my opinion, been negligent for failing to act.

---

[23] https://www.trevorcooperauthor.com/book-referenced-material

24

Silver linings and failure

Over ten years had passed since Nellie walked out the door. After the initial separation and my return to Australia, when I met new people, I would not want to tell them my story. It's such a big story, I felt judged on so many levels. I would feel at a complete loss and embarrassed by the situation and later by the bizarre situations I found myself in, still questioning what I could have done differently and wanting to be regarded as normal and without hang-ups or baggage. Occasionally, when forced to disclose, some people would understand perfectly and realise what some personalities are like, while others with a gendered ideology would ask "what did you do to upset her?" The layers of complexities, the bouncing around a pinball machine, never knowing where the next "ping" will come from, where it will push you and what will happen next has had a lasting impact on me.

When I do any standard test for anxiety, I invariably get top marks. This is my every day.

What began as a starting point for me to reach out and receive support is what keeps me going as no one should have to go through this and no child should suffer from such a poorly managed system. I have survived this horror, but now I still have to learn how to live again—to some extent anyway. This journey has taught me more about myself, my case and the cases of other men and women that suffer from parental alienation, have added to my understanding of what can happen. I have also found many ways in which I could help and support others by passing on my knowledge and experience. Some people I meet that are contemplating court are able to navigate themselves away from the adversarial route, while others that no longer consider suicide as they can see they have other options. It comes at a cost. I recall once chatting to a lady whose brother was subjected to typical strategies used within the separation industry, died by suicide ten years after not seeing his children and got her to put in a submission to the parliamentary inquiry. I relate closely to her brother that I have never met, but it is this ability to relate that at times makes me effective in helping people navigate the family court system.

I found a way I could help others, as was done for me, sharing experience and knowledge of the processes which lead to better outcomes, calming them down, discussing cases and legal documents and talking some down off their ledge. The silver lining, I guess you could say is that through my experience in this area, I could now help others. I became experienced by circumstance because of what I had lived through and survived. In helping others, I have been able to help myself as well. I will always have hope that my daughter will seek me out one day, by reminding her that she is loved, and the door is open even though she doesn't reply. Until then, I will support others and live as best I can.

I had an interesting visit to a psychologist, who I had been seeing to handle the extreme stress that resulted from the situation I found myself in. It was at one of those sessions where I was told that I cannot give up due to my personality and I needed to accept the loss of my daughter at this time. I have therefore learned how to accept the situation I am in, that I will not get the outcome that I desired in the short term and acknowledge that Jasmine and I have a long road ahead. I have to accept that the courts cannot, in their current form and current processes, provide what many believe to be fair for all, that justice will prevail or that they can deliver what is in the best interests of the children.

In terms of mental health, I have also learned that one cannot help someone that does not want to be helped (although sometimes you can teach someone to accept help and instil the desire to change). While I do not give up, I am one of the many who want to see the children placed first and foremost in the family court and end the abuse that children experience, being forced to sever the ties and alienated from a good and responsible parent.

Perhaps I will not see my daughter again due to past circumstances, which I cannot change. I understand that Jasmine would not want to see me based upon what I believe she has been told. It is not her fault for the position she has found herself in, but I will never give up on her.

My daughter may eventually question why I left and perhaps even read this book, so that a stronger than ever, father-daughter relationship will occur. It will not be in the short term, and the fact that Europe is where she has grown to know as home, may not be geographically close, but it will be reinstated.

I believe love will conquer bitterness and hatred.

Conclusion

M any men who come to our peer support groups come to share and talk because they can relate directly to others who are going through this same experience. I get asked why I stay in this space to help others? Many men initially refuse to see psychologists for several reasons such as, "It will be used against me," or they believe that "they just practice theory and as they have not lived through what I have," how could they understand? Many get what they need without a psychologist, while for others, we break down that barrier.

The answer is simple, I can't walk away from my daughter. I can't "write her off" as many have had to ... to simply survive. I can understand this, but I cannot do it. I cannot also just leave this space entirely and take up gardening for a hobby. Even though I am still lost from a personal perspective, have lost the most important person in my life, I am also in the perfect position to help others because I can relate directly to what they are going through and help Jasmine, the day she is ready.

My story is an insight into what the world of parental alienation looks like for one targeted parent. There is so much that needs to be done in this space to create real change. There must be a shift in prejudice and men need to be seen as important and equal parents. For some of the women I deal with, when they seek help from traditional services that do not understand parental alienation, they believe they were judged to be a bad mother as it simply wouldn't happen to a good mother. I know it can and does happen to good mothers which sets me apart from much of the social services industry. Many out there will relate to parts of my experience. Some will dismiss it as a man's perspective, but I know of many women who I relate to (more so than some men), as they share many of my experiences and the abuse. For the women who read this book and do see it as a man's perspective, it could easily be your brother, your friend, or even your new partner.

For fundamental change to occur, there may need to be a Royal Commission into Family Law with perjury and false accusations being a punishable offence. The fact that coercive and controlling behaviour is being perpetuated with the aid of the state (police/courts) in my opinion means that the state is complicit in criminal activity. There also seems to be a strong disconnect between three studies being:

- The largest survey in the western world on domestic violence being the "Partner Abuse State of Knowledge" (PASK project).[24]
- The Australian Bureau of Statistics – Personal safety survey Australia.[25]
- The Australian Institute of Family Studies.

When considering the police actions and the proportion of each gender charged. It should be noted that while domestic

---

[24] https://domesticviolenceresearch.org/
[25] https://www.abs.gov.au/ausstats/abs@.nsf/mf/4906.0 and http://www.oneinthree.com.au/infographic/

violence is challenging, when a significant proportion of domestic violence is mutual then perhaps both parties should possibly be charged, which only highlights the fact that the current system has a long way to evolve.

Above all, it is imperative to find a way to integrate the needs of the child suffering parental alienation and to reconnect with family.

Looking back, I have since realised that I have experienced horrendous behaviour through the family court, won and lost at the same time, faced parental alienation daily, and lost my daughter. If you had asked me fifteen years ago if this is what I would be doing with my life and with my hand on my heart, I could never have predicted this journey. But I have learnt key information, especially about our courts and laws and wished I had had someone to assist me when I first came up against it all those years ago before I left to go to the Netherlands and again before I returned to Australia.

Throughout all of this, I have found a way that I can help myself as well as helping others. By remaining active in Fathers Support group and a parental alienation group, occasionally still seeing a psychologist as I continue to address the on-going trauma, I have a much better handle on it these days and now I am continuing working towards helping others. Not just alienated mums and dads but lobbying for family law reform and hopefully bringing about a national suicide prevention organisation focusing on situational distress.

There is a branch of psychology known as "writing therapy" or "expressive therapy" that specifically believes that writing, even if no one ever reads it, is a good way to release one's feelings and is therefore therapeutic. I did not originally write the book for that purpose but as a record for Jasmine and that she is loved. The book was put down numerous times as the events were recalled and the nightmares took hold. My daughter is unlikely to ever read this book as written under an alias, she would need to be researching parental alienation to come across it and would therefore already be a part way through the reunification journey. Children are also trying to avoid the conflict and mainly want to know they are loved when they return and while describing the conflict was important to frame an understanding, I only hope the love for my daughter shone through.

The knowledge of the impact on the children of parental alienation was one driver that made me finish this book. I often hear firsthand and read the events that are happening to others suffering parental alienation. How poorly the government departments through social workers understand the dynamics. How the information is poorly presented to the family courts or the court mismanage the situation and it becomes clear that many of the interventions by government departments and the courts are counterproductive to the child's best interest. While Joe was older and did not appear affected, Jasmine was. I hear from parents how their children are impacted and read the research and hence this book needed to be finished.

Legislation prevents me from putting my real name and face to this real story. In my opinion not putting a human face to a story is one of the factors that has allowed a failed system, having intergenerational impacts to fester and continue. The relevant section of the Family Law Act that makes people anonymous may have been put in for good purpose, but should be reviewed as it may not even be serving its intended purpose. I hope that the emotional toll, the impact, and the futility of what has occurred in my case has been conveyed to you.

While I hope you cannot relate to this book due to your personal circumstances or to someone you know, if I have, then I would have achieved something. The person could be someone you care about and possibly someone you love, like a brother, sister, son, daughter or cousin, a colleague at work or someone you do not know, on the train or elsewhere. Hopefully, you will care about the people around you to do something about this failed system and addressing the underlying causes that has made the family separation industry so destructive and toxic to our society.

Epilogue

At the time of writing this, my daughter is now twenty-four years of age. From a girl who only wanted to draw (and I still have one she did for her nana on my wall), she went to university and studied arts/animation for one year, changed course and studied one year of law, and then found something she enjoyed and spent several years doing a literature course that I have no doubt she completed. My investigations on a travel site where you can post your name, looking for accommodation revealed that she is on a twelve-month trip, possibly backpacking around some dangerous areas of the world. It also provided me some photographs that I treasure and have a half-filled (or half-empty) photo display, but at least it's something.

I really do not know the impact of living with a parent that showed the level hatred that I experienced, being told by Nellie that her hatred for me was more important than ensuring Jasmine's future, all those years with a manipulative personality who displayed little care for others. I continue to send her monthly emails and while they do not bounce, they are also never responded to, and hence have no direct contact with Jasmine at all, at present. I wonder every day how she is, what is she like now as a young woman, and what might her future relationships look like?

Could the hatred toward me from her mother be the role model that shapes her life and behaviours? Could she be a radical feminist (that abuses the basic principle of equality and seeks advantage) now, hate just me or hate all men? While it was a mistake, in one exchange with Jasmine, well after she was twenty-one and during the time I was paying the equivalent of child support direct, I felt that I was forced to explain why I left the Netherlands. In one sentence I outlined the threats to lie and have me locked up, the recruitment of Samael and feelings that was unsafe to return. I did this communication in one sentence and reverted to asking about her and her needs. The response was, "That's profane," the definition of which is "treat (something sacred) with irreverence or disrespect," and at that time I was clearly not believed and Jasmine was defensive and I suspect protective of Nellie. Did that trigger her to look at what was going on? Possibly one day she will question why I left but at this time, I still do not know.

Perhaps she has gained insight into her mother and decided to move out and is angry at both parents, or hopefully she is old enough and packed up and left on the adventure of a lifetime. At present, I wonder if she is:

- A 24-year-old adventurer who is safety aware and off travelling?

- A 24-year-old who hates her parents, rebelled with high-risk behaviours and gone off the beaten track for a while?

Is she as lost as me, or has she healed? Maybe she realises her mother has a mental health condition or maybe she is fearful that she will develop it if there is indeed a genetic link—maybe she will think, "I know why Dad left!" ... or maybe she will just hate me?

I fought hard to have Jasmine in my life. I did not apply for custody as I knew that I would never have a chance as I was already alienated and would mean a change in country. Perhaps I should have fought knowing what I would lose, as a sign to my daughter I cared, but that is history. I focused upon what was realistic thinking, a sensible outcome would be just around the corner, so that I could survive and provide. I fought across two countries and two different types of courts and in two different languages, appearing personally or by legal representatives to defend myself and Jasmine before judges many times. Over $700,000 of the family wealth plundered in legal fees, spent in court proceedings to get some finality in the separation from Nellie and attain a sense of control over myself. Courts were misled, delayed, postponed and the many stalling tactics employed by Nellie that were used for coercive control, to prolong conflict and I suspect this was to solidify the parental alienation. The emotional and financial stress was extreme on myself and I suspect all of us. My only wish was to shield Jasmine from the conflict and for the children to have the right to have two parents, travel between us, be supported and develop into healthy and happy adults.

Believe it or not, I think when I set a firm boundary for Jasmine was the time I fell into my greatest depression. I said I wouldn't give her any more money unless we had some proper communication—she was twenty-three, after all—she said, "Stuff your money!" And this hurt the most, but at least when she was abusing me, hurling anger my way, or sending a meaningless one-line email, she was still communicating with me. But I can't reward bad behaviour and my peers helped me make the near impossible decision and a psychologist praised me for this choice.

As time goes on, there will likely be a lot of triggers for Jasmine that will have her asking questions about what occurred. This could be a new relationship or a breakup of a relationship, the birth of her child, may see a family breakup and realise how distorted perceptions can be or she may stumble across information she did not know. She may also mature and grow as time goes by, and want to learn from what happened in her past and see it differently.

Recently, I posted Jasmine a letter, written with the aid of a psychologist. I now know, as she has been travelling for six months and will be for another six months (according to an internet site), that she would not have received the present, the card and the letter I sent.

The original letter has not been altered apart from names to ensure authenticity. This was written solely by the author.

Happy 24th Birthday

Jasmine Cooper – (June 2018)

To my darling (princess you always loved animated films and travelling to Disneyland and hence the card) daughter. I wanted to wish you a happy 24th birthday on your special day and hope you have a great day. I have sent you separately a token present that you will receive separately.

Now that you are 24 there are some things I think that you are old enough to share with about my life.

Unfortunately, I have been through things similar to you and have never told you up until now. When I was about 20, my parents split up. Brandon at that time had behavioural problems and was not at home, Graham had left home as was older and as my mother having just walked out could not support me. I stayed in the family home with my father. My father was under tremendous stress from losing most of his family that one day he said in anger that "if you leave and take anything, I will ring the police".

I had worked in semester breaks so had a little bit of money and found somewhere to live and got a friend from university with a small trailer and took what was in my bedroom, (a really old fridge that was in the garage I think and an old black and white television and disappeared from his life for a while.)

I supported myself through my last year at university to achieve a Bachelor of Civil Engineering. My father was not invited to my twenty-first birthday party which Graham and his wife (Sean and Erica's mother) arranged at their place. He did post a birthday wish in the newspaper as it was before email and many of the modern ways to communicate. He was not invited simply because my mother had so much hatred toward my father of around 30 years marriage that was possibly due to how she viewed how her life had turned out.

As you know, my father and I re-connected or you would never have met him, and the relationship was just different. I attended his wedding to Denise but then I did a lot of travelling with work in large construction projects. Later, when I thought I had settled down and you arrived it was not long before we were all whisked off to Europe.

When I thought I would have to leave The Netherlands I remember saying to you that I understood that you wanted to stay in The Netherlands with your cats and friends and mother and said that is okay to make you feel better and now realise you may have taken that wrongly. You were sixteen and all I was trying to do is making the family split up easier for you but always wanted you with me and never thought there would be more than a year apart. There was so much I wanted to tell you but that didn't seem to happen or came out wrong with all the rush and remains unsaid. I have been finishing all correspondence with "Love Always" and I hope you realise I really mean it.

There are so many things that I miss regardless of it being taking you (and at times your friend from six doors down the street) swimming and hosting your birthday parties. I often tell people about your school friend when you were young at your birthday party that asked me something in Dutch to which I would respond in Dutch and another father would say exactly the same words (as he thought the little girl couldn't understand my crappy Dutch accent) and that happened 3 times in a row before another father burst out laughing. I miss the Black Forest cake that I would make for special occasions (as well as the birthday parties). I miss fixing up your rooms which seemed to need painting regularly as you changed from the small room, into the larger room on the 1st floor (that was Joe's) and then upstairs and fitting out with all the carpet and IKEA furniture including the huge wall of billy book cases with glass doors for your stuffed animals. I miss installing the cat flap and getting Dana (group secretary of the area I worked) to find Sindy for you and later other cats including Sooty. I also miss getting up at 3 in the morning to search for Sooty and having to get you out of bed as she came to you and jumped through the garage door opening (at about your shoulder height). I miss taking you to the cinema which we sometimes had to run all the way to get there on time and I think it was to Rotterdam we had to drive to once. I miss taking you to the doctors and especially pushing the doctors to see you one Monday morning when you had appendicitis and staying with you in the hospital each night. I miss making you angry when I talked to your teachers when you could not see the board at the front of the classroom and getting you your first glasses and the strange look, you had when you saw all the carvings on the side of the buildings. Most of all I miss having you around to find out what you wanted to do and talk you through matters even if it was giving up swimming and taking on singing or something else.

I will sign off as usual and hope that you know I mean it.

Love Always
Dad

CPSIA information can be obtained
at www.ICGtesting.com
Printed in the USA
LVHW081755220819
628599LV00012B/474/P

9 781925 935189